DATE DUE

MAY 18 '99	

GAYLORD   PRINTED IN U.S.A.

THE
MANAGER'S
HANDBOOK

THE MANAGER'S HANDBOOK

A practical illustrated guide to successful management

Arthur Young, U.K.
Special American Edition

CROWN PUBLISHERS, INC. NEW YORK

Conceived, edited and designed
by Marshall Editions Limited
170 Piccadilly, London, W1V 9DD

Editor: Erica Hunningher
Art Director: Paul Wilkinson
Deputy Editor: James Harpur
Assistant Editor: Pip Morgan
Picture Research: Sarah Wergan
Editorial Assistants: Tony Livesey
                        Louise Tucker
                        Pat Hunter
Managing Editor: Ruth Binney
Production: Barry Baker, Janice Storr

Copyright © 1986 by Marshall Editions Ltd. London

First American Edition

Published in the United States in 1986 by Crown
Publishers, Inc., 225 Park Avenue South, New York,
New York 10003 and simultaneously in Canada by
General Publishing Company Limited.

Reproduced by Reprocolor Llovet, S.A., Barcelona, Spain
Typeset by MS Filmsetting Limited, Frome, U.K.
Printed and bound by Usines Brepols, S.A. Turnhout,
Belgium

**Library of Congress Cataloging-in-Publication
Data**
Main entry under title:

The Arthur Young manager's handbook.

   1. Management – Handbooks, manuals, etc.
I. Arthur Young & Company. II. Title: Manager's
handbook.
HD31.A75 1986   658   85-26950
ISBN 0-517-56135-2

4

CONTRIBUTORS

Arthur Young is one of the world's
largest accounting and consulting
organizations. AY helps companies
resolve a broad range of business
problems, particularly in the fields of
accounting, auditing, tax, management
consulting, information technology,
corporate recovery, and education. The
book was prepared by Arthur Young in
the United Kingdom where it was
originally published.

Consultant editors
Joe Liddane BA, FCA., is Director of the
Educational Services Group with Arthur
Young, UK. His group provides practical
education and training to business
managers on the broad range of topics
covered by this handbook.

Keith Davis is a Senior Consultancy
Partner. He has had substantial
experience as a business advisor and
director of strategic reviews and major
projects in the UK and overseas.
Previously, he ran a major European
computer consultancy company.

Brian Chandler is Director of
Management Training in Arthur Young,
UK. With over 20 years' experience
covering strategic and management
issues, he specializes in devising training
solutions to the broad range of business
problems encountered by senior
managers.

Barry Ricketts is a public affairs
consultant to national and international
clients. He has held senior posts in public
relations with Unigate and Coca-Cola,
and worked closely with government and
UN agencies.

Authors
Leslie Atkinson, MA, FIPC
Joseph M. Berry, Dip. Com
Richard Buckley, BA, FCA
Tim Chessells, FCA
John M. Duncanson, B. Sc
John Gibson, FCA
Alistair Gray, MA, F. Inst. M., MBIM
Gerard M. Gray, BA (Econ), ACMA,
    MBIM
Timothy E. R. Jacobs, MICE, Ch. Eng,
    Dip. MS, MIMC
David Jardine, CA, ACMA
Niall Lothian, BA, CA
Martin Russell, ACA
Owen R. Scott, MA
Ronald S. Smith, MIIM
H. Beric Wright, MB, FRCS, MFOM
Iain Wylie, MA, Dip. PM, AMIMC
Ralph Zeuthen

5

CONTENTS

9	Introduction	58	Working capital management
		60	Cash forecasting
10–17	**KNOW YOURSELF**		
10	Who are you?	62–71	**Measuring the business**
12	What type of person are you?	62	The income statement
14	What do you value?	64	The balance sheet
16	Be aware of the future	66	Statement of Changes in
			Financial Position
18–39	**KNOW THE**	68	Valuing a company
	ORGANIZATION	70	Ratio analysis
18	Public image		
20	First impressions	72–5	**Providing business**
22	Size and scope		**information**
24	Corporate culture	72	Management accounting
26	Who really has power?	74	Budgetary control
28	Different departments/different		
	tribes	76–81	**Using business information**
30	What are the rules?	76	Costs and pricing
32	The winning team	78	Long-term planning
34	The heart of the business	80	Are things going wrong?
36	Adapting to survive		
38	Making the right choice	82–87	**The role of Personnel**
		82	Investing in people
40–127	**THE ESSENTIAL**	84	Supporting and advising
	FUNCTIONS	86	Operating successfully
40	What is a business?		
42	The anatomy of a business	88–93	**New technology**
44	The structure of a business	88	Keeping up to date
		90	Creating systems
46–49	**Strategic management**	92	Implementing systems
46	Planning future directions		
48	Analyzing your position	94–109	**Selling and marketing**
		94	Customer relations
50–55	**Management organization**	96	Developing a strategy
50	Essential features	98	Preparing a plan
52	Growth and development	100	Creating a structure
54	Choosing a structure	102	Prospecting
		104	Selling
56–61	**Funding the business**	106	Promoting the business
56	Equity and long-term debt	108	Distribution

110–127	**Materials management**
110	Getting the right balance
112	Buying
114	Receiving and storing
116	Controlling inventory
118	Production planning
120	Production control
122	Manufacturing management
124	Manufacturing strategy
126	Innovation, research and development
128–197	**THE MANAGER'S ROLE**
128	Achieving the right balance
130	Leading your team
132–143	**Communication**
132	Getting it across
134	One-to-one
136	Effective writing
138	Effective reading
140	Public presentations
142	Writing a memo
144–147	**Meetings**
144	Preparing and chairing
146	Achieving results
148–151	**Consultation**
148	Using internal resources
150	Seeking outside help
152–155	**Negotiation**
152	The formal approach
154	Internal bargaining
156–163	**Developing people**
156	Staff selection and interviewing
158	Planning succession
160	The need for training
162	Finding effective training
164–179	**Managing teams**
164	Selecting and shaping
166	Developing an approach
168	Understanding motivation
170	Creating motivation
172	Preparing to delegate
174	Making delegation work
176	Appraisal, counseling and promotion
178	Handling trouble
180–183	**Managing change**
180	Exploiting opportunities
182	Coping with crises
184–189	**Managing people**
184	Dealing with stress
186	Planning time
188	Using time
190–197	**Taking control**
190	Managing tough situations
192	Managing problems
194	Making decisions
196	Managing the boss
198–209	**MANAGING YOUR CAREER**
198	Planning your future
200	Creating the right image
202	Changing jobs
204	Getting to the top
206	Staying on top
208	Checklist to a brilliant career
210–215	Glossary
216	Bibliography
217	Arthur Young worldwide
218–223	Index
224	Acknowledgments

INTRODUCTION

Good managers are not born, they are made. They are fashioned by experience of business and the realities of the workplace. They grow in stature and managerial skill largely from their encounters with people and problems, not from studying the notes and theories cataloged in textbooks.

The Manager's Handbook is different. Rather than explaining the theory of management, it describes real life from the manager's point of view. In doing this it offers a uniquely illustrated, practical and concrete guide to conducting your business life more positively and to becoming a better manager.

Business life, and the job of the manager within it, have an apparent complexity but an inherent simplicity. *The Manager's Handbook* cuts through the complexity and lays bare the simplicity with checklists, guidelines, diagrams and charts.

It was once believed that all you had to learn to become a manager was how to organize, coordinate, command and control. It is now widely accepted that this view is simplistic. The target keeps moving; events and people do not always conform long enough to be planned and controlled. The ways and means of management, therefore, involve continual experimentation with new approaches to old and new problems. Remember the maxim: "Try it, fix it, do it."

You will grow and learn and be a better manager by observing, practicing, thinking and rethinking, experimenting and continually questioning. Worthwhile answers will come from the heat of the action, from dealing with the course of real business events as well as from the problems and personalities of those involved in them.

Management is about people not systems; people coming together to achieve the clear objectives of their organization. In a very real way you have a contract with your organization: everyday you give something of your life and receive something in return, not only a meal ticket but a genuine chance to achieve. At the end of the day, you and your subordinates should derive some meaning which reinforces and reaffirms your own values. This book gives some essential guidelines to help you achieve this difficult aim.

The practical approach of *The Manager's Handbook* means that it will be useful to managers at all levels. But it is those in their early years of management who are intended as its primary audience.

We recommend that, first, you observe business reality and then take the book, dip into it, and compare what you find with what you have perceived in the workplace. The reality should measure up to the way in which the book was conceived, written and illustrated – a distillation of the experience of a broad spectrum of consultants and practicing managers in the United Kingdom.

Who are you?

Self-knowledge is invaluable to any-one seriously intent on choosing the right life-path. If you, as a manager, don't know yourself, you will be led into making ill-advised decisions about your life and work from which it may be difficult or impossible to extri-cate yourself.

It would be wrong to suggest that self-knowledge is the key to manager-ial success. A good manager will need a range of skills and knowledge which come with experience. You will need to practice skills, take advice, use others' strengths and work hard. But self-examination is a good starting point and is rarely stressed when it comes to choosing the right job for you and doing your present job best.

The problem is that there is rarely time to stop and think: "Hold on, do I *really* want to do this?" There are powerful pressures to go straight from school into a job; these stem from a perceived shortage of good jobs, the need to pay the rent, the need to be socially acceptable, the desire to be of value to the community and the desire to finance outside-work activities.

Job mismatch can also happen if your natural areas of skill and enjoy-ment are obscured by the desire to achieve simply for achievement's sake; by a natural competitiveness; or be-cause it seems somehow wrong to con-centrate solely on what is enjoyable or comes naturally. Companies now spend more time on matching people with jobs, using sophisticated tests, assessment centers and career coun-seling. Their costs, when they get it wrong, are great; yours could be inestimable.

If you are not enjoying your job, look at situations in the past where you have enjoyed yourself and done well at something. The chances are that you have strayed away from your natural abilities and a move to recap-ture them will be rewarding for you and the company you work for.

Am I in the right job?

People's values and interests change. Every so often you should ask your-self the following questions to find out whether you are still satisfied with your job. There is no "right" answer except the truthful one.

● Do you begin to feel anxious in the evening at the prospect of work the next day?
● Do you talk obsessively to your partner about your work or about a member of staff? Or are you un-naturally reticent about them?
● Do you find yourself working late regularly or not taking your lunch hour because you feel you need to impress or because you have been given, or taken on, too much work?
● Are you offhand or short-tempered with your subordinates or peer colleagues?
● Are you enjoying your job and clear about where it is taking you?
● Do you feel your boss is incom-petent and that you could do his or her job just as well?
● Do you have pangs of envy when you hear your friends talk about their jobs? What do you envy? Their freedom? Responsibility? Opportun-ity to travel? Salary?
● Are you sick of being delegated to and not delegating?
● Do you feel run down or stressed?
● Have you had to give up hobbies or interests because of work?

The Ancient Greeks thought self-knowledge so crucial that they had the phrase "Know Yourself" carved above their temple entrances.

Is the job right for me?

If you feel dissatisfied in your work, ask yourself what you need:

- More money?
- Longer vacation allowance?
- Better contractual terms?
- More recognition for your efforts?
- More time for outside interests/hobbies?
- An office or a bigger office to yourself?
- A personal assistant?
- More challenging tasks?
- More responsibility?
- More variety in your work?
- An expense account?
- Less traveling for extended periods?
- Better refreshment facilities?

It may be that your current job cannot give you, say, more money or more responsibility. But the task of analyzing and focusing on what your needs are is crucial to an understanding of yourself.

Analyze your needs

To be an effective manager you must realize that your satisfaction requirements *change*. In the mid-1950s, A. H. Maslow, a pioneer in management psychology, put forward the theory that there are five basic needs which people aim to satisfy. How many of Maslow's needs does your job fulfil?

1 Physiological needs: the basic need for food, clothing, shelter.

2 Safety needs: the need for security, continuity, protection against anything that threatens an organized orderly existence.

3 Social needs: the need to belong and be accepted in a social context.

4 Esteem needs: the need to have status and others' respect.

5 Self-fulfilment needs: the need to feel fulfilled through the creative use of your natural aptitudes and practiced skills which leads to "self-actualization."

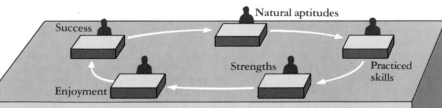

Success — Natural aptitudes — Practiced skills — Strengths — Enjoyment

What are you good at?

If you are unhappy in your job, get back in touch with what you enjoy and are good at. What are your natural aptitudes and skills? Try to list, analyze and rank them. Then ask yourself whether you are concentrating on the most important. It is not easy, so where do you start? At the beginning.

All of us are born with a natural aptitude for something, whether it be a fascination for words or a flair for ball games. We are encouraged to practice and develop that particular talent. As a result, we come to have a definite strength; it might be a technical skill such as playing chess, tinkering with cars or something like being a good talker, getting on with people, taking responsibility. Whatever it is, we are bound to get enjoyment and a sense of satisfaction from doing it. This, in turn, naturally leads to success.

What type of person are you?

To know how you function in the office, what you are best and worst at, is all part of knowing yourself. Some managers deal with people in just the right way: neither too bossy nor too appeasing, they handle staff with tact and sensitivity, careful not to overlook individual needs while ensuring that the team or the department thrives as a whole. They also tend to get the job done and everyone benefits.

Others are great at thinking or solving problems but don't know how to handle people. No two managers are alike. What type of manager are you?

Carl Jung pioneered the study of personality types at the beginning of the century. He thought that people oriented themselves toward the world in either of two basic ways. "Introverts" are most happy when they are by themselves, doing their own thing; they do not pursue social activity and often feel uncomfortable in it.

"Extroverts" give their lives meaning from interaction with people and can feel at a loss when by themselves. Human beings are complex and don't fit into boxes. But some theories are a useful starting point for the difficult task of self-analysis.

Jung thought that we receive and process data via four functions: thinking, intuiting, feeling, sensing. Each person has one predominant function, one or two that are semideveloped, and one that is underdeveloped. As a "thinker" you will be strong on clear, logical thinking; you will be methodical and be able to analyze problems.

As an "intuitor" you will be good at ideas, creative or lateral thinking – the imaginative approach. The "feeler" will see things according to personal values and not from a dispassionate weighing of pros and cons; "feelers" are warm, outgoing and thrive on social interaction. The "sensor" is down-to-earth, energetic and practical, preferring action to words or ideas. The "sensor" likes to get things done.

"With your creative ability, Peter's methodical approach and my analytical thinking, we make a great team!"

Concentrate on your strengths

● Try to recognize your basic bent or direction: it will give you belief in yourself, which in turn leads to motivation and energy.

● Work out what your strengths are – doing, organizing, analyzing or what? You will then be in a good position to avoid a job mismatch.

● Ensure that your weaknesses are covered. If you are part of, or running, a team, make sure that there are those whose strengths can compensate for your weak points.

● Keep out of situations in which your weaknesses are likely to be continually exposed.

● If you have been given a specific task that will show you up, pick the brains of a colleague or delegate the job to someone you can trust.

● Remember, however, that you cannot avoid all situations that challenge your weaknesses: sometimes you must cope the best you can or learn to improve.

● It may be necessary to make fundamental changes to your situation if you are continually under pressure and your natural strengths are not being exploited.

● If you decide that you lack challenge or are going in the wrong direction, it may be that the only solution is to change jobs. If so, seek advice and reflect long and hard on the wisdom of such drastic action.

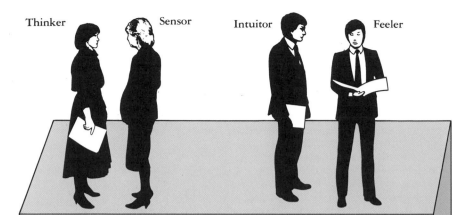

Thinker

Sensor

Intuitor

Feeler

Jung's four functions

As a manager it is useful to know whether you are an introvert or extrovert and which of the four functions is your strongest and which the weakest. Also, if you can spot the strong and weak functions of your subordinates, it will help you decide who will be most useful for different tasks and enable you to build effective teams.

Thinker
● Enjoys tackling problems with logic.
● Is strong on analysis but weak on implementing solutions.
● Is a methodical worker.
● Is skeptical of projects unless backed up with sound, rational arguments.
At work:
Good with facts and figures; researching; systems analysis; accounting; financial side of business.

Sensor
● Is good at getting things done, often impatient with the planning stage.
● Feels at home with routine work.
● Has a lot of common sense and is practical.
● Works hard and is usually well organized.
● Is energetic and single-minded.
At work:
Good at initiating projects; setting up deals; negotiating; troubleshooting; converting ideas into action.

Intuitor
● Enjoys playing with ideas and theories.
● Is good at seeing the "overview" but misses the detail.
● Is creative and has a strong imaginative sense.
● Will often get hunches about things that turn out correctly.
At work:
Good at long-term planning; creative writing; lateral thinking; brainstorming.

Feeler
● Enjoys human company.
● Assesses on personal values not technical merit.
● Is warm and sympathetic.
● Is perceptive about peoples' moods, feelings and reactions.
● May overlook blatant facts in favor of "gut feelings."
At work:
Good at cementing team relationships; counseling; arbitrating; public relations; will talk as easily with a clerk as with an executive.

What do you value?

"My aim is more money."

"I don't care what else the job has to offer, as long as I get to travel." "I started in Personnel, recruiting technical staff but realized I just had to get out to where the technical problems of production were actually being solved."

To what extent values are innate or brought about by social conditioning is a difficult question. As children we are bombarded with people's values. What makes us absorb some and not others is probably due to our psychological make-up. What is clear is that everyone has a personal value system and to be a good manager you should have a fair idea what yours consists of.

This is not always easy. It can take quite a time for dominant values to emerge. Also, people have many values and so it is necessary to work out your priorities – experience will help to show what they are. But be open to their changing.

Add your values to your natural aptitudes and strengths. Then you are well set to begin or continue a successful, happy career.

Review your personal balance sheet regularly and above all with an eye on tomorrow.

What do you value in your job?

● An ordered environment and security?
● The chance to help others?
● Freedom and flexibility?
● Being your own boss?
● The chance to achieve?
● Power, recognition or authority?
● A tangible finished product?
● Facts and figures to work with?
● Congenial people to work with?
● The chance to travel and meet people?
● A glamorous lifestyle?
● A high salary?
● A company car and other perks?

Do you value conformity and structure?
Conformity has negative connotations but many would admit to wanting it to some degree. To value conformity, order and structure is really to value security; a job that has a regular routine, in which roles are clearly defined and set procedures are used, can provide it. If you value security, look for a well-defined job that gives company benefits, such as health insurance and an adequate pension plan.

Do you value helping others?
It could be said that all jobs benefit mankind, if only in the smallest way; but clearly some do so more directly than others. If you want to help others but don't want to be a nurse, doctor, teacher or social worker you could join the personnel or training departments of large companies: all organizations need their share of "people" managers. Alternatively, you could use your managerial skills in the service of a charitable organization; philanthropy can compensate for a low income.

Do you value freedom and flexibility?
Some people hate regimentation in any form. A commuter-style routine, clocking in and out at specific times, may fill you with horror. If you value your freedom then make sure your job allows you a tolerable amount of flexibility. Can you come in 30 minutes late and make it up after hours? Can you wear more or less what you want? Does your boss fret every time you make a phone call?

Do you value achievement?

The need to achieve is often instilled in a child by parents and the need for parental approval can last into adulthood as an unconscious drive: a desire to achieve without really knowing why and without being satisfied. If you do value achievement, make sure it is recognized and rewarded. If it is not, are you in the right job? Realize, however, that you cannot achieve everything at once. Set your sights on short-term attainable goals.

Do you value power?

Most people value power but few will admit it. To want power may disguise a need to be in control of your immediate environment and therefore your destiny: to be responsible, independent, to give orders rather than receive them. If you value power, choose an industry or company where power is recognized as a legitimate goal. But be careful not to alienate yourself through manipulation and unscrupulous behavior.

Do you value a tangible product?

If, as a child, you loved making models, drawing pictures, building sand-castles, you may find that one of your priorities at work is to see something tangible produced. If you need the satisfaction of turning raw material into a finished product, avoid jobs, such as public service, that don't provide tangible results: you will be better off in an industry such as manufacturing, engineering or publishing.

Do you value facts and figures?

Accounting, computing and research oriented jobs are attractive if you prefer dealing with data than with people. It may be that outside the office you have a rich, emotional, if not turbulent, personal life and that in your job you need something that makes no demands on your inner resources. Or you may be an introverted "thinking" type who likes to work methodically through the day with minimal social interaction.

Do you value working with people?

For many, working with compatible colleagues has as much or more value than a high salary. If you interpret quality of life in terms of communication of ideas and rewarding friendships rather than material perks and incentives, you will be happiest in a job where it is no sin to chat with those around you. You might find journalism, public relations or local politics suitable.

Do you value financial success?

Some people grow up knowing nothing more than that they want to be rich. Money, what it can buy, the opportunities it affords are uppermost in their plans. If getting rich is your first priority, go for the big salaries and generous perks offered by large corporations or set up in business on your own. You are unlikely to become wealthy by working in public administration or professions such as teaching.

15

Be aware of the future

In the final analysis, knowing yourself, and therefore arming yourself with the equipment to make correct choices concerning your life and job, is not something easily acquired.

It is *not* simply a matter of answering questionnaires, adding up your scores and drawing glib conclusions. Self-knowledge, as sages from Socrates to the Zen masters have avowed, is a process that continues as long as you are alive. There is no beginning or end.

Questioning yourself about your needs, personality type, strengths and weaknesses, and your values, is just a start. You should now try to develop a day-to-day awareness of your behavior and attitude toward the myriad aspects of your life and work. Ultimately it is perception and sensitivity that determine whether you, as a manager, will be able to motivate, delegate, reprimand, negotiate, communicate and perform all the other managerial tasks.

Since life is a continuously flowing river and not a static pond, you should be aware that you are changing – your body, your thoughts, your attitudes – every moment. It is important, therefore, to keep up to date with yourself; to keep breaking the habit of thinking that you fit a particular mold.

You should keep a personal balance sheet, listing your strengths and weaknesses, values and desires, and then review it at a set date, every year or two years, to see how you have progressed. You may find, for instance, that on the debit side you listed "Take things to heart too much and am under too much stress" and then wondered, when reviewing it, why you ever thought it was a problem.

Be prepared to change. After gaining better awareness of your strong and weak points, concentrate on your strengths: winning is about giving your strengths full rein. That is not to say that you should ignore an obvious

weakness. It will have to be dealt with. Through effort, training and experience, most managers can become competent at all the managerial skills.

Finally, be aware that the rate of social change is increasing and that in

Facing up to the future

You should be aware of the fundamental changes in life that will affect you and your work, and be prepared to adapt accordingly.

Starting out
After leaving school or college, you face the challenge of trying to establish yourself in the outside world. It is likely that you will be relatively fit and eager to get on with making money to pay for your rent and leisure activities. You will probably have lots of confidence and energy born from a lack of experience of failure, and these provide the necessary impetus to get you into your working life.

Getting established
Later on, perhaps from the age of 25 to the early 30s, you will start focusing outside work on your personal and emotional life. Your job may not be as exciting as it first was but you have begun to establish a financial base and are now looking for a partner to share your life and a house to buy. Now is also the time when you may start looking for an alternative job.

Consolidating
From late 20s to late 30s you will probably be fairly set in your job, even if you have changed careers,

the future more people may be working at or from home, and there will be more leisure time and job sharing. Change and impermanence are part of tomorrow's world. Be ready to accept the challenge.

and may be living with your partner in bought accommodation. Security will be high on your list of needs and you will still be ambitious, having been promoted but with more rungs to climb. You might have started a family. If so, you might find that your job, at least temporarily, becomes of secondary importance.

Staying on course
You might also find that babies mean sleepless nights and, coupled with a tailing off of your leisure activities, it is harder to cope and more stressful at work. If this happens to you, check to see whether your workload can be lightened by, say, delegating more. Also, make sure that you are using your talents and have not strayed away from using your natural strengths.

Midlife turbulence
In their early 40s, men and women experience a phase of transition. The infamous midlife crisis may result in turbulent change for you and your partner. You may have anxious feelings about fulfilment, linked to concern about your career development.
Marriages can come under stress during these middle years. Couples may already have grown apart by

this time: a jet setter on an expense account, for example, is likely to grow away from a spouse with a less glamorous lifestyle; a middle-manager, dissatisfied with a humdrum job, may seek excitement at the expense of family commitments.
If you have children, their adjustment to adolescence may coincide with your problems at middle age, heightening domestic conflict.

Planning for retirement
If you have weathered the storm that follows the midlife crisis, you should be able to cope with the next phase of readjustment. Now you should have settled for your position in the company and be making the best of it. Retirement will be increasingly on your mind: "How will I cope? Should I be saving more? Shall I try to carry on working or negotiate a consulting position? Will I have the leisure interests to fill my day or will I be at a loss?" You will begin to take stock of your career and what you have and have not achieved.

Public image

If you know your basic direction, recognize what you need and value and are aware of your strengths and weaknesses, you will be in a position to sort out what kind of organization you should work for. Most important is to try to match your strengths with the company's needs.

Success in one organization does not necessarily guarantee success in another. The management whiz-kids who do well in the orderly environment of one company are often unable, for example, to cope with the hurly-burly world of another. There is a world of difference between working as a manager for, say, Bank of America, US Steel Corp., Apple Computers or Pan Am.

Each organization needs different kinds of people to run it: some thrive on the intellectual challenge of systems administration, while others prefer the more human aspect of the personnel department.

Thus you should look at an organization and the job it offers and consider whether it suits you: is it a large conglomerate or a small family-owned business? Will it provide you with scope to gain experience or move up the promotion ladder? Will you fit in with the corporate "culture?" How does it match your strengths, weaknesses, values and needs?

The way a company is regarded by its competitors, its customers, the general public and by its employees tells you a lot about the organization and its style of management.

Many employees in large companies do not understand the complexity of the organizations for which they work. They work in specialist departments and see only the details which make up their particular contribution to the whole activity. To them the detail *is* the company: the more ambitious you are, the more you should keep the wider perspective uppermost in your mind.

1

4

Does the organization suit you?

● What reputation does the organization have? Is it, for example, known for high-quality goods or for giving good value for money?
● How is it regarded by its competitors and by the financial press?
● What sort of people work for it? Is there an old-boy network? Will you suit the profile of those at senior levels?
● Is it optimistic, go-ahead and expanding? Or the reverse?
● Do employees seem to be happy? Are there good conditions of employment?
● Is there a history of good or bad industrial relations?

The corporate image

1 It is difficult to assess a company accurately from the outside. The products or services, the style of advertising, the buildings may all give a misleading or superficial idea of what life is like on the inside. You cannot tell what it is like to work for American Express simply from looking at its credit cards.

2 A company's literature is a poor indicator of corporate personality. Literature is often produced by groups outside the company whose job it is to create a desired image. But a company does not change every time a new advertising campaign is introduced.

3 A company's physical premises – its offices or factories – can indicate corporate personality. Small, spartan offices may show a down-at-the-heels company, but they could also be a sign of an efficient management anxious to keep overheads to a minimum.

4 It is important but difficult to assess what a company is like from its staff. At an interview, you should try to meet as many people as you can. Be aware of the back-up staff of secretaries and receptionists. How a company treats those on the bottom rung is a good pointer to how they treat those at the middle or the top.

5 A company with an advanced technological service/product does not necessarily have a progressive attitude toward management.

More important are the price, quality and reliability of that service/product. Is it the best in its field? Does it deal in a high volume of small transactions or a small volume of high-quality transactions? What future does the service/product have?

First impressions

The first link with a company often occurs when you read its recruitment advertisement in a newspaper. Such ads tend to glorify the company, the job and the person needed to fill the post. You need to find out much more about a company you are considering joining.

Talk to friends, colleagues, people who have previously worked for the company and, if possible, those who are currently working there: valuable information can be gained from those who know the company from the inside. Keep your eyes open to the media and especially the pages of the financial press.

Get hold of the company's annual reports from the last two or three years and those of its chief competitors and compare them.

Remember, however, that the report is prepared primarily for shareholders or potential shareholders, bankers and financial institutions and the financial press. Consequently, it tries to show the company in the best possible light.

If, for example, the company feels it necessary to present a balance sheet that shows a lot of cash, it will manage its transactions near the year end to produce such a situation. Read the financial press for a more objective view of the company's performance and management.

Company reports will contain much accounting jargon; don't let it put you off. With a careful reading and some common sense, you should be able to deduce a considerable amount about the company's products, people, customers, markets, physical location, objectives and financial strength.

The comparative analysis over several years is often the richest source of information. Is the company achieving what it sets itself as a target? If the profit graphs show increasing earnings, are they increasing as fast as those of competitors?

1 What is the company's reputation in the market place? Is it well known and successful? What does the financial press say about it?

2 How fast and how much is the company expanding? Is the company's expansion exceptional or typical of the industry it is in?

3 What exactly does the job require? How many staff will it involve managing/ supervising? What happened to the previous incumbent? Was he/she promoted or fired?

4 Don't be put off by high demands. You may not be perfect, but nobody else is either.

5 Does the company have a reputation for efficiency and profitability? Will you have the resources to achieve the expected results?

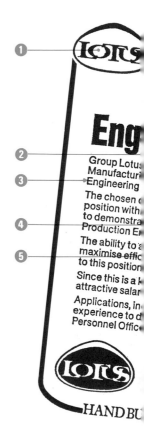

❶

IOTS

Eng

Group Lotus
Manufacturi
Engineering

The chosen
position with
to demonstra
Production E

The ability to a
maximise effic
to this position

Since this is a k
attractive salar

Applications, in
experience to d
Personnel Office

IOTS

HAND BU

❷
❸
❹
❺

1 **How big is** the organizational unit in which you will work? How big is the management team in your unit?

2 **Does the ad** tell you the full extent of the duties you'll be expected to perform?

3 **Where exactly** will you fit in the chain of command? Who will you have to report to?

4 **To what extent** will you be on your own? How much work will be done in collaboration with others?

5 **How generous** is the salary in comparison with other companies in the same field? What fringe benefits and bonuses are offered? How much do top managers get?

The annual report

From two or more annual reports you may be able to acquire the following basic information about a company:

● Ownership: who are the owners? What is the profile of those at the top?

● Corporate values and objectives: read the chairman's statements, bearing in mind what is not said.

● Products, services and investments: what exactly are they?

● Future plans and expectations: is it likely to diversify or take over another company?

● Financial position: study the accounts and the audit opinion.

● The relative profitability of the different business segments.

● Growth record: is it expanding? Is its market shrinking?

Size and scope

When it comes to choosing an organization to work for, size is important. There can be a world of difference between a small family company and a giant multinational conglomerate. The accepted wisdom is that there are more opportunities in larger companies but a greater variety of work in smaller companies; large companies are formal and heavily bureaucratic, while small companies permit a high degree of flexibility and freedom. In fact, there is only one rule: "Don't make a judgment on size alone – investigate." Giant organizations may be split into small vigorous units. Small stagnant companies are just as common as large monolithic ones. Size is relative and not static: Apple Computers, for example, employed only a handful of people in 1977. By 1985 they had a workforce of several thousands.

Choosing an organization also depends on yourself: what stage of your career are you at? Are you building or

Organization A produces bathroom fixtures for the wholesale trade. It has a workforce of 500 people. It started life as a family-owned company but was taken over by a large overseas organization, involved in the same trade. The parent company operates worldwide and has its base in its home country's capital city. Three members of the family are still employed at senior levels: the father, a well-respected local man, is still the chairman.

A number of foreigners have been installed at different levels. This local unit believes that it has autonomy and the authority to approve its own capital expenditure program. The production facilities have been slightly modernized as a result of the takeover.

Questions you might ask yourself include:
● How many foreigners are there and is the company merely a place to gain experience for them?
● What influence and power do the foreigners have? Is the chairman just a nominal head kept on for good public relations with the local community?
● What exactly is the relationship between the foreigners and former senior figures/family members/other employees?
● What management practice does the parent company believe in? Does it understand the local mentality and attitude?
● Is there a point at which you are likely to go no further in the company?
● Is the local unit safe if something drastic happens to the parent company?
● Are the local unit's profits measured in the currency of the parent? If so, what is the risk of a damaging currency fluctuation?
● Have the modernized production facilities contributed to profits? Will there be more modernization and, if so, is there a risk of layoffs?
● Can the local unit really authorize its own capital expenditure program?

consolidating? You must ask yourself exactly what you want: money, experience, a prestigious name to work for or a chance to develop new skills. Maybe you can find them all in one company.

It is more likely that you will have to compromise. If you want to build a career as quickly as possible, it may be best to go for a large company with a household name for an all-round training. Having got your blue-chip credential, you may then wish to take a risk with a smaller, less well-known firm where you are likely to have a greater degree of power and influence. But don't be put off by an unknown name: all the best-known companies have been unknown quantities at some stage.

Before making a decision about joining a company you should try to find out about its size and scope. Look at the two examples of organizations below and ask yourself the questions that follow.

Organization B deals in life insurance. It is publicly held and has a workforce of 1,500 people. The head office is based in a capital city. It has prestigious premises: a marble entrance, plush carpets, cafeteria and executive dining suite. It has grown rapidly in the last ten years, with turnover and profits increased by 500 per cent. It has offices in every major city in the country and an extensive overseas network. The chairman came up through the ranks and is knowledgable about the business. He is now 58 years old and due to retire.

Questions you might ask yourself include:
● How did the organization grow so fast – by merger/acquisition/real growth?
● What happens when the chairman retires? Is he the driving force behind the company? Does he set the management style? Has his succession been planned for?
● Is there a chance of the company being decentralized?

● Will you be based at the head office or sent out to a branch?
● Does its size suit you? Is it strong on systems? Does it have a bureaucracy that works?
● Does it have a formal, hierarchical structure?
● Will you get an overview of all the operations or will your knowledge be restricted to a few?
● Will you be near the seat of power? Will you pick up the rumors and undercurrents?
● Is there an old-boy network operating at senior levels? Do you match the profile of those at the top?
● Does the company practice equal opportunity? How many women are there in senior posts?

Corporate culture

As a manager, it is important for you to know the official company culture and to compare it with reality. Look at your company's recruitment brochure or annual report – it will be full of fine words giving a glowing picture of the company's performance together with its policies.

But have these establishment values really permeated through the company to all levels of the organization? Are they shared by top executives and middle managers? Are they just for public relations?

A company may state clearly that it believes in equal opportunity between the sexes. The actual presence of women in top management provides more compelling evidence that the company means what it says.

Company values take time to evolve into a shared, unwritten code of behavior. Although hard to define, this corporate culture *is* recognizable in management style, budgets, priorities, attitudes to employees and customers, even notepaper.

There is a world of difference between the culture of an advertising agency and a local government office, for example, which is illustrated not only in dress and language but also in the pace at which business is conducted.

You should know the culture of your own company as well as that of its rivals. The IBM corporation has a paternalistic culture: as an employee you are expected to devote yourself totally to the company and, in return for hard work and loyalty, you are looked after and well rewarded – both financially and with other substantial benefits.

By contrast, Apple, the computer company that has grown dramatically over a relatively short time, has a forward-looking, optimistic culture. Apple sees itself as a David continually growing in strength at the expense of a Goliath.

Are you aware of your company's culture?

- Is there a high turnover of staff?
- Is there a fast-moving, high achievement atmosphere?
- Are important decisions made at the top or does middle management run its own show?
- Is it bureaucratic or is there a high degree of freedom?
- What is its market strategy – to be a leader, follower, specialist?
- Is it R & D-oriented? Is it risk-oriented?
- Does it have a relaxed, first-name terms policy?
- Does it have a traditional, hierarchical structure?
- Does it have a systematic, predictable approach?
- Is it product-oriented and quality conscious?
- Is it bright, forward-looking and optimistic?

Culture clash

An example of the importance of "management culture" was illustrated with the 1983 break-up of the international financial venture, Becker Warburg Paribas Group.

Heralded as the vanguard of global banking nine years before, it brought together A. G. Becker & Co of Chicago, S. G. Warburg of London, and Cie Financière of Paris.

But hopes of such leadership were dashed in the spring of 1983 when Warburg pulled out of the arrangement. The biggest point of friction, by most accounts, was the disparity in the firms' self-images and individual styles. Primarily, Warburg's safety-first style clashed with Becker's aggressiveness.

Shared values

Corporate culture at McDonald's is summed up in their motto: "Quality, Service, Cleanliness and Value."

Employees are given precise instructions on the McDonald's view of QSC & V. Everything is spelled out – from the choice of prime lean beef to the requirement for cashiers to make eye contact with and smile at every customer.

The result is a workforce steeped in the company's philosophy, enabling McDonald's to run thousands of successful restaurants with a relatively small number of corporate managers.

This kind of employee commitment cannot be achieved through a system of management *controls* but only through a system of *shared values*.

Johnson&Johnson

Cultural identity

Changing corporate culture can be a difficult task. Johnson & Johnson, the maker of consumer products like Band-Aids and Baby Shampoo, embarked on an accelerated move into sophisticated medical technologies. To push successfully into these new areas, however, J&J had to tinker with its decentralized management structure – once the model for how to avoid a bungling corporate bureaucracy.

J&J wanted swifter corporate reactions to changes in the competitive health care field and closer cooperation among its units. Those goals, however, meant a loss of autonomy for division heads and an encroachment on the long-time dominance of marketing and sales executives.

Initially, J&J lost key division executives who could not adapt to the loss of autonomy, and had difficulty switching its emphasis from marketing to research and development.

Who really has power?

If you function entirely within the outlines of your job description, operating within a standard area of activity, handling routine crises, there may be no need for you to know who has power.

But if you want to extend your sphere of influence by, say, doubling your department's staff, or getting new policy accepted and implemented, you need to find out who has command of resources. You have to know where the real power lies.

An obvious starting point is your company's organization chart: a typical chart consists of a series of functions set in boxes of the same size with neat connecting lines showing how power and authority flow downward, through departmental heads to the lowest levels.

To find out who actually has power, you need to read between the lines, checking out the links between powerful figures. No organization chart shows who generates ideas, which managers are related to each other, who play golf together, or who was recruited or trained by whom. Power rarely lies with one person; there is usually a group, linked by common experience or values.

Power may lie outside the organization chart if your company is a subsidiary or if the chief depends on outside advisers. The owners may have the whip hand; but if the number of shareholders runs into thousands, power will be diluted and will, in effect, revert to the directors.

The clever company allows itself to be driven by people who have key knowledge and/or up-to-date skills. In not-so-smart organizations the boardroom is filled with people whose power bases were built in the past. During a recession, financial control is needed at the top; when the economy is growing, it is idea people who should be holding the reins.

To get new ideas implemented, you

Find out who has the power

● What sort of ideas are going to prove easy or difficult to get accepted?
● What criteria will be used to evaluate your ideas and you?
● Is the direct approach, via your immediate superior, always going to be the best one?
● With whom can you test ideas before launching them?
● Who should you get on your side before attempting to implement your ideas? Who is likely to be against them?
● In what order should you approach the people from whom you need support?
● Who is it best to speak to personally and who prefers memos?

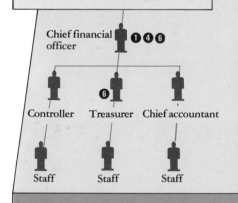

need to know who has influence or access to those with power. The chief executive officer's secretary may have little power but enormous influence. As well as knowing who makes decisions, find out who influences decision-making.

Before planting your idea, ask yourself whose opinion the boss is going to seek. An approach from the side, via someone whose views the chief executive officer respects, may be more effective than dropping a proposal directly on the boss's desk.

Holders of power and influence

Imagine you have recently arrived in the sales department, recruited by the sales director, interviewed by the sales and marketing executive. You saw the chief executive officer for five minutes before your appointment was ratified.

To operate effectively, you need to consider the realities about power and influence in the organization chart. Many of these will not become apparent, in the normal course of events, for some time.

A complex tangle of relationships and influences will emerge. You will need to study it and test it before you can begin to plan how to get your best ideas accepted and implemented.

You should also try to discuss where the tensions are. Who fails to get on with whom? Which people have mutual respect for each other? You will need to add what you know about the personalities of the key figures.

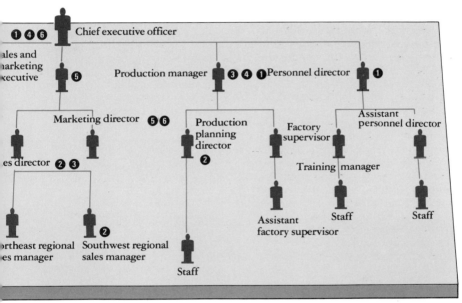

1 Social links
The chief executive officer, the chief financial officer and the personnel director's husband play golf together. The three wives socialize with the production manager's sister and are members of the same local political party.

2 Education
The sales director, production planning director and southwest regional sales manager went to school together.

3 Family ties
The sales director is married to the production manager's sister.

4 Company history
The chief executive officer, the chief financial officer and production manager have each spent more than 25 years in the company. In that time it has grown substantially and each has a 4 percent shareholding. The chief executive officer is an accountant and was formerly the chief financial officer.

5 Training
The marketing director was hired by the sales and marketing executive when the latter was marketing director.

6 Key skills
The treasurer's position is a recent creation. Cash flow questions are discussed every Monday by the chief executive officer, the chief financial officer and the marketing director. The chief executive officer's secretary usually takes notes.

27

Different departments/different tribes

No organization is simply one huge homogeneous mass of individuals who look alike and speak exactly the same language. Rather, there exists within it a number of different departments with different functions.

These "tribes" develop their own collective identities and protective mechanisms; they have their own common language, dress, culture, rituals and "watering holes."

None of this is overt. On the face of it the tribal differences are unspoken and largely unrecognized. Nevertheless they do exist and you should try to understand the make-up of different tribes and ask yourself whether your own tribe is in a healthy, productive state. Is there good communication between tribal members, with a common language evolved from working together?

Even physical location can be important. If a department is in a separate building down the street, it becomes even more isolated from the other tribal groups in the company. Isolation may mean that the tribe is removed from the center of power and is forgotten. But it can also give that tribe a sense of identity and the feeling of being an élite corps.

Knowing your organization means understanding which tribes exist, what functions they perform, which are the most powerful, the most and least efficient, which tend to get the biggest slice of the budgetary cake, and so on. You should know which tribes are central to the company's operations and which are peripheral.

You should learn what differentiates one tribe from another – in function, educational background, and language – so that you can overcome the barriers when having to deal with members of different tribes.

On a day-to-day level, you should establish contacts in other departments – people you can draw on for information or help. By trial and awareness you should ensure you know the politics of other tribes. Who is the chief? Who is waiting to become chief? Who is excluded from the inner circle? If you know the politics, you will deal with them more effectively.

Be prepared, if you want to get something done, to listen to the ritual tribal moans. It may mean that you have to massage the ego of a salesperson, reassure a production chief that you know he/she is overworked or let Finance know that you respect their painstaking approach.

Tribes make up the organization and the link between a tribe and the company's power structure can have an impact on promotion prospects. If the head of your tribe becomes head of the company, everyone in the tribe will feel more important. If no one from your tribe ever gets anywhere near the top, ask yourself why.

What Finance may think of themselves	What others may think of Finance
"We are the custodians of the company's money; we control costs and protect the profits. We are meticulous and prudent and stop the company from making costly mistakes. If Production had their way, we would have ever-more expensive machinery eating up profits; as for Sales, they would pour far too much into unprofitable advertising."	"They are routine-minded plodders who lack vision. They are far too cautious and obsessed with the business of measurement. They might be good at controlling costs, but they don't make the profits."

Tribal stereotypes

"We sell to the customers and know exactly what they want."

"The company's survival hinges on Sales."

"Those customer modifications agreed to by Sales will be impossible to implement."

What Production may think of themselves

"We are in the boiler room of the company, getting our hands dirty, making it happen. We are constantly being dictated to by Sales and Finance, who don't appreciate the problems we have, nor that the buck stops with us. We work hard, uncomplainingly, but without enough recognition. After all, we actually come up with the goods; without us there would be no business."

What others may think of Production

"They are obstructive and obstreperous; closeted away in their own self-centered world, they are ignorant of the real needs of our customers. Their myopic outlook prevents them from seeing that the company survives because of other tribes apart from theirs. They're obsessed with deadlines, schedules, raw materials, quality control and goodness knows what else!"

What Marketing may think of themselves

"We *are* the business. We look at the direction it's taking and make the decisions to steer it on course for prosperity. We have the necessary vision to cope with the ever-changing environment and plan for future success. We have to fight against the entrenched, obstructive attitudes of Finance, Sales and Production who can't see beyond today. The company's future is safe with us."

What others may think of Marketing

"They are the visionaries who are so busy looking at the stars that they don't see the pot holes ahead. They're out of touch with the day-to-day reality of the business, so busy are they planning for its future. They could do with rolling their shirt sleeves up and getting down to some honest work."

29

What are the rules?

When you join an organization, you cannot survive as a manager without knowing the rules and norms by which it operates.

To begin with you should read and follow the organization manual, if there is one. Note the physical manifestations of your company's corporate culture: use of first names, expected style of dress, executive dining-rooms, makes of company car, etc.

You need quickly to gather enough verbal and non-verbal information to know the ropes. The more you value security, the more important will be the rapid establishment of your exact role – agreed objectives, precise tasks to perform and codes of behavior.

Different organizations have different conventions and, within them, departments and employee levels have their own operating codes. Even individuals can have their own personal rules. At first, you may question the relevance of certain practices, but it may be wise to conform initially so as to be accepted by your colleagues.

Soon, you will be able to work out the norms that will apply to your department. But keep an eye on those who are in a position to promote you. If, say, you wish to be treated as an executive, think and act the part.

Once you feel in tune with your colleagues, you should try to distinguish the important rules and

Sophia Collier, co-founder of American Natural Beverage Corporation of Brooklyn, N. Y., was determined to create a beverage without artificial ingredients. She experimented in her kitchen with mixtures of sparkling water and natural fruit extracts, and began marketing a bubbly fruit punch in 1978.

The product has since been copied by major beverage companies and national sales of natural sodas are expected to reach $200 million by 1990. Collier flouted the maxim that natural foods have a limited market.

Richard Branson, ruler of the Virgin record and entertainment network, and the airline of the same name, has a reputation for being unconventional. His style is unorthodox, his image flamboyant.

When he founded the Virgin Group, Richard Branson set four rules and stuck to them.

First he kept overheads low. Second he encouraged entrepreneurship. His third rule was to buy, not make. Virgin's pervasive, youthful style obeys the fourth rule: don't stray from your core market.

Decide which rules can safely be
ignored, circumvented or deliberately
broken.

norms from the insignificant.

Be sure you know which rules are considered so important that breaking them would get you into real trouble. Many companies, for example, are fairly relaxed about checking employees' expenses but, in others, irregularities in claims may get you fired.

In some organizations, such as banks, you will not go far unless you are prepared to follow the rules, both official and unofficial. In others, there will be a better chance of succeeding if you break the rules ... carefully.

In all organizations, there are times when more damage is done by slavishly adhering to the rule book than by disregarding its contents.

Breaking the rules

If you plan to break an important rule, weigh the risks and seek approval or protection from influential people. Ask yourself:

● Will flouting convention cause disapproval among those in a position to promote you?

● Will non-conformity draw attention to your innovative qualities?

● Will breaking the rules be interpreted as rebellion or creativity?

● Will breaking the rules bring trouble from your subordinates?

● Could you increase your influence by setting personal norms and expecting others to conform?

Janice La Rouche, career counselor and author of *Strategies for Women at Work*, believes that success for women in the business world depends on playing the corporate game the way men do.

She became convinced that women must take control of their careers and be completely self-sufficient, by acquiring the crucial attributes of leadership and self-confidence.

Instead of taking the apparent rules literally, she advises women to grasp the principles by which work structures really operate.

Donald C. Burr, founder of People Express Airlines, has made a career out of breaking rules. He seized on airline deregulation in the late 1970s to create an airline from scratch. He then astounded the industry by viewing travel as a commodity business and offered no-frills, low-priced, air travel. His profits came through volume.

Burr offers big stock options and profit-sharing as an incentive to all employees and expects them all to take turns in doing low-status jobs, such as baggage handling.

The winning team

If you are building a career in a company, you want to be associated with success. Winners will often be working for the team whose function is critical to the company's success. Winning teams have strong, visible leadership.

Look carefully at the departments in your organization. Work out which function is dominant.

Don't be misled by fashions in organizational thinking. A company may decide that better marketing is the key to success. The marketing department is expanded, budgets increased, and promotion prospects enhanced. Meanwhile, in purchasing, the staff is unable to get authorization for the new typewriter it needs. But fashions come and go. Don't commit yourself to a department without questioning whether or not it is a long-term winner.

Star billing, like fashion, has nothing to do with efficiency, or with justice. A department that is doing its job well and making no demands on top management may be taken for granted. A less efficient department which is good at selling itself to top management may get both kudos and a bigger budget. If it is also coming up with good creative ideas, it may deserve its privileges.

Success may lie with the department that is on the rise rather than the one at the top which is about to peak. What would happen if it lost its leader? A declining department may offer better opportunities if it has a potentially important contribution to make to the business. An effective leader may be able to build it up to become a winner.

Above all, it is department leaders who set the style. The best leaders marshal the functional expertise without losing sight of the corporate mission. They make winners of all they lead. To win, you need to be a good leader, or to work for one.

How to be in the right place at the right time

Consider which functions/departments in your organization:
- Are growing and which are declining in importance.
- Have been set up recently.
- Have the easiest time getting their budgets approved.
- Provide top people.

Ask yourself:
- Is this emphasis right for the company?
- Is it in line with its critical success factors?
- Will it take the company into the future?

Then ask yourself:
- Do you have the key skills/knowledge the organization needs?
- Am I able to use them as a manager in a department that is, or should be, growing in importance?
- If so, get your act right and build your department into a winner.

To create a winning team:
- Recruit employees of high caliber. (But remember that moderate people can perform miracles if correctly led – and conversely a collection of stars is not necessarily a team.)
- Generate enthusiasm so that they believe in themselves.
- Believe in yourself and your people.
- Use your management skills to build a team where individuals work for one another.
- Establish high standards.
- Make sure that your department delivers what it promises and does not welch on commitments.
- Avoid empty publicity which is not backed by solid achievement.
- Take time to have your group's successes known and talked about throughout the organization.
- Build relationships with influential people.

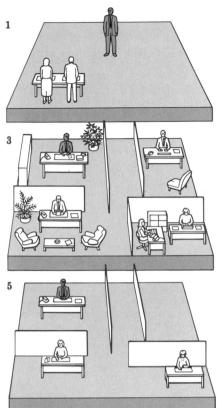

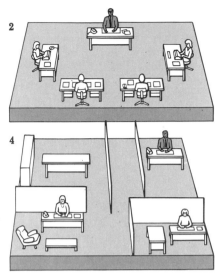

The rise and fall of a department

Consider the following scenario. Use this example to test whether your department is rising or falling.

1 The data processing (DP) department of a large organization had sunk to an all-time low: it lacked strong leadership, there was a high turnover of staff and morale was rock-bottom. But then the chief of the department left, and his successor, a dynamic, inspirational type, breathed new life into it. Its bad reputation was arrested, and it began to recruit high-caliber graduates attracted by the leader's vision.

2 The department's efficiency improved dramatically. Optimism pervaded the air. On the strength of its results, it managed to secure better offices, budgets, equipment and recruits of an even higher standard.

3 DP then became *the* department of the organization. The leader was the golden boy of the company and the envy of others. DP now had the plushest premises, the best recruits and a sizable budget. But then, with his department on the crest of a wave, the leader decided to leave the company.

4 The new head of DP was competent but unable to match his predecessor. Earlier achievements could not be duplicated and top management became less well disposed. Budgets were reduced, staff began to leave and recruits were no longer high-caliber.

5 DP had sunk back to mediocrity. It was becoming stagnant and moribund. There was no sense of tribal identity. The few remaining long-serving staff romanticized about the "good old days."

The heart of the business

The best organizations have a clear view of what makes for success. Excellent organizations make sure that their critical success factors are understood by all employees.

But accurate identification is not easy and it is common to find survival confused with success. Without looking after its survival factors, a company could be left on the rocks. Without concentrating on its critical success factors, it will not *win*.

Reducing the myriad activities of your organization to a few essential operations is an excellent way to get to the heart of a company and find its driving force.

The activities that contribute to big profits or big losses point to critical success factors. All companies – whether large and complicated like oil companies or small and apparently simple like a grocer's shop – have a heart. Everything else is a sideshow.

For the Mobil Oil Company success depends on finding the right holes in the ground and owning them. Mobil's ability to refine the oil, though essential, is not critical to its success.

Critical success factors lie somewhere in what Michael Porter in *Competitive Advantage* defines as the "value chain" – research/design, development, production, marketing/sales and distribution. Emphasis on success in one or more of these five areas enables a company to create and sustain an advantage over its competitors.

If big profits depend on consumer awareness, critical success lies in the marketing/sales section of the value chain. The quality of the product may determine survival, but for the manufacturer of cola drinks or beer, success depends on reaching the parts other advertisers have not reached.

Successful companies keep in touch with the fundamentals of their business and concentrate on promoting and developing existing strengths. They diversify only when all other options have been exhausted.

Even with the emphasis still on the same section of the value chain, companies can run into trouble if they have failed to recognize their particular critical success factor.

When Quaker Oats extended its well-established sales and marketing strategy to include toys and restaurants as well as foods, their original products lost their market dominance.

The collapse of large companies can often be blamed on innovation that drains their life blood without regard for the heart of the business.

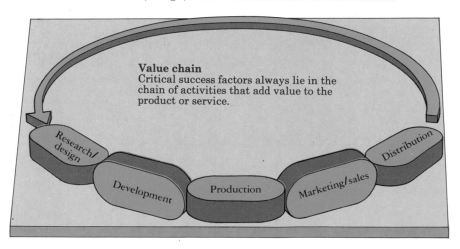

Value chain
Critical success factors always lie in the chain of activities that add value to the product or service.

Research/design

Development

Production

Marketing/sales

Distribution

Before it merged with General Electric Company in late 1985, RCA, in the early 1980s, was plagued by mounting debt and shaky earnings. It embarked on a divestment program and sold businesses that did not contribute to its core strategy or ones it did not have the expertise to manage. That included a $1·5 billion sale of CIT Financial Corporation to Manufacturers Hanover Trust Company and a $587 million sale of Hertz Corporation, its rental car subsidiary. Afterward RCA became a straightforward electronics and broadcasting company – just like the old Radio Corporation of America was before it set out to diversify nearly two decades before.

From the mid-sixties through the late seventies, the car industry was largely in stasis. Technology was not moving, the markets were unchanged. The race would be won by the organization making the product for the least money. During this period, the rise to prominence of the finance function at Ford Motor Company was the evidence of this critical success factor and gave rise to company sayings such as, "We don't make cars, we make money." But the game is changing rapidly in the eighties: fuel economy and concern for environmental pollution have pushed auto makers into computer management of the car's power unit, with a consequent shift of critical success factors away from production cost into research.

Sears, Roebuck and Co retained their critical success factor in the distribution section of the "value chain" by adapting to changing circumstances. They did so with such resounding success that it took them right through two world wars and the Depression. Until the mid-1920s success was based on providing quality goods by mail order to the isolated American farmer. "Satisfaction guaranteed or your money back" remained critical to success. But the change in markets brought about by the automobile made the company switch the emphasis from distribution by mail order to retail stores in cities. Thus, Sears served the motorized farmer as well as the city dweller with limited purchasing power.

Adapting to survive

Your organization's critical success factor may be different next year and then again the year after. Markets and environments do not stand still, and critical success factors must work toward a future goal.

A company's ability to adapt to change is the key to its long-term success. Strength in the marketplace is of direct concern to someone who is looking to build a career in a particular organization.

If a company is to be consistently successful in adapting to new circumstances, its power structure has to be in tune with the realities of a changing marketplace, a changing world economy and shifts in society.

Is your organization recruiting high-caliber young people with leadership potential? Are those in charge of your organization clinging to outmoded themes?

Is your organization's future policy based on fashion, which starts in the center, moves outward and dies? Or is it in tune with trends that start at grassroots level and grow?

Some organizations are flexible enough to respond to new circumstances. Others are too short-sighted or too cumbersome to adapt to change.

The Minnesota Mining & Manufacturing Company makes 45,000 different products, among them the highly profitable Post-it™ note pads. The secret of success lies in 3M's ability to nurture creativity: change is an essential part of the company's corporate philosophy. National Cash Register left it almost too late to adapt to the electronic age of computerized calculating machines. The once-great retailer, W. T. Grant & Company confused customers by trying to adapt to too many consumer trends and is now extinct.

Does your organization shrink from the prospect of change? Or does it embrace change as a means of gaining competitive advantage?

Signs of an organization heading for problems

- Diminishing market share.
- Low profit margins together with low volume.
- Aging products.
- Consistent dissatisfaction of customers.
- Quality/reliability problems.
- Consistently late deliveries.
- Heavy dependence on one or two customers/suppliers.
- Long-term fixed-price contracts.
- Heavy borrowing requirement.
- Production methods which are old-fashioned.
- Poor industrial relations.
- High turnover of employees.
- Management out of tune with commercial realities.
- Top-heavy organization.
- Inflexible management.
- Lack of communication between management and employees.
- Inward-looking management.

Signs of a forward-looking company

- Awareness of competition.
- High investment in research and development.
- Regular flow of new products.
- Careful use of consumer research and test marketing.
- Rapid response to complaints of customers.
- Dedication to the quality the customer wants.
- Concern for customer service.
- Pricing that is appropriate to the customer.
- Enthusiastic employees.
- Accessible management.
- Flexible organization.
- Decentralized decision-making.
- Concentration on critical success factors.
- Supportive financial controls.

No business is more competitive and more subject to change than the computer industry, and few companies have been quicker on their feet than Apple, whose founders spotted a new market and exploited it before anyone else. Their 8-bit personal computer, the Apple II, was a tremendous success. When IBM came along with its 16-bit personal computer the company's huge resources and business customers posed a serious threat to Apple's survival. In 1985, Apple looked like succeeding with the user-friendly Macintosh, along with "Jazz", the integrated business software package.

Traditional shipbuilding industries in the developed countries of Europe and America have been squeezed out of business by world labor forces. The need for developing countries with largely unskilled labor forces to employ large numbers of people led their governments to support such heavy industries by subsidizing them. The more forward-looking Western shipbuilders saw that a market remained for specialist ships and for sophisticated engineering components such as automated steering systems. Their ability to adapt to changing world trends ensured their survival.

In 1950, Britain made 80 per cent of the world's motorcycles. Now it makes less than one per cent. Even Triumph, which lingered on as a workers' cooperative, finally succumbed, although, by 1984, the famous name was revived by the UK company, Racing Spares. Triumph was badly hit by inefficient and old-fashioned production methods, poor marketing and product development and, of course, Japanese competition. The Japanese modernized the motorcycle and produced it cheaply and to a high standard.

National Intergroup, like many other American integrated steel companies, had fallen on hard times because it could not compete against low-priced Japanese imports. Under the leadership of Howard M. Love, the company closed much of its steel-making operations and teamed up with the Japanese to revitalize the remainder. More importantly, the Pittsburgh-based company embarked on a radical diversification plan and branched out into financial services and aluminum.

Making the right choice

Choosing the organization that is right for you is never easy. To be sure what life inside any organization is like is impossible without actually being part of it for some time. Even if you get the answer right initially, situations can change. The loss of a major customer, a takeover, financial difficulties or the departure of your immediate boss can bring dramatic and often unexpected change.

Once inside and working hard there is still no guarantee that success is yours. The social maelstrom of business (often as complex and uncompromising as family relationships) can cause frustration and failure.

Factors which ought not, perhaps,

Its public image
- Are you comfortable with the face your organization presents to the world?
- Does the advertising and other literature give an accurate picture?
- Do you feel your organization earns its reputation? If not, can you see why?
- Is it reflecting where the organization is going?

Size and shape
- Does the size of your organization suit the point you are at in your career?
- Is it providing you with the right experience?
- Are you a big fish in a small pond? If so, is that the way you want to stay?
- Is it time to seek a different organization and another range of issues?
- Can you quantify clearly what you have learned in this organization in the last 12 months?
- Are your particular talents being exploited?
- Is the organization run from the center or do you have local autonomy for important decisions?
- Is it growing or in decline?
- Is it characterized by leanness, efficiency and profitability or is it bureaucratic and hampered by its own systems?

Culture
- Can you believe in what your company is doing or making?
- Is it positive or negative, backward-facing or forward-looking?
- What behavior patterns are valued? Loyalty, respect for authority, conforming? Diligence, meeting deadlines, holding within budget? Generating new ideas? Questioning the status quo? Seeking new directions?
- Is this operating atmosphere appropriate to the market?
- Is it one into which you can fit?
- Are your values in tune with those espoused by the organization?
- What is the reaction of your spouse/friends to your definition of this culture?

Power structure
- Do you know who has real power? Do the holders of power know you? If not, are they likely to in the foreseeable future?
- Can you point to those who have influence but may not have power?
- Do *all* the most senior figures actually have power?
- Could you draw the unofficial links (family, education, social, etc) on the organization chart?
- Do you have access to enough influence or power to do your job effectively?
- What are the backgrounds of the top management group?
- Do you respect them?
- Are the skills, knowledge and/or contacts of those in power relevant to today's business ... and how about tomorrow's?

to be a part of a respectable commercial organization are often, in reality, the essential factors in individual and corporate success and failure. Envy, spite, greed, cunning may all have to be countered! Enthusiasm, energy, determination, skill, competence, conscientiousness will have to be generated.

And yet, once the cultural and tribal issues are recognized, when you sort out how to handle the rules, deal with power, concentrate on basic business transactions, management becomes much easier.

Coming to grips with these issues will involve your answering regularly the following types of questions:

Tribal features
● Can you recognize the tribes (groups or cliques) and their features (language, dress, rituals, etc.) that exist in the organization?
● Which are the most powerful tribes in the organization at the moment?
● Which are the tribal features that make your department stand out?
● Do you have a clear view of your own department's contribution to the organization? Is it important to the core of the business, necessary or just nice?
● Is your department consulted first on new ideas? If not, should it be?

Rules
● Does your organization have a rule book? Is there any indication that it is a working document or merely a rarely consulted reference book?
● What are the unwritten rules and operating codes?
● Do you know what the important rules are and can you justify them in the light of the critical success factors of the business?
● To whom would you look for cover and support if you needed to break them?

Winners
● Can you identify the leaders of winning teams in your organization?
● Is yours a winning department, full of enthusiasts? Is their enthusiasm directed at profitable activities?
● Could they survive losing the person who leads them?
● Does it suit you to be one of the winning pack?
● If your team is less valued than others, how could it be improved?
● Would you know how to create a winning team if you were given a chance?

The heart
● Can you define what makes your organization tick?
● Do you know *what* makes its profit?
● Do you know *who* makes its profit?
● Can you describe your organization's critical success factors?
● If you don't know your organization's critical success factors, how can you find out? Is it possible that no attempt has been made to define them?
● Is there any opportunity for you to take the lead in getting them defined?

The future
● Is your organization responsive to change?
● Where do you fit into tomorrow's organization?
● What significant changes are on the horizon? Define them under "environmental influences," "legal changes," "sociological conditions," "political influences," "technological advances."
● Are the people your organization recruits now going to become chief executive officers in the 21st century?
● Have you prepared a list of those signs that may indicate that your organization is well equipped for the future? Or on its way into trouble?

What is a business?

The enterprise in which you operate as a manager is unique. Nevertheless, every corporation, foundation, government department, even a small business, has a number of common features.

An organization comes into being and continues to function as a result of internal and external influences.

It must have objectives, explicit or implicit. These can range from maximization of return on investment to provision of a service to the community.

There must be owners. These may range from shareholders to the electorate who vote in a government. The owners provide the initial funding for the organization, which can then attract or generate additional funding.

The owners always have the right to influence the organization's objectives and its direction. (Even a tax-payer has the right to vote for a change in the direction of a democratically elected government.)

To operate effectively, the organization also needs a management control structure, usually of hierarchical form. Even in the apparently equal partnerships of some financial institutions, there is usually a structure of command and a system of ranking hidden from public view. Organizations always contain people who lead and those who are led.

With funding and a management structure, the organization can operate and put its objectives into effect. Operations, whether the manufacture and production of goods and materials or the provision of services or financial resources, are usually carried out by a team of people. They are responsible through the management structure to the owners. The responsibility

	Corporation (public/private)	Public utility
Objective	To make profit by providing goods or services	To provide service to the public at a profit
Owners	Public shareholders or private owners	Government unit or private shareholders
Control structure	Board of directors elected by shareholders	Board of directors
Operations	Chairman, chief executive, managers	Chairman, chief executive
Prime activities	Manufacture of product or provision of services	Provision of service
Business emphasis	Maximization of profit, return on investment	To provide a reliable service at a fair profit

for the day-to-day operations is therefore nearly always delegated to the executive management.

The operations of any organization are influenced by two further common factors: the organization's prime activities and the stress placed on certain business functions (e.g. selling, quality control, recruitment, purchasing).

Prime activities are the achievement of the owners' objectives and are as varied as the organizations themselves. In every organization, however, these core activities form the mainstream of the business and the reason for being in business.

Although operational management may have some degree of flexibility in developing the growth and direction of these activities, they nevertheless remain the essential function of the organization until such time as the owners change their objectives.

The amount of emphasis placed on individual functions, however, can be influenced by the management structure. There are always a number of routes or strategies by which the objectives of the organization can be achieved. The ability to direct the way in which a business develops is one of the prime motivational factors for executive managers.

Where there are different degrees of success in achieving the organization's objectives, this can often be attributed to the abilities of the individuals within the management structure to direct the emphasis and thrust of the business to achieve the best results.

Within any organization, which is set up to manage a business, these elements are always apparent to a greater or lesser degree.

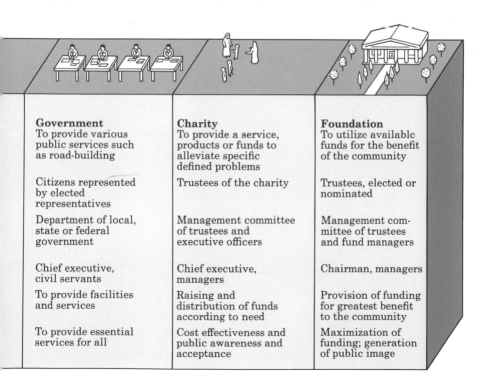

Government	Charity	Foundation
To provide various public services such as road-building	To provide a service, products or funds to alleviate specific defined problems	To utilize available funds for the benefit of the community
Citizens represented by elected representatives	Trustees of the charity	Trustees, elected or nominated
Department of local, state or federal government	Management committee of trustees and executive officers	Management committee of trustees and fund managers
Chief executive, civil servants	Chief executive, managers	Chairman, managers
To provide facilities and services	Raising and distribution of funds according to need	Provision of funding for greatest benefit to the community
To provide essential services for all	Cost effectiveness and public awareness and acceptance	Maximization of funding; generation of public image

The anatomy of a business

A business is an enterprise created for the purpose of trading for profit and other assets it generates. Essentially it consists of groups of people joining together for the common purpose of achieving a reward in return for contributing money and skill to the enterprise.

The groups of people are owners and employees. Trading activity consists of three core functions:
● Buying: the acquisition of materials and resources for use in the business.
● Making: changing the state of the materials and resources (i.e. adding value).
● Selling: the disposal of the materials and enhanced resources.

Subsidiary activities within the business include:
● Management, which provides direction for the business and its parts.
● Control, including planning, scheduling, monitoring results and reporting.
● Administration, which provides the functions and systems supporting the organization and all communications between the constituent parts.

The success of the enterprise is defined by the profit it generates (or sales income less the cost of achieving it). The quality of success is measured by comparing the ability of the enterprise to generate profit with the performance of other enterprises in similar industries.

The markets
Each business coexists with its competitors in four marketplaces:
● The customer market in which customers and potential customers exist.
● The ownership market, in which investors buy and sell shares based on their judgment of a company's future profitability.

Businesses exist in a complex of markets consisting of the people and organizations with whom a business interacts, within an environment (*outer ring*) containing organizations, factors and attitudes which affect the markets.

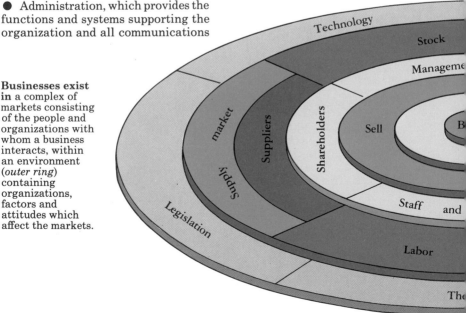

● The supply market, where physical assets may be obtained including loan capital, fixed assets, supplies and consumables.
● The labor market, which supplies workers.

The environment
The markets exist within an environment which contains thousands of companies. Most do not compete directly with your company, but they affect your operation because they influence:
● The economy
● Legislation
● Technology
● Ecology/pollution
● Public attitudes toward business

The business organism

A business is a living entity. Its anatomy and physiology can be described in terms of:
● The heart: buying, making and selling are the heart of a business. Heart failure, from lack of management blood or the collapse of individual functions, causes death.
● Blood supply: management is the life blood of a business, carrying life-giving oxygen (ideas of direction).
● The skeleton: businesses are vertebrates. Their structure is defined by organization. As the business grows, its skeleton should change in shape as well as in size.
● The nervous system: communication is carried out by the nervous system. The brain issues instructions, plans all schedules. The nerves detect variations of behavior, measuring them and reporting back to the brain, which analyzes the signals, modifies them and issues revised instructions.
● Behavior: businesses are social animals whose behavior ranges from contributory to predatory.

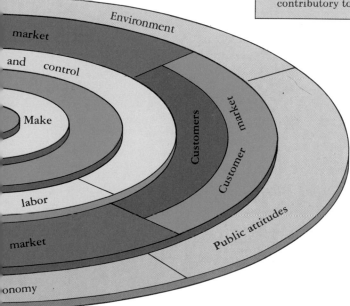

The structure of a business

In order to achieve its objectives, every organization must continually keep in balance the external and internal forces that affect it.

Most organizations carry out this balancing process by means of some form of management committee, or board of directors, coordinated by a chief executive.

Depending on the type of organization, the board may be two-tiered, i.e. having a policy-making body made up mainly of outsiders elected by shareholders and a second operating committee made up of top company executives.

This combination of non-executive and executive officers provides the mechanism by which the external and internal forces are balanced at the highest level within the organization.

The board or committee then provides the policy guidance and directional control for the organization's operating management.

The operating management is responsible for the day-to-day running of the business, usually through a hierarchical structure of subordinate managers down to foremen and supervisors.

These managers are then organized divisionally and by departmental disciplines but cannot function independently in a vacuum.

In consequence, in almost every organization there are also a number of key sub-committees which, collectively, are responsible for the overall coordination of medium- and short-term strategies.

The ever-constant interplay between the separate functions, particularly in the transfer of data and information, allows the organization to function cohesively.

Although no two organizations are identical and their objectives and business emphasis may widely differ, each will nevertheless function in this same way.

The functions of a typical organization

The central framework of a typical business (*right*) is affected by external and internal forces.

External forces include:
Shareholders: private individuals purchase a share of business equity with the expectation of a share of distributed profits.

Financial institutions invest funds in the business to create more wealth.

Banks: these provide cash funding for the operation of the business, based on agreed security, to generate wealth from interest levied.

Legislation: including corporation and trade union law, environmental and other national statutory legislation. It dictates the framework in which the operations of the organization can be conducted.

Auditors: independent accountants elected by the shareholders to verify the accuracy of corporate financial information and performance and compliance with statutory or regulatory financial requirements.

Internal forces include:
Operating committees: comprising nominees from the board of directors and senior management. Responsible for formulation of policy and directional control for activities such as:
● Product policy
● Finance and treasury
● Corporate strategy
● Human resources
● Quality

Division heads: heads of divisions responsible for direction and performance against objectives and budgets for areas such as:
● Finance
● Sales
● Production
● Product development
● Information systems

Managers: executives contracted by the organization to coordinate, manage or provide specialist skills. Operate within specific parameters laid down by the board and division heads. Control day-to-day operations and management of staff and labor.

44

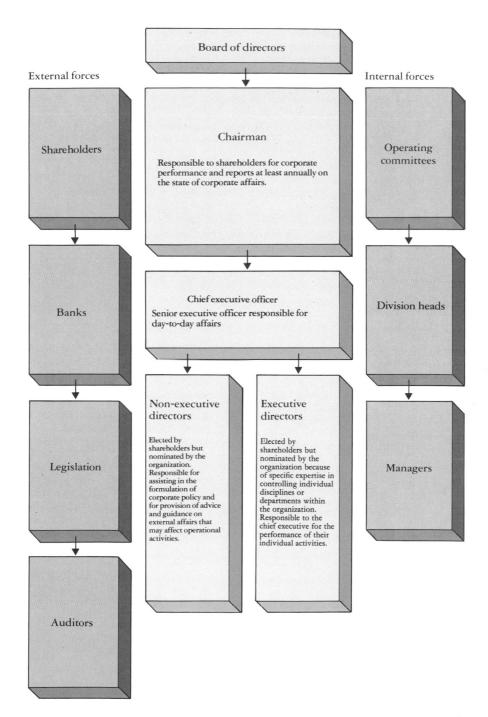

Board of directors

External forces

Internal forces

Shareholders

Chairman

Responsible to shareholders for corporate performance and reports at least annually on the state of corporate affairs.

Operating committees

Banks

Chief executive officer

Senior executive officer responsible for day-to-day affairs

Division heads

Legislation

Non-executive directors

Elected by shareholders but nominated by the organization. Responsible for assisting in the formulation of corporate policy and for provision of advice and guidance on external affairs that may affect operational activities.

Executive directors

Elected by shareholders but nominated by the organization because of specific expertise in controlling individual disciplines or departments within the organization. Responsible to the chief executive for the performance of their individual activities.

Managers

Auditors

Planning future directions

Strategy was originally a term applied to warfare; it was defined as "the art of planning and directing larger military movements and the operations of war." In business, strategic management is now accepted as the discipline of managing any organization's resources to achieve long-term objectives.

The origins of strategic business management are to be found in the long-range planning used in the fifties and sixties when markets were expanding and company policy was based on a belief in growth.

The stagnation of the early seventies highlighted the growing awareness that the then available planning techniques were inadequate to deal with business problems.

The new concept was that the fundamental strength of a company could be related to the development of strategic success potentials.

Strategic success potentials

A company's potential for strategic success may depend on those company objectives which are expected to result in above average long-term profits. They are generally related to products and markets and are commonly perceived as high product quality and service standards, favorable public image, low production costs or distribution advantages.

Traditionally, success potentials are identified from analysis of:
● The company's characteristics compared with its competition.
● The competitive environment and the potential for success that it offers.

More recently, it has become accepted that there are two further key attributes:
● Flexibility, or the potential for changing strategy on short notice in a rapidly changing environment.

The development of a strategic success position (SSP)

Defined by Professor C. Pümpin, one of Europe's leading exponents on strategic management, this has three stages:

Information analysis
● Establishing the project team and introducing the SSP concept.
● Collection and interpretation of the basic corporate data, internal and external.
● Determination and assessment of the current corporate strategy.
● Identification of key problems concerning strategy.
● First draft of possible SSPs.
● Determination of measures to be taken immediately.

Developing a strategy
● Reinforcement of the basic data by means of detailed analysis of the company; analysis of the environment, the market, competitors, customers, and of other relevant aspects.

● Development/definition of SSPs.
● Elaboration of basic strategy.
● Determination and ordering of SSP-oriented measures to be taken immediately.

Implementing the strategy
Specific activities and employees must be geared to the plan by:
● Definition and specification of SSPs for each section or department and each employee.
● Deducing the capabilities to be developed.
● Development of plans of action for each branch and each employee.
● SSP-oriented time management.
● Allocating company resources to the SSPs.
● Launching and supervising SSP-projects.
● Adjusting the company's organizational structures and management systems to the SSPs.
● Monitoring the SSPs.

● Implementability, or the compatibility of the strategy with a corporate culture.

Strategic phases

The strategy of an organization has a life cycle: a dormant phase, and a development phase. Because long-term issues are often neglected or minor adjustments are made to strategy after periodic reviews, organizations spend most of their time in the dormant phase.

From time to time, however, organizations recognize that they have a need for a fundamental reappraisal of where the business is going. Upon recognizing the need for fundamental change, management then embarks on the development of a strategic success position (SSP).

Strategic planning

Strategic planning should include:
● Setting objectives, or redefining what "success" should mean to the organization.
● Information analysis or reviewing the characteristics of the organization and the environment to link internal strengths to external opportunities.
● Strategic choice, or making decisions on the direction of the company and formulating a plan.

Implementation of strategy

The most important aspect of strategic management is the organization and control of implementing the business plan. The "best" technical plan will not succeed unless it is appropriate to the culture of the organization. Failure to communicate the strategy will mean that there is little chance of operational managers recognizing the direction of the company and making appropriate decisions. The priorities of the company should be demonstrated to operational managers.

The strategic cycle

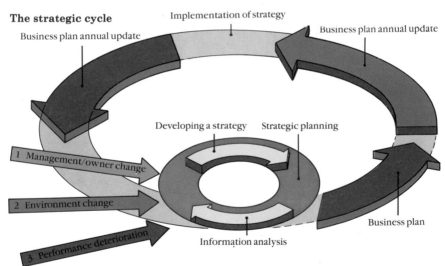

Implementation of strategy

Business plan annual update

Business plan annual update

1 Management/owner change

2 Environment change

3 Performance deterioration

Developing a strategy   Strategic planning

Information analysis

Business plan

The strategic changes normally occur because:
1 The aspirations and requirements of the owners and managers have changed (or the individuals themselves have changed).
2 The environment has changed:
● Market opportunity has increased or decreased.
● Technology offers increased opportunities or threats.
● Economy has improved or declined or led to a modified distribution of wealth.
● The social and legislative background has altered.
3 The present plan is failing to meet its objectives because of competitive activity or poor performance.

Analyzing your position

Strategic analysis is best carried out by the organization's own management in conjunction with external consultants. Management must be involved if it is to believe the output of the analysis and provide detailed knowledge of the organization.

Consultants provide the special analytical skills and an independent view to ensure management does not believe its own propaganda.

Strategic planning

All strategic planning first involves setting objectives and matching the organization's strengths with opportunities that arise. It then has to take into account strategic analysis and strategic choice.

Strategic analysis means measuring the organization's strengths and weaknesses and the opportunities and threats presented by the environment. Strategic choice involves the development of an operating plan encompassing all functions and disciplines within the organization reflecting the strategic choice.

SWOT

The SWOT (strengths, weaknesses, opportunities, threats) approach to strategic analysis forces management to analyze every aspect of the operation so that objectives can be assessed as attainable and a strategic plan adopted to achieve them.

All organizations have strengths and weaknesses. The best way to identify them is to have groups of senior managers brainstorm. Once the key factors have been subjectively identified, detailed objective analysis is required.

Organizations tend to be either too optimistic or pessimistic and this is usually reflected in managers' perceptions of their own companies. Some companies have a tendency to believe their own propaganda, whereas others often see only their own faults.

External events are regarded as an opportunity or a threat depending on

---

Your organization's strategy

● What are the objectives of your company? Are they primarily related to health or wealth?
● What rates of growth and return on investment are expected from the company? From your department?
● Which markets are expected to provide growth?
● Which products are expected to provide growth?
● Where is research and development being concentrated?
● If you don't know, or you are not in a growth area, *what are you going to do about it?*

By comparing words and actions, the perceptive manager can work out the organization's strategy. Ask yourself:
● Is your company telling you what you need to know to make the right decisions?
● Do the words and the actions match?
● If the words and actions do not match, were the right decisions made?

---

the organization's ability to exploit them. A progressive company welcomes technological change but a conservative one will feel at risk.

Secret strategy

Failure to implement strategies may be due to poor communication, because the strategy has not been fully developed. However, care should be taken that such failure has not been caused by confusion between the organization's two strategies: one public, the other secret, intended for senior directors only.

There is nothing wrong in having a secret strategy. In fact it is often essential when dealing with acquisitions, managers and competitive positioning. But once action is taken, you should explain its relevance to the overall strategy.

Strategic analysis: what management consultants can contribute

Consultants can help management identify and gather the information needed for successful strategic analysis. Their objective views are particularly helpful when attempting to interpret it as the basis for longer-term direction setting. You should work closely with them on:
- Validation of findings
- Description of internal processes and capacities
- Review of management skills
- Quantitative market research
- Competitive analysis
- Review of technological innovation
- Organization review
- Survey of customer opinions and attitudes
- Validation of all management claims
- Preparing comparisons of managers' reports

SWOT, the acronym of strengths, weaknesses, opportunities and threats, is a summing up of the factors affecting strategic analysis.

Strengths represent the basis on which success can be built.

Analysis may reveal weaknesses, such as obsolete machinery, which can be remedied if financial resources are strong.

Opportunities should be sought, recognized and exploited as they arise.

Threats must be acknowledged and steps taken to deal with them.

SWOT Evaluation

Internal – strengths and weaknesses

People	– skills, training, attitude
Organization	– structure and relationships
Systems/ Communications	– formal/informal, manual, computer and telecommunication
Products	– quality, life, cost
Production	– nature, capacity, quality
Finance	– balance sheet, profit and loss account, cash flow
Credentials	– reputation, track record, customer perception
Knowledge	– technical, market, competition

External – opportunities and threats

Market	– growth, decline, movement, fashion
Technology	– product development, substitution, production technology
Economy	– export/import climate, dollar strength
Society	– sales, employment, trade union practices
Legislation	– pollution, consumer protection, product liability tax
Ecology	– energy, raw materials, recycling, environmental protection

Essential features

The successful management of any large enterprise, be it the construction of the pyramids or the running of one of today's giant multinational conglomerates, depends on the development of a soundly based structure and the application of clear organizational principles.

Business management has become increasingly complex with a bewildering choice of products, some highly specialized production processes and sophisticated marketing practices. Facilities and operations are progressively more capital intensive, financial structures and funding more complex, and government interference more extensive.

The pressure on the workforce has increased as business has become more exacting. Organizations of all types are now effectively part of a global market with its attendant currency and trading complications.

In today's commercial environment, organization, and its related principles, is therefore more important than ever.

While most business managers accept that effective organization is crucial to business success, opinions differ as to the exact nature and significance of organization.

Obviously, a basic objective of most business enterprises is to survive in a competitive market. The ability to do so can be measured in terms of profit growth and return on capital.

Individual companies have their own particular targets concerning the types of goods or services produced, the degree of diversification of products and the market sector in which to operate; but all are directed toward survival.

Attaining this objective depends on the coordination of the main elements of a business operation: people, capital, facilities and information.

In addition, an organization's structure fulfills secondary but important requirements: it must be low cost and economical; it should be as simple as possible; and it should permit the development and testing of managers of the future.

The essential features of a structured organization

In every complex environment, good organization:
- Forms a "route map" through which the affairs of the enterprise can be planned, directed and controlled.
- Highlights and isolates key activities that need resources and control.
- Provides for orderliness in human affairs, which otherwise would almost certainly degenerate into confusion.
- Enables each member of the organization to understand his or her role, duties and relationships.
- Helps to eliminate both duplication of effort and unnecessary activity.
- Provides a practical means for the allocation and control of costs, budgets and human resources.
- Permits the objective measurement of results in terms of achievement of goals, profit, and other agreed criteria.
- Facilitates the communication of data and instructions to the people required to take action.
- Provides identity and a sense of belonging to a group that has a common objective, and thus supports the members' morale.
- Speeds up the response of the business to external events or pressures in its environment, such as new competitive products, price changes or labor shortages.

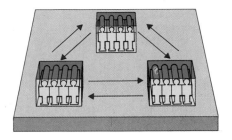

Reach of management

It is generally accepted that the maximum numbers of subordinates who can be adequately supervised by one manager is in the region of 8 to 10. The number of direct relationships and subrelationships created by numbers beyond this level means that it is usually necessary to create additional layers of management to control them effectively. The Roman army recognized this need by organizing itself into cohorts (ten soldiers) and such principles are still valid in modern business.

The number of departmental functions that can be effectively controlled by one manager is also limited. Working groups should be manageable, economic and of optimal size.

As the number of subordinates increases, so does the number of relationships that have to be handled. The resulting complexity of relationships should be taken into account when determining the optimal reach of management, as should the following factors:
● Degree of interaction between the unit or personnel being supervised.
● Extent to which the manager or supervisor carries out nonmanagerial work.
● Similarity or dissimilarity of the activities being controlled.
● Degree of delegation which is possible considering the abilities of those people being managed and the complexity of the work.
● Incidence of new problems.
● Extent of standardization procedures.
● Degree of physical dispersion of the activities to be controlled.

The application of organizational principles

An organization's leaders should seek clarity and simplicity. In doing so, the following key principles should obtain.
1 The grouping of activities
● Separate organizational components should be established only when they comprise logically separable functions.
● Separate functions should as far as possible work toward a common objective or leading function.
● Each individual in the organization must be accountable to only one superior.
● The optimal reach of management should be determined.
2 Authority and responsibility
● Responsibility should be defined

clearly and assigned to one person.
● Responsibility should be matched with the appropriate authority.
● The number of levels of authority should be kept as low as possible.
● Clear lines of authority and accountability must run from the highest to the lowest levels.
3 Working relationships
● Working relationships must be clear and logical.
● Reporting relationships should be consistent with the nature of the responsibilities exercised.
● Higher authority must be held fully accountable for the acts and duties of its subordinates.
● An organization should provide for the development of leaders.

51

Growth and development

Every enterprise is unique. It comprises individuals directed toward survival and success in a given market or environment, within defined locations and resource constraints, and growing from a variety of origins.

However, there are typical organizational traits in all enterprises. These are expressed either singly or in combination.

The elements influencing organization growth and structure affect authority patterns and styles of operation.

Origin and foundation

A partnership established by two or more individuals requires collective decision-making. This is typical of, say, professional firms of lawyers, accountants and architects. Rapid decision-making on commercial issues may not be easy to achieve.

In a company established and developed by one strong individual, as in a family firm, his or her influence is likely to remain pre-eminent. The key to understanding the company is to analyze the links within management.

An enterprise founded as a trust or by a benefactor reflects the original intent for which it was established. It might be paternalistic toward its employees and make some decisions on a basis other than a commercial one.

Growth pattern

In theory, a company's growth may be classified as organic or acquisitive. In practice, companies exhibit features of both.

Organic structures are those which, having originated as a single company based on one or a range of products and services, have grown through internal expansion, new products and the establishment of new operations integral to the existing business.

Acquisitive or conglomerate structures are those which started out as single product enterprises but which have expanded by acquisition and absorption, either of related businesses or as part of diversification of different operations.

These organizations may encounter greater difficulties in the control and integration of a variety of management styles and company cultures. They tend toward decentralized control from a central point.

Stage of development

As in human life, an enterprise has several "ages." The particular stage a company's evolution has reached is reflected in its organization. Within large conglomerates with decentralized control several subsidiary operations may be found to coexist at different levels of development. The main stages are start-up, growth and consolidation, followed by either expansion or standstill.

Physical location

A company with dispersed manufacturing, sales or distribution activities will tend to decentralize control over operations. It may retain centralized control over product policy, standards, credit and finance, especially if it has grown organically.

Markets

The structure, size and nature of markets require particular organizational responses from a company, such as a split of organization between domestic and international, or major and minor customers.

Products/services

A company may organize along logical product lines such as automobiles and trucks, or may centralize certain product aspects such as engines.

The nature of the product and the process by which it is manufactured will influence the shape of the organization's structure.

Social environment

The social values within the company's operating environment influence its structure. For instance, local employment customs or laws create requirements in terms of manning and therefore management.

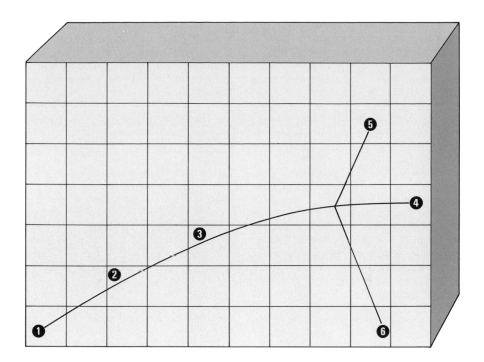

How a company evolves

1 Start-up may be unstructured or project-oriented. At birth, an organization generally consists of a limited number of people with individual tasks and roles. To survive, it requires strong leadership and people with a high level of flexibility.

Many enterprises do not get past this stage and either disappear altogether or have their assets (mainly product ideas and skills) acquired by larger commercial companies.

2 In the development stage the organization goes through rapid growth and change and begins to define its structure, operating mores, and the roles of its employees. Expansion forms or changes the culture of the company. Emphasis is on product development and sales orders to support growth plans. This can create a crisis because the company may lose its sense of autonomy.

3 Consolidation is a period during which the organization considers its gains and losses and further development while consolidating its present position.

This period needs strong direction and should be marked by planning for new products, future growth and/or acquisition. At this stage a company may suffer a crisis of control. Decisions made now determine whether a company reaches a plateau or expands.

4 A company reaches a plateau when little or no change is made to its profile and products. This may be because no new proposals or ideas are generated, or because the skills are not available, or because the company's existing product success overrides considerations of alternative strategies. It may continue for long periods with the same or slightly modified successful products, but eventually it will decline or expand.

5 A company expands either through the development and introduction of new or modified products or by acquisition.

6 When a company declines, a larger company may acquire it or rising costs and uncompetitive products will force it out of business.

Choosing a structure

When considering the optimal structure for itself, a business will seek:
- Consistency of quality of service or product.
- Adherence to agreed corporate directions and standards.
- Cost effective methods of administering itself.

In order to achieve these it needs to:
- Avoid duplication or conflict of effort.
- Exercise control to ensure that various parts of the organization stay within agreed boundaries (budgets, regions, product ranges, etc.) or seek approval before going outside them.
- Establish good information flow on customer satisfaction, local market conditions and competitor activities.

The business, therefore, usually has to ask itself how much control a few senior people should have.

Consciously or otherwise, all businesses consider the question of centralization versus decentralization.

This question will concern the division of power between head office and branches. At another level it will involve, for example, deciding how much autonomy the production department should have to decide its own buying patterns, etc.

At an even lower level it will be a question of whether or not a purchasing supervisor should make decisions about, say, buying in greater bulk to get a higher discount.

Many organizations never come to terms with the natural tension between the center and the periphery and alternate between centralized and decentralized approaches. They will usually need a mixture of both.

With the increasing rate of change, greater competition from unexpected sources (department stores selling insurance, food supermarkets selling clothes), increasing demands and rising expectations, organizational structure can have a significant impact on a business's profitability.

Organizational patterns

There are a number of different issues to consider when establishing an organizational structure, such as: top management's desire to exercise close control, size of operation, diversity of product range, quality of middle management, and geographic spread. The more common organizational patterns include:

Centralized organization
Authority is concentrated in one central point or position. Major decisions are made by one controlling body. Delegation generally operates through formalized procedures and authority levels, or by recognized custom and practice.

Decentralized organization
Decision-making is dispersed into small units. Decentralization may be necessitated by geography, product mix or market.

Functional organization
Resources and authority are assigned on the basis of recognized industrial or professional skills, such as marketing, finance, sales and personnel. The heads of these functions are responsible for control of their resources, professional standards and liaison and communication across functions.

Matrix organization
Project-oriented authority draws its resources from a number of different departments. Thus a researcher or project leader can call on, use and direct resources from another part of the organization to achieve the project's goals.

Line and staff organization
Essentially, line management has direct control over a process that involves staff from many disciplines: a production, sales or research team.

Managers in staff functions are essentially the advisors, providers of recommendations to senior managers, reviewers and analyzers of policy. They have line control only over their own personnel.

ERICSSON ≋

Balancing corporate needs

Large international companies need to be flexible enough to respond to changes in their many markets. At the same time, they must find ways of varying the needs of each local market so as to rationalize the use of their resources (e.g. production, distribution, sales, marketing).

LM Ericsson, the Swedish makers of telecommunications equipment, have managed to achieve this difficult balance (see Y. Doz and C. K. Prahalad, *Journal of International Business Studies,* Fall 1984). Top management encourages independent perspectives at all levels, but it also creates close understanding and a common culture.

Functional corporate managers, such as marketing managers, occupy key positions and control the two-way flow of data between top management and subsidiaries. This ensures that varying views converge and strategic decisions are handled effectively.

Overall, decisions are managed by subsidiary boards: corporate executives and prominent local nationals maintain the balance between subsidiary interests and corporate priorities.

LM Ericsson are able, as a result of this organization, to be responsive to market needs at a subsidiary level yet manage the integration of both manufacturing and technology centrally.

Advantages of centralization

● Broad overview of business is easier to achieve. Strategic direction setting may be easier.
● Gives absolute and clear control.
● Makes administration easier.
● Common standards can be monitored.
● Provides certain service or expert functions cost effectively.
● Inconsistent or conflicting decisions are easier to avoid.
● Can eliminate possible competition which may be undesirable, e.g. a similar product being sold at different prices by two parts of the same organization.
● Enables you to have an overview of the business because it avoids, for example, differing priorities and information systems.
● Economies of scale (e.g. bulk buying) can be achieved.

Advantages of decentralization

● Local management can react to changing local conditions so that the business can act quickly.
● Decision-making is quicker, clearer and based on more precise understanding of local conditions.
● Local responsibility and authority develop managers in greater volume and quality.
● Higher involvement and motivation can lead to greater productivity and increased profits.
● The greater likelihood of innovation, creativity and nonacceptance of a status quo will make for a healthier business.
● Administration and paperwork are minimized.
● Functional departments (personnel, legal, etc.) are more in touch and leaner. It is easier to control their operations.

Equity and long-term debt

Business needs cash to get going. Premises need to be rented or purchased, plant and machinery have to be leased or bought, raw materials must be purchased, and the workforce has to be paid from the day the business starts.

Few entrepreneurs can afford to start up using only their own savings. They need to know where to go for other capital and what costs and benefits may result.

The capital of the owners is equity. This is the most exposed form of finance because the owners receive a return on investment only after all others – employees, tax authorities, creditors, bankers and other lenders – have received their legal entitlement.

Should the business face bankruptcy, equity will be repaid only after everyone else has received what is owing.

Should the business prosper, however, the owners can claim all of the profit after the interest charges on the debt have been met.

A company need not limit its equity to the cash contributed by the founders: venture capital, institutions and the stock market provide more equity financing.

Another form of funding is long-term debt, which can vary in amount, purpose and legal entitlement.

Providers of long-term debt usually seek first claim on the assets of the business. This is precisely what happens in the domestic mortgage market when a savings or commercial bank lends against the title deeds of the property for which the loan is required.

Long-term debt must be repaid at the end of the stated term unless both sides are willing to renegotiate terms for another period.

Lenders must be paid interest periodically at a rate which is normally linked to bank base lending rate. When the profits of the business fall, this interest commitment can be a burden.

Equity

The owners' equity in a company is a residual interest, a claim on the assets not required to meet the claims of lenders and creditors.

Equity comprises the amounts originally contributed by the owners, together with profits from previous years not distributed by way of dividend.

Equity is represented by the net assets of the firm which it has helped fund.

Long-term debt

Where a business needs funding for a long period, it may approach one or more of the following providers:
- Commercial banks
- Insurance companies
- Pension funds

The most popular forms of long-term debt are:

1 Senior or subordinated debt or convertible bonds. Senior debt has first claim on assets while subordinated debt or 'debentures' have second claim.

Convertible bonds entitle the holder to exchange the debt for an equity stake at some future date.

2 Sale and leaseback: a business can sell a valuable asset, usually a building or piece of land, to a financial institution for a capital sum and then lease the asset back at terms favorable to the business.

A badly constructed financial package can seriously damage the health of the company. Take professional advice before committing to long-term debt.

Leverage is the relationship between equity and long-term debt. Companies should keep a reasonable balance between the two. Generally, lenders will not provide more money than the owners have provided.

Leverage has an impact on the owner's return; a company without extensive debt will weather an economic storm better than a highly leveraged one.

(Figures in dollars)	*Highly leveraged Company*	*Low leveraged Company*
Equity	40,000	80,000
10% Long-term debt	60,000	20,000
	100,000	100,000
Leverage	60%	20%

	Year 1	Year 2	Year 3	Year 4
Income before interest	15,000	10,000	7,500	6,000
Highly leveraged Company				
Interest	6,000	6,000	6,000	6,000
Income	9,000	4,000	1,500	0
	15,000	10,000	7,500	6,000
Low leveraged Company				
Interest	2,000	2,000	2,000	2,000
Income	13,000	8,000	5,500	4,000
	15,000	10,000	7,500	6,000
Return on equity				
Highly leveraged	22.5%	10%	3.75%	
Low leveraged	16.25%	10%	6.88%	5%

The fall in owners' earnings is less dramatic (16.25% to 5%) with low leverage than with high leverage (22.5% to nil). But if corporate profits were rising, the highly leveraged owners would enjoy a much steeper climb in their return on equity.

More equity financing?

Each of the three main sources of fresh capital has advantages, depending on the growth profile of the company and on the motives of the existing owners.

1 Venture capital is supplied by venture firms specifically set up by institutions, individuals, banks or even government agencies,to provide equity for companies showing potential for high growth. Because of the high risks involved, these firms tend to look for high returns. They expect to realize their investment when the company grows. They leave operational control to existing management, but expect to be involved in major decisions.

2 Entry into the National Association of Securities Dealers Automated Quotation Systems (NASDAQ) is a natural stage in the development of a successful company from a private one to a public one. NASDAQ allows companies to raise money from outside investors and for founders to unlock some of the capital tied up in the business. Companies must be fully registered under the 1933 or 1934 Securities Acts and have $2 million in assets and $1 million in equity. To list on NASDAQ, a company must issue at least 100,000 shares to 300 shareholders.

3 A domestic company qualifies to list on the 'Big Board' (the New York Stock Exchange) if: the aggregate market value of publicly-held shares is at least $16 million; if it has a minimum pretax net income of $2.5 million in its current fiscal year and $2 million in each of the two previous years. The company must have issued at least one million shares to at least 2,000 shareholders in blocks of at least 100 shares.

Working capital management

A business will collapse without funds generated from within. Sooner rather than later a company must generate sufficient funds from normal trading operations to maintain the existing level of business and to provide the backbone of future expansion.

Profit must be the starting point for internally generated funds. Profit is the surplus left when the costs of producing and selling have been deducted from the revenue derived from sales. But a company does not keep all of its profit. Taxation takes a percentage and shareholders want a return on their investment. Skillful managers attempt to keep these two amounts at the lowest possible level. The role of the company's tax advisors is to minimize the taxable profits.

Shareholders receive a modest return on their capital – enough to prevent their seeking alternative investment opportunities. By and large, they appreciate that profits retained in the core of the business are used to sustain and expand the company's operating capability.

With an underlying trend of internally generated retained profits, the company has a future.

But beware! Profit is not cash. Profit is measured by using a number of accounting conventions, some of which have no bearing on cash flow. For example, depreciation, a non-cash item for the business, is charged on the property and plant and thus reduces profit.

Managers tend to be more concerned with cash, or liquidity, than with profits. Wages, dividends, taxes, the heating bill are all cash leakages, not profits. So-called profitable companies have gone out of business because they ran out of cash.

Managers should be able to understand how cash is pumped around the business, where the pressure points are for more cash and where surplus cash can be drained off.

Cash flow pressure points

To control the amount of cash needed by normal operations of the business, astute managers make sure the flow is as fast as possible. They keep tabs on three pressure points:

Accounts payable: raw materials and supplies are needed for manufacturing operations. Every attempt should be made to use suppliers that allow a generous credit period before requiring cash payment. Often a company is better off to forego a discount for quick payment so that it can hold on to its cash. But it is seldom worth keeping important suppliers waiting—they could go out of business and leave you without a source of supply.

Inventories and manufacturing work-in-process: stocks of raw materials are held to prevent disruptions in production or to avoid an imminent price rise. The levels of partially finished and finished

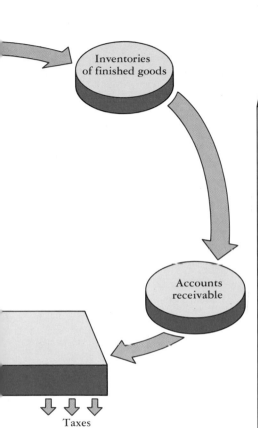

Inventories
of finished goods

Accounts
receivable

Taxes

goods are determined by the volume of production required to meet future sales. Inventory managers avoid being out of stock as it is disruptive, expensive and damaging to customer goodwill. But inventories are costly. Managers must ensure minimum levels are carried in order to minimize the cash outlay. In a recession, one of the first actions a manager takes is to cut inventory so that cash can be squeezed out of the system for critical use.

Accounts receivable: unless you operate in the retail sector where cash sales are a significant part of operations, credit sales are unavoidable. If your competitors offer credit terms then so must you. The more generous the terms, the more expense for the seller. You must strive for a balance between giving good terms, which attract customers, and having a strict collection policy, which minimizes cash outlay.

The treasury function: the big company's answer to cash management

A company involved in international sales increases its problems. Treasury departments within international companies concern themselves with the complete range of issues surrounding cash movements and holdings. Ask:

● Does the company have any bank accounts with credit balances? Idle balances on current account with banks earn no interest. Efficient treasury systems arrange to use cash as it becomes available.

● Has the company optimized its collection system to obtain the same value as its customers?

● Does the company know the bank charges associated with each aspect of the business? Is it using the bank best equipped to handle each aspect of the business?

● Is the company familiar with the full range of borrowing and deposit instruments available? Borrowing overseas with a full currency hedge may be a viable alternative.

● Does the company monitor its currency exposure to keep the risk at acceptable limits? Is it covering the risk at the lowest cost? The volatility of foreign exchange markets can put at risk even the most advantageous of overseas markets.

● Does the company have a system which effectively controls investment in working capital at operating levels?

Cash forecasting

An essential component of working capital management is negotiating a credit line with the company's bankers. Most banks insist on a cash flow forecast for 6 or 12 months. This laborious procedure is simplified by the use of a microcomputer spreadsheet, which allows for automatic re-working of all subsequent numbers following a particular adjustment or correction.

Sample cash flow forecast

Three graduates in computer science are planning to form a company in January to design, manufacture and sell a range of floppy disks for micro-computers.

Each graduate will contribute $15,000 in cash. The bank they have approached for a credit line of $30,000 has insisted on a cash forecast for the first six months' trading.

● A suitable factory has been located costing $24,000 but the local development corporation is prepared to accept $12,000 immediately and offer a mortgage on the balance with interest payable at 10 percent per annum on the last day of each month.

● Equipment, plant and vehicles costing $30,000 must be acquired and paid for within the first month of trading. It is anticipated that one of the vehicles will be sold during June for $500.

● Each disk made will cost $3, comprising $2 for factory wages and $1 for materials. Selling price will be $6, and

CASH FORECAST for period January to June

2 Salaries
January:
disks for inventory 2,000
disks for February sale 2,000
_____
4,000 @ $2 = $8,000

February:
disks for March sale 2,500 @ $2 = $5,000
_____
and so on for the following months

3 Raw materials paid in the month following supply:
January purchases:
for finished goods inventory 2,000
for February sale 2,000
for raw material inventory 1,200
_____
paid in February 5,200 @ $1 = $5,200

February purchases:
for March sales paid in March 2,500 @ $1 = $2,500
_____
and so on for the following months

1 Sales @ $6 each	Jan	Feb
Invoiced sales	—	$12,000
Cash sales 10% this month	—	$1,200
Debtors 90% next month	—	—

4 This set of cash outflows is typical of a start-up situation when substantial sums are spent in advance of sales. Provided the company is selling a profitable and needed product, this outflow will soon be reversed.

5 The graduates will need to renegotiate their credit facility in the first six months; they need at least $32,100 all together. Provided subsequent months indicate a constant cash recovery, most banks would agree to an increase such as this.

OPENING CASH BALANCE

Paid-in capital
1 Cash sales
Cash from credit sales
Asset Sales

RECEIPTS

2 Salaries
3 Raw materials
Production overhead
Administrative overhead
Selling & distribution
Advertising
Factory
Equipment, plant, vehicles
Interest on mortgage
Architectural services

PAYMENTS

MOVEMENT IN CASH

4 CLOSING CASH BALANCE

CREDIT LINE
5 SURPLUS/DEFICIT

expected sales are as follows, in units: January Nil; February 2,000; March 2,500; April 3,000; May 3,000; June 3,000; and for each month thereafter, 3,000; 10 percent of sales will be for cash. The balance will be sold on credit for settlement in the month following delivery.

● Materials, production and administration overheads will be acquired from suppliers who will expect to be paid in the month following that of supply of the goods or services. Production overheads are likely to be incurred at the rate of $1,800 per month and administrative overheads at the rate of $1,700 per month. All other expenses are paid in the month in which they are incurred.

● Sufficient materials will need to be purchased in January both to manufacture the disks to be sold in February, and also to maintain a level of raw material inventory of 1,200. The inventory of finished goods will be maintained at 2,000 disks during the six months under review and the production level for any month is that of the next month's sales.

● Advertising is to be used: $1,500 in January, $1,000 in both February and March, and $500 per month thereafter.

● Selling and distribution costs will be: $600 in March, $700 in both April and May, and $800 in June.

● Each of the three graduates has agreed to withdraw a salary of exactly $1,000 per month.

March	April	May	June	(Figures in dollars)
$15,000	$18,000	$18,000	$18,000	
$1,500	$1,800	$1,800	$1,800	
$10,800	$13,500	$16,200	$16,200	

January	February	March	April	May	June	Total
0	(9,600)	(26,200)	(30,600)	(32,100)	(30,900)	0
45,000						45,000
	1,200	1,500	1,800	1,800	1,800	8,100
		10,800	13,500	16,200	16,200	56,700
					500	500
45,000	1,200	12,300	15,300	18,000	18,500	110,300
8,000	5,000	6,000	6,000	6,000	6,000	37,000
	5,200	2,500	3,000	3,000	3,000	16,700
	1,800	1,800	1,800	1,800	1,800	9,000
	1,700	1,700	1,700	1,700	1,700	8,500
		600	700	700	800	2,800
1,500	1,000	1,000	500	500	500	5,000
12,000						12,000
30,000						30,000
100	100	100	100	100	100	600
3,000	3,000	3,000	3,000	3,000	3,000	18,000
54,600	17,800	16,700	16,800	16,800	16,900	139,600
(9,600)	(16,600)	(4,400)	(1,500)	(1,200)	(1,600)	(29,300)
(9,600)	(26,200)	(30,600)	(32,100)	(30,900)	(29,300)	(29,300)
30,000	30,000	30,000	30,000	30,000	30,000	
—	—	600	2,100	900	—	

The income statement

Public companies prepare a set of financial statements periodically and at the year-end. For those companies, the Securities and Exchange Commission (SEC) regulates what items must be included and how they should be presented.

Many parties are interested in these statements: investors, employees, creditors, bankers, tax authorities and consumer groups. It is essential for managers to know how they are prepared and what they disclose.

The three principal financial statements are: the income statement, the balance sheet and the statement of changes in financial position. The examples on these pages are taken from the accounts of a group of retail companies.

The income statement is a measure of the operating performance of a business over a given period of time. Companies do not necessarily use the calendar year as their reporting year. They usually prefer the natural business year in an attempt to measure performance at a time when most earnings activities have been concluded. But business is a continuum; it may not be easily divided into annual pieces.

The income statement measures the normal operating activities of the business. Specifically, it matches revenue for the year against the cost of goods sold and other expenses.

This statement also discloses revenues arising, or costs resulting, from non-operating activities, e.g. the profit from selling a piece of land. Such items should be kept separate from the ongoing operating results to provide a true impression of the underlying trend in operating profitability.

After provision has been made for taxes, the income statement discloses how the net income will be used: as dividends to the shareholders and the balance retained to expand the company's future operations.

Accountants: a cautious breed

Accountants do not like taking the risk of reporting profit before it has been earned and is collectable. Therefore they record costs at the earliest possible moment and revenues when they are assured.

For instance, if a company is engaged in a long-term construction contract in an unstable part of the world, it will not record income while construction is in process, in accordance with the percentage of completion method, unless profit from the contract is probable and collection is reasonably certain.

Companies should be consistent in the way they account for their transactions. For example, they should not keep changing the way they depreciate their assets or record sales transactions.

Assessing the income statement

The accruals basis of accounting (as opposed to the cash basis) reports costs incurred as expenses in the year when the revenues to which they relate are recognized. Items in annual accounts have not necessarily been received or paid in cash by the end of the financial year. For example, a company pays $12,000 annual factory rent, in advance, halfway through the year. The income statement would include $6,000 cost this year and $6,000 next year. Similarly the revenue figure includes sales which have not been paid for at the year-end.

Pretax profits are a good indicator of corporate performance. After tax profits can be deceptive because of tax benefits.

Interpreting the income statement

1 The cost of sales figure for a wholesaler or retailer includes the cost of merchandise purchased for resale. A manufacturing company's costs would include raw materials, labor and manufacturing overheads.

2 Selling, general and administration expenses include staff salaries and costs not included in cost of sales: rent, property taxes, energy and security costs, professional fees, depreciation on fixed assets, repairs to furnishings, equipment and vehicles, and interest payable on loans and overdraft.

3 The income statement indicates a company's operating results, including those of its subsidiaries and equity investments. Minority interests are shares in subsidiaries owned by outsiders. Minority shareholders are allocated their proportional share of the total group's operating results.

4 The net income is the amount earned for shareholders. The retained earnings (end of year) is the amount retained in the business.

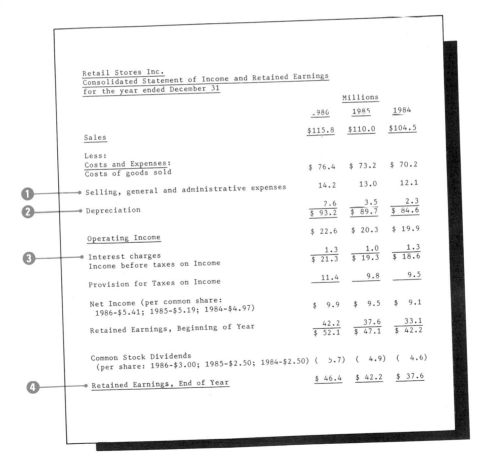

Retail Stores Inc.
Consolidated Statement of Income and Retained Earnings
for the year ended December 31

	Millions		
	1986	1985	1984
Sales	$115.8	$110.0	$104.5
Less:			
Costs and Expenses:			
Costs of goods sold	$ 76.4	$ 73.2	$ 70.2
❶ Selling, general and administrative expenses	14.2	13.0	12.1
❷ Depreciation	2.6	3.5	2.3
	$ 93.2	$ 89.7	$ 84.6
Operating Income	$ 22.6	$ 20.3	$ 19.9
❸ Interest charges	1.3	1.0	1.3
Income before taxes on Income	$ 21.3	$ 19.3	$ 18.6
Provision for Taxes on Income	11.4	9.8	9.5
Net Income (per common share: 1986-$5.41; 1985-$5.19; 1984-$4.97)	$ 9.9	$ 9.5	$ 9.1
Retained Earnings, Beginning of Year	42.2	37.6	33.1
	$ 52.1	$ 47.1	$ 42.2
Common Stock Dividends (per share: 1986-$3.00; 1985-$2.50; 1984-$2.50)	(5.7)	(4.9)	(4.6)
❹ Retained Earnings, End of Year	$ 46.4	$ 42.2	$ 37.6

The balance sheet

The balance sheet of a company is a statement of what it owns (assets) and what it owes (liabilities) at a particular time, usually the last day of the company's financial reporting period. It is composed of three major elements: assets, liabilities and shareholders' equity.

Assets are resources of the company that have the potential for providing it with future economic services or benefits. An asset can be an amount receivable from a third party or a future benefit.

Financial assets such as cash and accounts receivable are shown on the balance sheet at their cash equivalent values. For instance, if it appears that one of the company's customers is not going to pay, the assets must be reduced by the amount that is deemed not collectable.

Other assets (raw materials, land, buildings and equipment) are ordinarily stated at acquisition cost.

Assets are usually split into fixed assets (such as land, buildings, plant, vehicles), intangible assets (such as goodwill) and current assets (such as inventories of raw materials, work-in-process and finished goods, accounts receivable, short-term investments, prepaid expenses and cash).

Liabilities represent obligations of a company to make payment in the foreseeable future for goods or services already received. Companies usually distinguish between amounts which require payment within one year and those due after one year.

Liabilities include long-term debt, loans and obligations under long-term leases, and deferred tax.

Shareholders' equity is a residual interest: it comprises the original capital that was contributed together with any profits which have not been distributed by way of dividend. The owners' equity is represented by the net assets of the company.

The basic balance sheet equation
Assets = liabilities + shareholders' equity.

Start-up Inc. was incorporated on January 1 with an issued share capital of $1,000, paid for in cash by the founding directors. The first day balance sheet would be expressed:

Start-up Inc.	**$**
Assets	
Cash-in-hand	1,000
Shareholders' equity	
Common stock	1,000

During the first week of operation the company bought raw materials for $600, half of which were supplied on credit, and some machinery for $300. At the end of the first week the balance sheet would look like this:

Start-up Inc.		**$**
Current assets	Cash-in-hand	400
	Inventories	600
		1,000
Fixed assets	Machinery	300
		1,300
Current liabilities		
Accounts payable		300
Shareholders' equity		
Common stock		1,000
		1,300

The above balance sheet is obviously a very simple example. In reality companies will have much more detailed balance sheets accompanied by explanatory notes.

Notes to the financial statements
To help the reader understand the three principal financial statements, companies provide detailed notes which explain the bases on which the more important numbers are determined. The first note is generally a list of accounting policies adopted by the company.

Balance sheet analysis

1 The value of inventories of unsold merchandise is at times difficult to determine. Accountants insist that inventories be valued at the lower of either cost or market. Market value is an approximation of replacement cost. Reported profit is affected by the valuation a company places on its inventories. Auditors pay particular attention to clients' procedures for counting and valuing inventories.

2 When a company issues shares, it usually decides on their nominal (or face) value and the price at which they will be offered to the public. If the company offers shares of $10 nominal value for $10.25, the 25 cents is the share premium and is kept in the additional paid-in capital account.

3 Fixed assets are normally valued at cost and are shown less an amount for accumulated depreciation.

4 A company normally retains some profits each year to fund future growth and expansion. This figure indicates the cumulative build-up in these retained earnings.

```
Retail Stores Inc.
Consolidated Balance Sheet
as of December 31
```

Assets		Millions	
Current Assets		1986	1985
Cash		$ 9.0	$ 6.2
Marketable securities		-	2.0
Accounts and notes receivable		12.4	11.4
Inventories ❶		27.0	24.6
Total Current Assets		$ 48.4	$ 44.2
Property, Plant and Equipment ❸		104.3	92.7
Buildings, machinery and equipment, at cost		27.6	25.0
Less accumulated Depreciation		$ 76.7	$ 67.7
		.9	.7
Land, at cost		$ 77.6	$ 68.4
Total Property, Plant and Equipment			
Other Assets		4.7	3.9
Receivables due after one year		.2	.2
Surrender value of insurance		.6	.5
Other		$ 5.5	$ 4.6
Total Other Assets		$131.5	$117.2
Total Assets			

Liabilities & Shareholders' Equity			
Current Liabilities		$ 6.1	$ 5.0
Accounts payable		3.6	3.3
Accrued liabilities		1.0	.8
Current maturity of long-term debt		9.6	8.4
Federal income and other taxes		1.3	1.1
Dividends payable		$ 21.6	$ 18.6
Total Current Liabilities			
		3.6	2.5
Other Liabilities			
Long-Term Debt		32.0	26.0
5% Sinking-Fund Debentures, due July 31, 1997			
Shareholders' Equity			
Common Stock ($10 par: authorized-2,000,000			
outstanding-1,830,000		18.3	18.3
Additional Paid-in Capital ❷		9.6	9.6
Retained Earnings		46.4	42.2
Total Shareholders' Equity ❹		$ 74.3	$ 70.1
Total Liabilities, and Shareholders' Equity		$131.5	$117.2

What a balance sheet is not

The total shareholders' figure in the balance sheet does not represent the real market value of a company's net assets.

The figures in the accounts are based on the acquisition or "historical" cost of the assets.

With the land and buildings, the acquisition may have happened years ago and bear little resemblance to the amounts the company would realize if it sold any or all of them: the balance sheet is not a statement of values.

65

Statement of Changes in Financial Position

The Statement of Changes in Financial Position (SCFP) helps explain how and why the company's financial position has changed during the year. It shows where the financial resources (funds) have come from and how they have been used. The SCFP provides the answers to the following:

● Are normal company operations generating funds?

● Are the funds generated from operations sufficient to enable the company to continue paying dividends?

● Where did the money for the purchase of new assets come from? From operations or from borrowings?

● Does the company have sufficient funds to meet its short-term obligations?

● How can the company be earning profits but still be short of cash or working capital?

Funds are more than just cash. They are the working capital, defined as the surplus of current assets over current liabilities. Current assets, e.g. inventories, are constantly converted into cash to pay current liabilities.

A company's main source of funds must come from operations. If it cannot generate sufficient internal resources it will not survive. In order to determine funds generated by operations, the net income as disclosed in the income statement must be adjusted for non-cash items, such as depreciation. These funds are usually applied in purchasing fixed assets, repaying long-term debt and paying a dividend to shareholders.

Other sources of funds are the proceeds from the sale of fixed assets, long-term borrowings, and issues of new shares.

The difference between sources and applications of funds is reflected in the net increase in working capital components. These consist of cash, inventories, accounts receivable and payable, accrued liabilities, and other current assets and liabilities.

The audit

Shareholders of public companies usually approve the management's recommendation of a firm of independent accountants to report to them each year on their examination of the consolidated financial statements. The report states whether, in the auditors' opinion, the financial statements have been prepared in accordance with generally accepted accounting principles (GAAP). And whether, in their opinion, the statement fairly presents the operating results for the year and the financial position at the year-end.

The auditors must ensure that the books, records and internal accounting controls have been satisfactorily maintained during the financial year. They will therefore:

● Examine the accounting system to ascertain whether internal accounting controls are present.

● Compare the accounts with the underlying records to see that they are in agreement.

● Verify the ownership, existence and book value of the assets, and the amount of the liabilities in the balance sheet.

● Verify that the results shown are fairly presented.

● Determine whether all transactions and accounts that should be included in the financial statements have been included.

The audit report of Retail Stores Inc. is "unqualified" because the auditors have no material reservations. If they were doubtful about any important item included (or not included) in the financial statements they would have to give a "qualified" report, stating the reason and the extent to which they were not satisfied. Corporate management always does its best to avoid a "qualified" report.

What is happening at Retail Stores Inc.?

The company required $19.4 million during the current year for major items of expenditure. $12.5 million of this came from operations, $7 million from the proceeds from long-term debt. A further $1.2 million in cash was used to fund an increase in working capital, notably a build-up in inventories.

1 To convert net income into funds generated from operations, it has been adjusted for the non-working capital item – depreciation.

2 Build-up in inventories from the previous year ($2.4 million) is more than double the build-up in 1985 over 1984 of $1.0 million. Inventories require cash that could be used for more critical purposes. Always ask: is the increase justified by higher prospective sales?

Retail Stores Inc.
Consolidated Statement of Changes in Financial Position
for the year ended December 31

| | Millions | | |
	1986	1985	1984
Sources of Funds			
Net Income	$ 9.9	$ 9.5	$ 9.1
Depreciation	2.6	3.5	2.3
Funds provided by operations	$12.5	$13.0	$11.4
Increase in other liabilities	1.1	2.0	1.4
Proceeds from long-term debt	7.0	6.0	-
Total funds provided	$20.0	$21.0	$12.8
Applications of Funds			
Additions to fixed assets	$11.8	$ .5	$ 6.2
Dividends on common stock	5.7	4.9	4.6
Payments on long-term debt	1.0	15.0	-
Increase in non-current receivables	.8	.1	.3
Increase in other assets	.1	-	.2
Total funds used	$19.4	$20.5	$11.3
Increase in working capital	$ 1.2	$ .5	$ 1.5
Changes in Components of Working Capital			
Increase (decrease) in current assets:			
Cash	$ 2.8	$ 1.0	$ 1.1
Marketable securities	(2.0)	.5	.4
Accounts receivable	1.0	.5	.8
Inventories	2.4	1.0	1.3
Increase in current assets	$ 4.2	$ 3.0	$ 3.6
Increase in current liabilities:			
Accounts payable	$ 1.1	$ .9	$ .6
Accrued liabilities	.3	.5	.2
Current maturity of long-term debt	.2	.1	.5
Federal income and other taxes	1.2	1.0	.8
Dividends payable	.2	-	-
Increase in current liabilities	$ 3.0	$ 2.5	$ 2.1
Increase in working capital	$ 1.2	$ .5	$ 1.5

Report of Independent Accountants

The Board of Directors and Shareholders Retail Stores Inc.

We have examined the accompanying consolidated balance sheets of Retail Stores Inc. at December 31, 1986 and 1985 and the related consolidated statements of income and retained earnings and changes in financial position for each of the three years in the period ended 31 December 1986. Our examinations were made in accordance with generally accepted auditing standards and, accordingly, included such tests of the accounting records and such other auditing procedures as we considered necessary in the circumstances.

In our opinion, the accompanying consolidated financial statements present fairly the consolidated financial position of Retail Stores Inc. at 31 December 1986 and 1985, and the consolidated results of operations and changes in financial position for each of the three years in the period ended 31 December 1986, in conformity with generally accepted accounting principles applied on a consistent basis during the period.

New York, 15 February 1987
Arthur Young & Company

Valuing a company

Value, like beauty, lies in the eye of the beholder. Companies are valued for takeover, merger, initial public offerings and for capital taxes.

Since two parties – the owners of the shares and the outsiders – are always involved, valuation is part technical calculation, part negotiation.

There are several ways to value a company, of which the three examples outlined here are the simplest.

The valuation will be influenced by the needs of the buyer and seller, and also by the size of the holding.

Size of shareholding

Large shareholders have the power to influence the management of the company and thus exercise an element of control over its decisions and resources.

Shares that give the buyer control over investment decisions and dividend policy will probably carry a higher price than their technical valuation.

Potential buyers of such a shareholding will look further than the company's book value. They will be interested in issues such as management strength and style, customer base, products, patents, market penetration, image and potential growth.

A smaller shareholding may be easier to value – and cheaper to buy. The technical valuations may be enough to answer questions regarding the investor's preference for income or capital growth which is the potential increase in the shares' market price.

The needs of the buyers and sellers

As well as deciding how well the acquired investment will complement their existing holdings or how well the acquired business will complement their existing activities, buyers may also be considering how saleable the acquisition will be in the future.

The price that buyers are willing to pay for a business depends on how badly they want to own it. The differ-

---

Technical valuation of shares

Technical calculation is based on:

1 Balance sheet valuation. Retail Stores Inc. has $106.3 million of net assets in the balance sheet. Its share capital comprises around 1.83 million ordinary shares. Each is therefore worth $58.08 in terms of net assets. But two significant features cause an analyst to be wary of this assets per share: the assets are valued at cost in the balance sheet and are worth much more in current value terms; and good management make their assets work for the business – dynamic earnings potential is favored more than static asset values.

2 Market valuation. If the company has a Stock Exchange listing (Retail Stores Inc's is $60) it is simple to value relatively small blocks of shares. However, if a sizeable block of shares, say that held by a pension fund, is sold (or

---

ence between the technical valuation and any higher purchase price could reflect, among other things, the strength of the buyer's desire or their view of the business's potential. The difference between the book value and its actual purchase price is usually known as goodwill.

Buyers may pay more than the technical value to protect markets by buying a competing company, or to protect its supply lines, or to improve margins with economies of scale.

The sellers' primary concern could be the original cost of their investment, and thus a desire to maximize a profit or minimize a loss on it.

But sellers could equally need cash in order to take advantage of another investment opportunity or to meet cash flow problems. Speed of sale may take precedence over their own technical valuation.

purchased) this action alone will disturb the equilibrium between supply and demand and the price will fall or rise. The market capitalization valuation is the current market value per share multiplied by the number of issued shares: 1.83 million shares × $60 = $108 million.

3 Earnings valuation. A company's stock market value is based on a combination of factors but probably the major factor is the earnings potential of the company. This is assessed taking into account future growth in new products and markets, known cost reduction programs, and quality of management. Potential earnings are then multiplied by the company's Price Earnings ratio (P/E) which expresses the number of years that a company would have to continue generating earnings at their present level to accumulate sufficient earnings to equal the current share price.

P/E of Retail Stores Inc.

$$=\frac{\$60}{\$5.41}=11.1$$

Current earnings of Retail Stores Inc. = $9.9 million

Potential earnings next year + 10% = $10.9 million

Earnings valuation = $10.9 million × 11.1 (years) = $121 million or $66.1 per share.

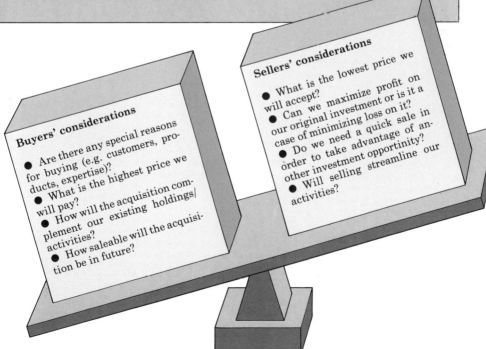

Buyers' considerations

- Are there any special reasons for buying (e.g. customers, products, expertise)?
- What is the highest price we will pay?
- How will the acquisition complement our existing holdings/activities?
- How saleable will the acquisition be in future?

Sellers' considerations

- What is the lowest price we will accept?
- Can we maximize profit on our original investment or is it a case of minimizing loss on it?
- Do we need a quick sale in order to take advantage of another investment opportinity?
- Will selling streamline our activities?

Ratio analysis

Once you understand how a set of accounts is constructed, you need to be able to analyze them to find out what they really disclose. Interpreting and analyzing financial statements will enable you, as a manager, to compare the performance of your company this year with last year, to compare your company with its competitors, and to detect weaknesses which you can correct.

Absolute figures in financial statements do not tell you much. For example, to be told that Retail Stores Inc made $21.3 million income before tax is not a useful piece of information unless it is related to, say, the sales which produced the income or to the capital employed in the business.

Ratio analysis is a useful tool with which to interpret financial accounts.

Liquidity

Your first concern as a manager is to ensure the short-run survival of the company. Is the company able to meet its short-term obligations?

Current ratio

$$= \frac{\text{Current assets}}{\text{Current liabilities}}$$

$$= \frac{48.4}{21.6} = 2.24 \text{ times}$$

Most analysts prefer to see a company with more current assets than current liabilities. But in the retail sector, companies have substantial cash sales, which may make for healthy liquidity.

Quick ratio

$$= \frac{\text{Cash} + \text{marketable securities}}{\text{Current liabilities}}$$

$$= \frac{9}{21.6} = 0.42$$

In some manufacturing companies inventories contain products that are not readily marketable and accounts receivable can contain items which may be difficult to collect. To provide a more rigorous test of the company's ability to meet its short-term obligations, these items are removed from the calculation.

Capital structure

Companies can be financed by a mixture of owners' equity and long-term debt. Debt ratios analyze this mixture by measuring the contributions of shareholders against the funds provided by lenders. Retail Stores Inc. has little long-term debt; but the significant ratio is:

$$= \frac{\text{Long-term debt}}{\text{Shareholders' equity}}$$

The income statement provides another useful angle on the capital structure. Is there a healthy margin of safety in the net income to meet the interest payments on its debt? A highly leveraged company may show signs of running out of funds to pay this burden.

Debt coverage

$$= \frac{\text{Pretax income} + \text{interest charges}}{\text{interest charges}}$$

To be sure that their dividend is safe, shareholders will want profits compared with the dividend payable:

Dividend cover

$$= \frac{\text{Net income}}{\text{Dividend payable}}$$

$$= \frac{9.9}{5.7} = 1.64$$

But for ratios to be meaningful, they must be compared with equivalent ratios calculated for previous years and with those of the industry in which the company operates. Industrial ratios are produced by a variety of commercial banks for industrial statistics.

Ratios reduce the amount of data contained in the financial statements to workable form. This aim is defeated if too many are calculated. You must learn which combination of ratios will be appropriate to your needs.

Ratios lead you to ask the right questions; however, they seldom provide conclusive answers. In the examples on these pages, no attempt is made to compare Retail Stores' ratios with these industrial averages for the retail sector.

Activity and efficiency

The ratios showing inventory turnover and average collection period of accounts receivable help managers and outsiders to judge how effectively a company manages its assets. The figure of sales is compared with the investment in various assets. The following inventory turnover is more typical of manufacturing companies which tend to show a much slower turnover than do retailers.

$$\frac{Inventory}{turnover} = \frac{Cost\ of\ goods\ sold}{Inventory\ average\ for\ last\ two\ years}$$

$$= \frac{76.4}{25.8} = 2.96\ times$$

The following collection period is not typical of the retail sector which tends to discourage lengthy consumer credit terms. Manufacturing companies' collection periods can creep up to 60 days and more.

$$\frac{Average}{collection}_{period} = \frac{Accounts\ receivable}{Sales\ per\ day}$$

$$= \frac{12.4}{115.8 \div 365} = 39\ days$$

Similarly, managers should aim to extend the period of credit taken to pay suppliers.

Profitability

This ratio shows management's use of the resources under its control, excluding extraordinary items.

$$\frac{Profit}{margin} = \frac{Operating\ profit}{Sales}$$

$$= \frac{22.6 \times 100}{115.8} = 19.5\%$$

Profit is closely related to the assets employed by the company. The calculation below is based on total assets, but some analysts calculate the return on specific assets.

Return on total assets

$$= \frac{Net\ income + interest\ charges}{Total\ assets}$$

$$= \frac{11.2 \times 100}{131.5} = 8.5\%$$

If a public company fails to earn a decent return, the stock price will fall and prejudice chances of securing additional capital or long-term debt on beneficial terms.

$$\frac{Return}{on}_{equity} = \frac{Net\ income}{Shareholders'\ equity}$$

$$= \frac{9.9 \times 100}{74.3} = 13.3\%$$

Management accounting

Money is the common denominator used to evaluate alternative business decisions and to measure a company's performance. Most business transactions are recorded, analyzed and presented in financial terms; they are coordinated within the finance function.

Finance provides an important service to the operating activities in managing their resources. It is not, however, an unlimited source of management information. The same information can be analyzed and presented in many different ways. It is up to you as a manager to ensure the system is providing you with the information you need.

The structure of the finance func-

tion varies from company to company. The typical structure in large organizations is shown below. The role of the financial accounting and treasury departments, collectively responsible for external reporting and cash management, is described on pages 56–67.

Management accounting is the department to which you will have most exposure as a manager. It is here that financial information is analyzed and disseminated to form the basis for decision-making. The department also provides an early warning system for the planning and controlling of the business.

The role of management accounting is essentially to do three things:

The activities of the finance function

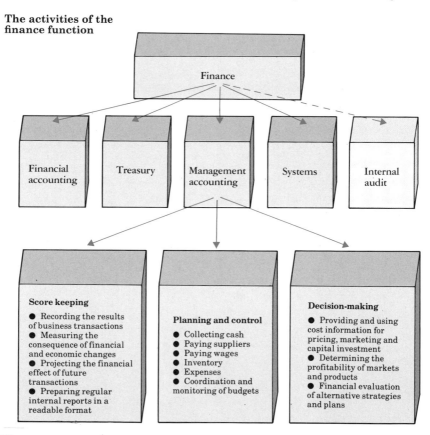

Finance

Financial accounting | Treasury | Management accounting | Systems | Internal audit

Score keeping
- Recording the results of business transactions
- Measuring the consequence of financial and economic changes
- Projecting the financial effect of future transactions
- Preparing regular internal reports in a readable format

Planning and control
- Collecting cash
- Paying suppliers
- Paying wages
- Inventory
- Expenses
- Coordination and monitoring of budgets

Decision-making
- Providing and using cost information for pricing, marketing and capital investment
- Determining the profitability of markets and products
- Financial evaluation of alternative strategies and plans

● Score keeping: keeping track of transactions and the subsequent impact on the health of the business.

● Planning and control of essential functions, including the overall framework of planning, budgeting and tracking actual peformance.

● Decision-making: providing sufficient information for managers to determine future activities.

Management accounting information is provided on a regular basis, usually monthly or quarterly. At the senior level, this will be in the form of an income statement and balance sheet for the period, and at the lower level in the form of departmental performance against prior targets. Many companies include projected results for the full year, updated with the same regularity.

The level of detail, including the balance between financial and non-financial information, is a matter for discussion between you and the accounting manager. Don't assume that you must manage with the information provided; it should be geared toward your requirements. You are the best judge of your specific needs.

Many organizations allow operating managers access to financial information via their own personal computers. This makes the question of user needs even more important and demands database designs that allow easy and efficient access to important figures.

1 Financial accounting
● Recording business transactions.
● Collecting income/paying debts.
● Preparing statutory financial statements.

2 Treasury
● Ensuring the business receives the best return on idle cash.
● Providing enough cash to pay debts.
● Foreign exchange transactions.
● Providing information on cash flow for reporting and budgeting.

3 Management accounting
Recording, interpreting and analyzing financial information for internal planning, control and decision-making.

4 Systems
● Planning computer strategy.
● Reducing complexities in the availability and flow of information.
● Providing database financial and non-financial information.
● Selecting computer equipment.
● Implementing computer systems.

5 Internal audit
To preserve its objectivity, IA often reports directly to the chief executive or another senior officer.
● Examining and reporting on the effectiveness of policies, procedures and programs.
● Advising on new control procedures.
● Examining areas of the business for improved value for money.

Working with the accounting function

The success of the accounting function depends on its relationship with those that use it. Both the accountant and the user need to understand what is being produced and why.

● Be careful of jargon, Most of the terms used by accountants have common, widely accepted definitions. It is a good idea to ask your accountant to explain to you the accounting techniques and concepts in your organization.

● Test and question the assumptions the accountants are making. Different financial measures produce different outcomes.

● If you require *ad hoc* information from accounting, state your requirements. Don't merely ask for a figure. Be precise and explain exactly what you are trying to do. The accountant will then be able to provide the data most relevant to your particular needs.

Budgetary control

Budgets help to make an organization run more smoothly and profitably. The overall budget is the master budget, made up of departmental budgets. Anyone who influences cost should be given a budget against which to measure actual expense. Every person with authority for a budget must exist in a well-defined structure to avoid overlap of responsibilities.

Individual budget targets can be dictated by senior management or negotiated so that they challenge rather than constrain.

Budget methods vary depending on the organization, department and type of expense, and include: standard costs revised annually for production costs; prior year level adjusted for administration costs or selling expenses; and zero-based budgeting for research and development.

Zero-based budgeting assumes that expenditure is nil, and each cost element has to be justified separately.

However, if budgets are always based solely on prior year expenditure, inefficiencies and overspending may be carried forward from one year to the next: a zero-based budget produced every few years is a useful method of budget checking.

Flexed budgeting allows for changes in the activity level of a business. It assumes that additional sales mean more profit and managers should not be penalized for the normal cost of producing the extra units.

Costs, the prime ingredients of budgets, can be classified as variable or fixed. Variable costs vary directly with the level of output. For example, the cost of sheet metal for car body panels increases with the number of panels produced. Fixed costs, e.g. depreciation and rents, are independent of volume level and change with time.

Budgets are flexed by adjusting the allowance by an amount equal to the variable cost of the incremental or decremental volume.

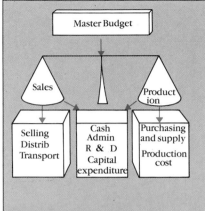

Budget coordination

If one aspect constrains the activity of the organization as a whole, it must be budgeted first. Budget coordination is normally undertaken by the senior accountant or through a budget committee.

All subsidiary budgets should be balanced to adjust targets for limiting factors imposed by one function on another. The principal limiting factor is usually the level of sales.

The budgeting process

Budget preparation begins with sales forecasts and information on external factors, such as inflation. Departmental targets are set or negotiated.

Departmental budgets are consolidated to eliminate inconsistencies between them and the company's overall profit objectives.

When budgets have been accepted by senior management, the flow of costs, revenues and capital expenditure is scheduled. Each budget manager receives a monthly target against which to measure expenditure.

Variance (the difference between budget and actual expense) is analyzed. If necessary, corrective action is taken which is fed into the overall planning process and ensures the company stays on course to achieve its financial targets. It is always crucial to understand the nature of variances so that corrective action is not superficial or short-term.

Controlling the budgeting process

Successful budgeting is essentially people-oriented and depends on:
● Cooperation and communication between budget managers.
● Targets that are perceived to be realistic and achievable.
● Managers' individual objectives being consistent with the overall objectives in the master budget.

Feedback should be constructive, not punitive. Reports for individual budget managers should highlight significant variances.

Budget reports should also be:
● Designed for each user in a format that is easily understood.
● Produced on a timely basis so that the user can relate the information to recent events.
● Accurate, to maintain the budget manager's confidence in the system.
● Increasingly detailed through lower levels of the organization.
● Supported by regular meetings between managers and their subordinates to review progress.

Advantages of budgets

Budgets can be time-consuming to prepare and review and, if imposed from above, they may constrain individuals. However, budgets do have significant advantages.
● The organization's objectives are clearly defined in financial terms.
● Key actions which the organization may need to take are highlighted.
● Responsibilities and yardsticks against which to measure performance are defined.
● An overview of the organization's entire activities is contructed and decisions about trade-off of resources and priorities can be made at a high level.
● Inter-departmental conflict is reduced.
● Early warning of problems is given so that corrective action may be initiated.
● Correctly performed, the budgeting process can be a positive, motivating stimulus.

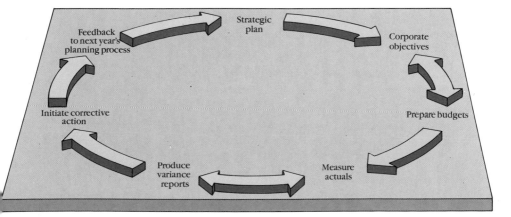

Costs and pricing

Your organization will have costing systems which collect and classify costs into different categories, at different times and, in some cases, in different currencies. You, as a manager, must understand the cost structure of your business well enough to know the financial implications of the decision you are making.

Some costs such as labor and materials can be charged as direct costs to a particular product or process. Other costs, such as heating, lighting, maintenance and depreciation, have to be apportioned as indirect costs.

The basis for apportioning costs varies by cost category and type of business. Different methods present different product costs and therefore must be taken into account when deciding which manufacturing process is used. Your accounting department will tell you which basis of cost apportionment it uses.

All decision-making requires cost information to evaluate choices. If, say, you visited a car showroom you would want to know how much each car cost before deciding to buy.

Cost information is used in pricing decisions. Price determines a firm's short-term profitability and a product's long-term success.

If the price is too high, sales will be lost. High prices that generate high profits attract other firms to join the competition. But if the price is too low, the firm may not recover its costs.

Pricing decisions tend to be either cost based or market based.

Cost based pricing

In cost based or cost plus pricing, a profit mark-up is applied to the total unit cost of the product. The amount of profit mark-up varies. For example, a product may be premium priced because it is technologically advanced or because it has a reputation for quality and reliability.

Alternatively, the profit mark-up

Costing systems

Costing systems are used to determine the cost of a unit of output. The most popular systems are process costing, job costing and operation costing.

Process costing is used where large volumes of identical products pass through a continuous production operation. The total cost of the operation is calculated for a given period, then divided by the number of units produced to give an average cost per unit.

Job costing is used in industries which produce to order. Costs can be identified for each job at every stage of the production cycle, with direct and indirect expenses allocated separately.

Operation costing is used to develop the cost per unit of services rendered.

---

may be set to achieve a target rate of return on capital employed, for a given level of sales. This is common with component suppliers whose prices are influenced by their dependence on a single manufacturer.

Market based pricing

Pricing decisions are based on the perceived value to the customer, or "what the market will bear." They depend on awareness of the customer, the structure of the market and the price and the quality of competitors' products.

Costs are of secondary importance in determining how low prices can be set. In the oil and motor industries, for example, prices are based on that of the market leader, adjusted for product feature differences.

Variants of market based pricing include price discrimination where the same product is offered to different customers at different prices. Competitive pricing is based on the assumed pricing strategies of competitors.

Costs are a fundamental tool for decision-making but, like profits, can be expressed in many different ways.

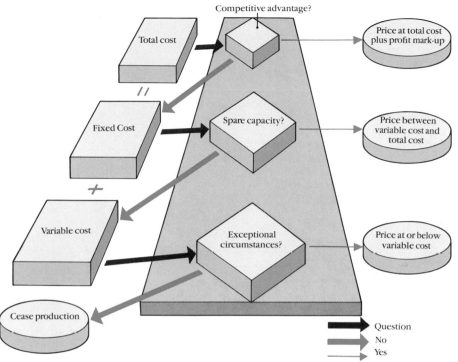

Pricing decisions

1 Competitive advantage: the first question you should ask is, does the product have a competitive advantage? It may be technically advanced or innovative, or your organization might be the market leader with an established brand image.

If the answer is yes, you can use cost plus pricing to develop the selling price. The mark-up will depend on the market and on the product's level of competitive advantage.

If the answer is no ...

2 Look at spare capacity: do you have enough to produce the product without incurring additional fixed costs, e.g. additional machinery, extra staff or more warehousing facilities? This question might arise in a competitive pricing situation where the objective is to price as low as possible yet make some contribution to fixed costs already incurred.

If spare capacity is available, you can afford to price the product at variable costs, plus some mark-up respresenting a contribution to fixed costs.

If the answer is no ...

3 Exceptional circumstances: you are really now taking pricing decisions at the margin. If you don't recover your variable costs, you are not even getting back the additional costs you will incur in producing these units.

There are exceptional circumstances that might make this avenue viable. Such exceptions depend on the other objectives of the firm, against which profitability can be traded off. For example, the firm may wish to establish a brand image, or to attract sales of other highly profitable products in the range, or to generate high profits in the after-sales market through service and supply.

If there are no exceptional circumstances, then you should immediately cease production, since that product will never be profitable to the firm.

Long-term planning

Cost information is used not only to make decisions about the day-to-day running of the business, but also to assist long-term plans. Managers need cost information to compare revenue or profits generated in the future with costs incurred today.

As part of the strategic and business planning process, accountants will help to:
● Evaluate future alternatives and measure the profitability of projects spanning a number of years.
● Project the firm's income statement and balance sheet over the next five or ten years.

Areas in which sound financial planning can play an important role include:
● The launching of new products.
● The replacement of existing equipment or buildings.
● Whether to make or buy a particular component.
● Where and when to locate new production facilities.

But no one knows with certainty what will happen in the future. As-sumptions have to be made so that costs and benefits, not easily expressed in cash terms, can be measured. How would you measure, for example, the benefits of an improvement in your firm's market image, or in employee morale?

You are the best person to predict the outcome of decisions affecting your department. So, while you should trust your accountants' skill and expertise, you should not rely solely on their judgments. Make sure that they take into account all the non-financial benefits you expect to accrue from a particular project.

Decisions should not be based on financial criteria alone. Financial evaluation is one aspect of the decision-making process, along with other factors, such as the validity of the assumptions and the sensitivity of the costs to change.

Financial evaluation techniques

	Original investment	1st year
Cash flows	(1000)	300
Cumulative (net) cash flows	(1000)	(700)
		⌐———— Payback ———
Discounted cash flow (DCF) 10% rate	(1000)	273
Cumulative net cash flows	(1000)	(727)
Discounted cash flow (DCF) 25% rate	(1000)	240
Cumulative net cash flows	(1000)	(760)

Capital investment budgeting involves decisions about how to invest money in projects now to maximize cash returns. Is the project profitable in its own right? Will it generate a rate of return at least equivalent to investing the money elsewhere at the same risk?

Imagine your company is considering whether or not to invest $1 million in a new production line (see example *above*). How should the company decide whether to go ahead?

If, by making certain assumptions about future cash flows, your accountants measure the profitability of the project, on what basis would they have to make their decision? There are three common approaches:
● The straightforward payback method asks: How quickly will the initial

(In thousands)					
2nd year	3rd year	4th year	5th year	Total cash flow	Average cash flow
300	400	400	600	2000	400
(400)	0	400	1000	$ARR = \dfrac{400}{1000}$ $= 40\%$	
248	300	273	372 *		
(479)	(179)	94	466 ↑ NPV		
192	205	165	198 *		
(568)	(363)	(198)	0 ↑ NPV	* Discounted cash flows can be obtained from specially prepared tables.	

Financial modeling

In the calculations (*left*), many of the figures are estimated and subject to significant variation.

Computer models can be constructed which allow extensive sensitivity analysis, enabling the variables to be changed and a number of different scenarios to be selected.

Such models often use discounted cash flow calculations to project future profitability patterns. You can then ask: "What will be the outcome if any of the assumptions were changed?"

Remember that the figures are only predictions and are sensitive to many fluctuating forces. If the accountants turn down your project on the grounds of their calculations, try your own sensitivity analysis. Examine the numbers again and again.

And what about non-financial factors: can your company afford not to invest in a new product, especially when competitors' actions make it imperative? Supposing your plant is becoming obsolete? Do not hesitate to question the accountants' calculations when your business sense disagrees with theirs.

investment be repaid? In this example, it is paid back after three years. And the quicker the payback, the less the risk to the project. However, this method does not take into account the cash flows after the payback date.

● The Average rate of return (ARR) method averages out the cash flow over the life of the project, five years in our example, giving a percentage figure for the average return on the initial investment. Here it is 40%. And the higher the figure, the better the profitability.

● The Discounted cash flow (DCF) method accounts for more variables and so is more complex but more accurate. Unlike the payback and ARR methods, DCF measures the time-value of money by translating future cash flows into their

net present value (NPV).

A discount rate is selected which represents the company's desired rate of return. It will normally equate either to the projected cost of borrowing money or to the return earned on present projects. Often this figure will be increased to allow for risk.

At 10% the project shows positive cash flows and at 25% it breaks even. The decision to go ahead or not would use these estimates and all the other business related factors known to one's company.

A 10% rate, probably an underestimation, gives a net profitability of $466,000 after 5 years. A 25% rate, probably an overestimation, means the company would be breaking even over the life of the project. These figures are known as the internal rate of return.

Are things going wrong?

Major financial problems rarely occur overnight and do not always mean that a company will fail. They do, however, indicate that top management has problems to deal with that, if they are left uncorrected, could ruin the company. If management does not respond to the problems and fails to manage the accounting function and/ or has poor budgetary control, then it is heading for trouble.

Company failures are management failures. Lack of success is reflected in the accounting information, but it is a symptom of ineffective management not a cause.

Top management needs to deal with present problems and future plans. Financial directors are essential participants. They must ensure that the

Signs of major financial problems

Companies do not usually have major financial problems without warning signs, some of which will be apparent from the accounts.

Further inquiry will be called for if these show:
● The company's net worth is negative or that two years' operations at last year's levels would put it into deficit.
● The assets, minus the long-term secured borrowings, are less than twice current borrowings.

If two or more of the following situations have also occurred, there are clearly major problems:
● In the past three years, the company has lost more money than it has made.
● Sales have declined in two of the past three years.
● The gross profit percentage has declined in two of the past three years.
● Interest and financial costs are greater than profits after tax.
● Debtors or inventory have increased more than 10 percent faster than sales in the past two years.

Lack of management action

If it is clear that management is not controlling the company, it is probable that they are not planning ahead. Likely symptoms of this include:
● Lack of specific plans to solve problems.
● Failure to identify market developments in advance.
● Hope for a general economic recovery rather than specific management action.
● Failure to identify the precise area of performance failure.
● Policy and operations are unreasonably dominated by the personal views of a single individual – often the owner-manager.

Additional danger signs include:
● Complacency or a lack of a sense of urgency, despite the appearance of major problems.
● If a mistake has been made, an inability to recognize it as such and take remedial action.

information which management needs is provided. They should explain the financial consequences of company policy and emphasize the effects of indecision and delay on any proposed changes.

Without effective management, companies cannot react to problems or rectify mistakes. The most common mistakes are:

● Overexpansion, i.e. growing beyond the financial capacity of the business.
● High leverage, i.e. too much cash borrowed to run the business.
● A "mammoth project" is undertaken without considering whether the company has the financial and management resources to see it through to a successful conclusion.

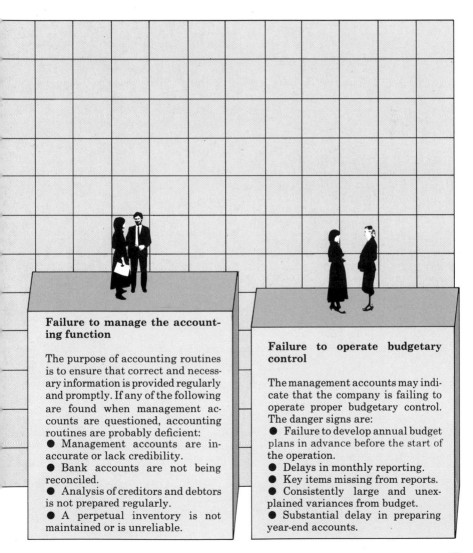

Failure to manage the accounting function

The purpose of accounting routines is to ensure that correct and necessary information is provided regularly and promptly. If any of the following are found when management accounts are questioned, accounting routines are probably deficient:
● Management accounts are inaccurate or lack credibility.
● Bank accounts are not being reconciled.
● Analysis of creditors and debtors is not prepared regularly.
● A perpetual inventory is not maintained or is unreliable.

Failure to operate budgetary control

The management accounts may indicate that the company is failing to operate proper budgetary control. The danger signs are:
● Failure to develop annual budget plans in advance before the start of the operation.
● Delays in monthly reporting.
● Key items missing from reports.
● Consistently large and unexplained variances from budget.
● Substantial delay in preparing year-end accounts.

Investing in people

Personnel concerns are one of the most important aspects of any organization. The aim is to get the most out of manpower resources.

As a manager, you are responsible for good relations with your staff. It is important that you recognize Personnel as an integral part of the management process and understand how the function can contribute to your effectiveness.

The development of Personnel

Since the early years of this century the personnel function has passed through various stages.

Personnel began as a concern for the physical and social welfare of working people. The next development of Personnel responsibility was the recruitment of staff to perform specific tasks and fill particular vacancies in the company.

Personnel has also been traditionally responsible for providing on-the-job training and rewarding employees for increased output.

Increasing levels of regulations, procedures and controls, and the use of coercion and money as the primary tools of motivation, led to widespread workforce militancy. In the negotiation of salaries, bonuses and working agreements, Personnel operated as intermediaries and conciliators.

Since the 1950s behavioral science has been included in the personnel function.

In the 1970s employment legislation brought a new role for the personnel function as legal adviser to ensure the company complies with a plethora of new rules.

Modern Personnel

In the 1980s the role of personnel departments is still interpretive, advisory and administrative. They are still the "people experts." The purpose so often prescribed for Personnel is one of getting the best return for an organization on its investment in people. That task has now become crucial to modern industries.

Recruitment

Personnel's role includes manpower planning and should cover:
● Liaison with the appropriate manager to agree on job description and specification of the type of employee required.
● Preparation of recruitment advertisements and screening of replies.
● Help with candidate interviews.
● Associated administration, including reference checks.

As a manager, use Personnel to help you find the best recruits.

Clearly define your needs so that Personnel can draw up a job specification. Leave Personnel to sift applicants and draw up a short-list. Take advantage of their interviewing expertise to help you with final interviews.

Personnel ought to help reduce the differences between the managers and the managed.

You and Personnel

The primary responsibility for good staff relations rests firmly with you, the manager. However effective the personnel department, it cannot do as much good as you can.
● Ensure that you are closely involved in issues affecting your staff.
● Demonstrate your commitment and loyalty by solving your group's personnel problems or by making sure they are dealt with correctly.
● Seek advice from Personnel on how to apply the organization's formal procedures to everyone's benefit.
● Don't hide behind procedures laid down by the personnel department. If you have to resolve questions that don't fit the guidelines, work out your own solution.
● Avoid searching for a rule that determines what you might do before thinking out for yourself what is best.
● Don't think, "I cannot do this because Personnel won't allow it." Rethink your particular problem.
● If Personnel's answer is right for your staff, consider the decision as yours.

Hiring

Personnel's objective in the last stage of the recruitment process is to help managers familiarize new employees with the company and its environment quickly. They should provide information on:
● Physical layout and facilities of the workplace.
● Key company rules, procedures and philosophies.
● Products and services.
● Key personnel.

Functions of Personnel

The functions and duties are to:
● Supply expert and up-to-date advice, interpretation and support on managing people.
● Run comprehensive administrative back-up, such as reference checks or physical fitness exams.
● Provide expert recruitment support.
● Provide advice and support on the hiring of recruits.
● Help identify training and development needs and set up the required programs.
● Understand and apply the principles of job evaluation.
● Provide a framework for assessing staff performance which allows the company to identify training needs and promotable people, and enables individuals to identify their career prospects.
● Ensure that all departures, whether by resignation, retirement or dismissal, are managed in accordance with statutory provisions.
● Have a detailed understanding of employment legislation and its implications for the organization.
● Give authoritative information on personnel-related company procedures and agreements.
● Ensure a consistent development and implementation of remuneration and benefits policies.
● Handle company welfare provisions, including the counseling of staff on personal problems.
● Have a general knowledge of government social services, how they apply to employees and how benefits are claimed.
● Understand the ways in which common, civil and criminal law affect the employment contract.

Supporting and advising

In speeches, in the annual report, at stockholders' meetings and on other occasions when the chief executive officer assesses the performance of the company, you are likely to hear these words: "Our most important asset is our people."

Finding, hiring and training these all-important people is the responsibility of the personnel department. Theirs is a unique role. Unlike virtually everybody else, they do not directly contribute to the product or service the company sells, or to the company's grand strategies.

But personnel work has become an important science of its own – the science of finding the right people, hiring them, placing them in the jobs where they can make the best contribution, and helping them deal with problems that threaten to keep them from doing their best work.

Links with the organization

The potential strength of the personnel department comes from its support and advisory roles. These bring it into contact with all line and functional heads. Credible individuals can therefore wield considerable influence.

Typically, a well-developed personnel department will report through its senior executive to the head of the organization without necessarily being represented on the board of directors. If it reports to a manager at any lower level, it will probably have insufficient credibility and weight to achieve anything worthwhile.

To perform its support functions, the primary administrative responsibility of the department is to maintain accurate records of individual employees. These should contain both personnel and detailed operational information.

Training of some sort will be required for every employee, however informal, at some stage of their career with a company.

As a manager, you should seek support from the personnel department for training your staff in basic or specialist skills, and for supervisory and managing training.

To appraise the job performance of your subordinates, you need sound understanding of what each job is about: its purpose, goals and targets. You should find out how well people are doing their jobs and if action is needed to improve performance.

To appraise job potential, consider whether subordinates are challenged, whether they accept responsibility and can view their jobs in relation to others.

Support function

To get the best return on the investment in people, Personnel must recruit higher qualified people and ensure that they are better trained and developed.

From the employee's point of view, Personnel can provide advice and assistance with personal problems, for example domestic, financial and legal difficulties, acting as a sort of in-house citizen's advice bureau.

More money is wasted on training and development than on any other aspect of the personnel department's work. There are only two reasons for training anyone: to make them capable of performing their job to a satisfactory standard, and to equip them to handle changed responsibilities either as a result of promotion or of redeployment.

Getting the right people trained in the right things is a difficult (and expensive) process. It requires the company to define its manpower needs now and in the future. It also requires individuals to know their strengths, to indicate their interests and ambitions and to analyze their shortcomings with complete honesty.

The department is frequently the designer of, and usually the coordinator or the advisor on, the appraisal system. Performance reviews should allow the organization to identify the good, the bad and the average and thus to plan the future use of resources at its disposal.

In the process, individuals should be helped to agree on tasks and objectives and advised on how they are themselves perceived by the organization and what their future holds. It is important that employees know both their duties and their prospects.

Training and development

A straightforward procedure should be applied before committing any funds to training:
● For all employees involved, identify what they need to do and what they are not qualified to do.
● For each need identified, specify on-the-job or off-the-job training and design or locate an appropriate program.
● Agree on criteria in advance for assessing the results of the training. This can be very difficult for management development courses, many of which rely on the gesture of faith that "some good will come of it."
● Ensure that senior management will support rather than thwart employees who return from training courses charged with new ideas.

Performance and promotion

A constructive appraisal scheme helps managers to improve their performance and that of their staff by:
● Demonstrating the value of all work done.
● Ensuring that managers and employees appreciate each other's position.
● Showing staff how to build on personal strengths.
● Identifying training needs.
● Drawing attention to employees with potential.
● Identifying any staff disharmony and rectifying it.
● Providing information on which to base future manpower plans.

Operating successfully

Companies have widely varying ideas on what their personnel policies should be and how they should be applied. The case studies (*opposite*) are not intended as ideal approaches to resolving these issues. Instead, they are indicative of what can be done, given commitment and vision by managements and workforces.

The procedures, rules and contractual arrangements surrounding the employment of staff inevitably deal with sensitive legal issues and have a potential for disaster if they are misunderstood or misapplied. Personnel has a clear function to interpret the written word and to know the precedents for its application.

Government legislation has increasingly affected the formulation of personnel policies and procedures and has introduced financial and other penalties for companies that fail to comply with its requirements. This has become important for personnel specialists who now need to understand the underlying statutes and their interpretation in the courts to be able to steer the company away from trouble.

Of particular relevance are the rules relating to layoffs and other dismissals and the anti-discrimination laws relating to sex and race.

Industrial relations
The most obvious involvement of the department is in the negotiating process. This is conducted either by direct involvement with the delegated authority of the chief executive, or Personnel acts as adviser to other managers who are seeking to resolve disputes or reach agreement on issues. Because interests are normally highly polarized, the process itself has become highly formal and proceduralized.

Other activities under this heading include joint consultation, employee participation programs, handling of grievances and disciplinary matters.

Departures

Whether due to dismissal, layoffs, retirement etc., departures involve Personnel in an advisory and administrative role to ensure:
● All benefits and entitlements are explained and paid.
● All internal procedures have been followed.
● The file on the individual is updated and retained for future reference.
● Statutory requirements have been met.

Most managers are happy to allow the personnel department to handle staff departures. Make sure that Personnel has all the relevant facts.

To minimize disruption to your department, arrange short-term cover for the vacancy or reorganize so that the vacancy disappears.

If a replacement is needed, start the recruitment process as quickly as possible.

TOSHIBA

Creating staff commitment

At Toshiba, positive staff relations are based on a recognition that, in employing somebody, a relationship has been entered into. Management expects commitment to the company in return for treating every employee as a valued member.

Employees are selected for their enthusiasm, idealism, attention to detail and expertise, as well as for their commitment. All are given the title "production employee," which allows for flexibility.

There is no job grading and evaluation scheme. Every employee is expected to wear a company-issue blue jacket at work and to eat in the same restaurant.

Everyone cleans their working area. All operators are given drawings showing clearly what their process involves. Each working day begins with a five-minute meeting to discuss problems, ideas and solutions.

Employees are trained to be quality conscious and self-checking. Production figures and quality level performances are freely displayed.

The result is low staff turnover, low absenteeism, minimal lateness, a cheerful workforce and production on target.

The belief that each person should feel important has brought Toshiba enviable production results. Their corporate philosophy and attitude to personnel work as well, if not as naturally, in Plymouth (UK), Tennessee and Singapore, as they do in Tokyo.

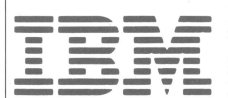

Supporting the manager

At IBM, the personnel function has little real power. Its role is to provide line management with a framework of personnel policies and practices. Ultimate responsibility for the management of IBM's people lies with the line managers.

Trust and confidence have been built up at all levels of line management. Managers are committed to IBM's personnel policies.

Full employment is offered to everyone. Employees whose jobs and skills are eliminated by economic or technical change are offered alternative jobs. In return, employees have to be prepared to move.

Most IBM employees have the same conditions of service and benefits; every employee's performance is assessed against objectives; everyone is paid according to merit.

A central communications department ensures that information reaches all line managers, who are encouraged to hold departmental meetings. Copies of the minutes are sent to the personnel manager. Opinion surveys are conducted on a regular basis.

Only if the system fails is the personnel function called on to adjudicate or make recommendations.

IBM recognizes that the company's aspirations will be realized only with the help of a workforce whose own aspirations are recognized by the company.

Keeping up to date

Keeping up to date with new technology is no easy task given the pace of development in information processing, office systems and communications. To be effective, managers need to harness new technology to meet their needs. To ensure efficiency is maintained, they need to keep what is available under constant review.

Technology stretches a manager's role as a decision-maker. To make the right decisions, managers need to put what is available to effective use. Peter Ueberroth, briefing his senior team members who were managing the Los Angeles Olympics, had one main message: never lose control. The same principle applies to all those managers using and developing technology systems.

Information processing

Commercial data processing originated with large computers, usually located at the head office to support the accounting operation of the business. On-line systems grew from the need to capture data at source, and the rapid development of the microchip allowed managers to use desk top computers in their offices.

The rapid growth in new technology resulted in increased demand for information systems which central data processing functions could not satisfy. Managers had either to line up for new systems or develop their own information systems.

Instead of making managers superfluous, as was once thought probable, technology has extended the role of managers, increasing the demands made on them.

The manager who has assumed a role previously undertaken by the central data processing function must apply the same standards expected of that function to the planning and control of information systems.

Office systems

Until the 1960s, most offices carried out specific functions, such as accounting, payroll or personnel. They were supported for general clerical needs by a large centralized office such as the typing pool or print room.

In the past twenty years, new technology has altered the tools of the office. In the last decade the changes have been dramatic. For example, the simple adding machine has given way to the calculator and microcomputer. Paper files are being replaced

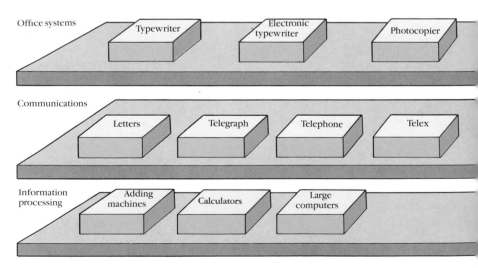

by microfilm/fiche and the laser disk. The typewriter and carbon paper are competing with the word processor, laser printer, intelligent photocopier and facsimile transmission.

With the new technology has come the dispersal of the centralized office functions. The office services function now finds its role converging upon that of the data processing function. This is reflected in the confusion facing today's managers who wish to choose a word processor. Do they talk to office services or data processing?

Although managers have accepted responsibility for their own office systems, they must conform to certain standards to enable their systems to communicate with others in the enterprise.

The pace of development within office systems, combined with the communications revolution, means that the paperless office is not far away.

The communications revolution

The old electromechanical analog telephone exchanges are giving way to modern digital exchanges. Information is being transmitted around the world by means of fiber optic cables and microwave links as well as an ever-increasing number of satellites.

The effect of this communications revolution on the business is not limited to the telephone system. The conversion to digital communications methods, coupled with the existing digital computer systems, has opened up countless opportunities.

Vastly increased transmission speeds now allow huge volumes of data to be sent. Organizations, using this technology to create a network of its offices, can still capture and retain data at the source but allow all offices to share the data.

This communications revolution has acted as the catalyst in bringing together the processing of data, text and voice. Businesses can now think in terms of information technology, and the effect of this convergence can be seen in the combining of responsibilities for information processing, office systems and communications into one function – that of information technology management (*see below*).

But within this framework, line managers must manage and control their existing systems and ensure that they acquire the new systems to meet their needs.

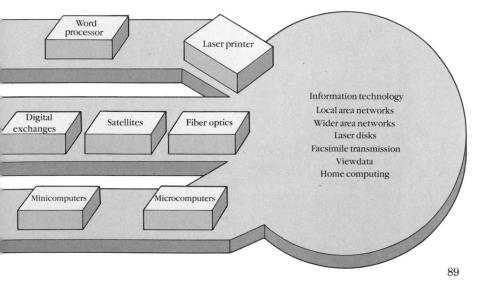

Word processor

Laser printer

Digital exchanges

Satellites

Fiber optics

Minicomputers

Microcomputers

Information technology
Local area networks
Wider area networks
Laser disks
Facsimile transmission
Viewdata
Home computing

Creating systems

If, as a manager, you are responsible for creating systems, or you take over someone else's methods and procedures, you must deal with what is important, not necessarily what is the most urgent.

To do so, you need to find out why the systems are there in the first place; the criteria for their performance; the need for, and the extent of, security measures (to ensure against loss/duplication), and the need for future enhancements to the systems, as they become necessary.

You should conduct a review of the system, carrying out the various tasks in a well thought out and structured manner.

It is crucial for managers to understand the business's objectives before establishing the information-processing objectives. Establish an order of priority to ensure that the system's objectives, if achieved, will satisfy those of the business.

Find out what systems plans exist, and when you have discovered who is responsible for carrying out the plans, determine the best way to communicate with them.

You must clearly establish the role and responsibility which you will assume for your own systems. Where the facilities directly support your business function or performance, knowing the ground rules becomes crucial to your success.

Reviewing a system

● Determine the objectives of the business and the system.
● Order objectives by priority.
● Establish how system performance is measured.
● Identify security procedures.
● Establish responsibility for system operation.
● Establish formal communication between the user and the provider.

The performance of an automated system

System performance should be examined according to the following two headings:

User satisfaction
Determine the system's level of user satisfaction by finding out:
● How much the system costs to run.
● If the system produces the planned benefits.
● How frequently it has been changed.
● How much changes to the system cost.
● What relationship users have with the computer function.

When you have done that, you should then go on to:
● Review the methods by which computer charges are calculated and passed on to users.
● Find out what support, such as training and advice, has been set up and then make sure that it is followed.
● Ensure that you are kept completely informed of all plans, progress, variances, problems and reasons. Monitor all the various costs and benefits.
● Establish quality control procedures; make sure that your objectives are met.

Checking performance
Examine the reports of the system's performance level. If they do not exist, initiate them on a regular basis and make sure that:
● Reports are, as far as possible, produced on time.
● Users who need to share data are able to do so.
● Terminals are available as planned and response times are adequate.
● Maintenance and breakdown procedures are adequate and that they are working as quickly as is necessary.

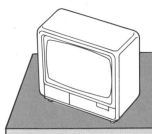

System management

To manage a system effectively, and be in control of your business area, you should try to:
● Focus on the critical information technology (IT) issues (e.g. response time and what information or level of detail is needed).
● Be aware of the status of all IT matters.
● Increase the awareness of senior management as well as that of your subordinates.

If you can achieve the above, you will be back in the driver's seat of your business area.

You can then go on to:
● Put into action plans to upgrade your automated systems to meet your demands.
● Address problems in the IT area effectively through the correct channels and methods.
● Test the adequacy of all new applications and procedures supplied by the computer function before you accept them.

Security for the system

Examine the physical and data security procedures for the system:
● Identify threats to hardware, software, data, networks and manpower.
● Ensure adequate documentation is available.
● Take protective measures, e.g. by making certain you are insured.
● Check back-up and security procedures; make sure they are working.

Draw up a disaster contingency plan by:
● Working out the critical business functions serviced by the computer and plan to be without them.
● Plan and test out recovery procedures.
● Set up a system of regular monitoring to ensure that you are not caught out by any unexpected changes in systems.

Implementing systems

Selection of information technology equipment, hardware and software requires similar disciplines to those applied to building a house or a new plant, for example.

Since the equipment will be incorporated into the business's systems and procedures, its implementation demands the wholehearted commitment of management and staff.

Whether managers are leading a project to install new systems within their departments, or are part of a wider project, it is essential that there is a disciplined approach to the selection and implementation of systems.

Developing a strategy

The development of new systems should be part of an overall plan to meet the business's objectives. A business plan from which an information technology plan can be derived is thus always essential.

Top management must be committed to the information technology plan and must ensure that each new

The stages of an IT project

1 Strategy
● Establish an information technology working group of senior management.
● Confirm business objectives and and also the critical success factors of the business.

● Prepare long-term system plans to meet needs.
● Prepare a mechanism for the approval, management and monitoring of the IT project.

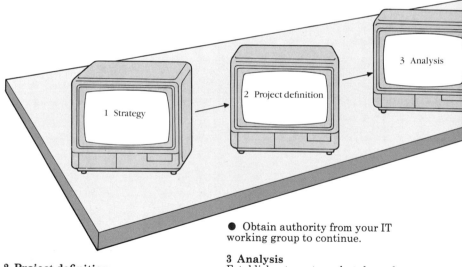

1 Strategy

2 Project definition

3 Analysis

● Obtain authority from your IT working group to continue.

2 Project definition
● Prepare a detailed project plan: to ensure objectives meet overall strategic requirements.
● Ensure adequacy of resources, timetable, management and monitoring mechanism.
● Define systems in broad concepts and clearly identify benefits and costs.
● Appoint a project manager with specific terms of reference.

3 Analysis
Establish a team to undertake and document detailed analysis of current systems including:
● Volume
● Staff employed
● Filing needs
● Timing constraints
● Input and output with other applications.
Establish future requirements and constraints of your proposed system.

system meets planned objectives, satisfies cost and benefit criteria, and is acceptable to the enterprise.

A high-level systems committee needs to be formed, meeting regularly to review all aspects of the business's information technology activities.

As each IT project is approved by this high-level committee, an individual project committee should be set up, with representation from all parties concerned with the project, having authority to commit staff and resources to the project.

Managers must ensure that both they and other users obtain training in how information technology systems are defined, developed and implemented.

Good project management is, of course, essential to the success of any development plan.

Progress from one stage of development to the next should not be permitted until the project committee has accepted the previous stage.

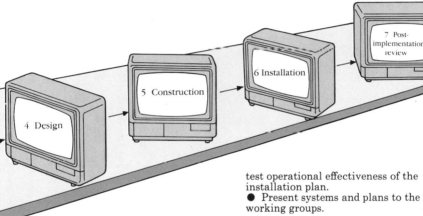

4 Design
5 Construction
6 Installation
7 Post-implementation review

test operational effectiveness of the installation plan.
● Present systems and plans to the IT working groups.

4 Design
● Ensure close involvement of potential users in any proposed system, especially screen and report design.
● Determine need of User Reference Manual and user training.
● Confirm that system specification, costs, timetable and benefits still meet original needs.
● Obtain approval from IT working group to begin construction.

5 Construction
Make sure that:
● Systems documentation is thorough and complete.
● A training package is developed.
● An installation plan is prepared and that it includes timetable and costs and resources required.
● Check actual costs and timetable against original plan.
● Where possible, use a pilot plan to

6 Installation
● Train staff in installation procedures.
● Implement installation.
● Test acceptance of the installation and (if pilot test used) complete installation.
● Confirm all documentation is available and that the system to update and change the system is operable.
● Report completion to IT working group.

7 Post-implementation review
● Measure actual achievement against budget and cost benefits proposed.
● Check that the system actually achieves the objectives originally established.
● Report to IT working group.
● Arrange annual reviews thereafter.

Customer relations

Marketing is surrounded by mystique. Definitions vary from "corporate planning" to "the preparation of a media schedule for advertising." In the game of business one-upmanship, you will score heavily by getting the definition right.

The simplest answer to "What is marketing?" is that it is the "process by which a company satisfies the needs of its customers at a satisfactory profit." The word "marketing" is associated with the street market, where vendors compete vigorously and use the simplest of strategies in order to sell their goods.

When K Mart opened its chain of cloned, no-frills discount stores, it displayed all the necessary constituent parts of a successful marketing strategy. K Mart was able to sell:
- The right products
- In the right place
- At the right price
- Promoted in the right way
- To the right people.

Today, K Mart is America's No. 2 retailer – behind Sears, Roebuck and Co – and it is applying the same marketing discipline to its move into upscale merchandise.

Yet in many companies marketing is the part of the organization that is developed last or cut first during cost-pruning exercises.

Companies will occasionally mount advertising and sales promotional campaigns without developing an adequate marketing strategy. These campaigns fail because the company has not asked itself what business it is in; what kind of business it should seek to enter; and how it should try to enter it.

In preparing a marketing strategy for products and services, you will succeed if you concentrate on one thing – the customer. It may seem obvious to say that without customers all other aspects of a business are superfluous; but ask any group of

---

The end product of marketing

To achieve the right mix of products and markets for the company and its customers, you need to:
- Analyze opportunities by asking: Who needs our products? What are our strengths? What are our customer needs?
- Select realistic objectives by using a consistent background for decision-making and planning. Then define roles and provide a sense of purpose.
- Develop strategy by recognizing internal strengths and weaknesses and external opportunities and threats. Develop tactics to beat the opposition.
- Formulate plans by drawing up your game plan according to resources.
- Implement and control: make it happen.

---

executives what is the most important success point on which a business should focus its attention and they will answer: profit, efficiency, productivity, management information, sales turnover or technical innovation. Customers, it seems, are regularly taken for granted.

Any business which does not satisfy its customer needs now and in the future, will cut itself off from its customers and its essential life-support system. It should ask its customers (directly or indirectly) what they think of existing products; what improvements/additions they would like to see; what unfulfilled needs they have; and what about value for money.

Marketing nurtures the essential relationship between the company and its customers, and the marketing function defines the methods by which a company selects the appropriate mix of products and markets with which to achieve its objectives.

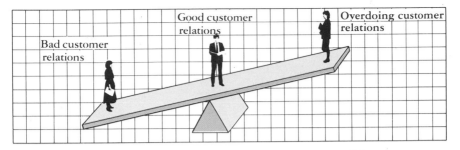

Good customer relations are essential for the success of a business. They are achieved by:
● Good customer service.
● Product margins that meet the company's objectives and give the customer value for money.
● Relevant product development and innovation to meet customers' needs.
● Regular sales calls and entertainment proportional to sales potential.

Overdoing customer relations can mean:
● High service costs.
● Low margins.

● High development costs of products with limited market.
● Late payments.
● Too many sales calls.

Bad customer relations are due to:
● Poor service.
● Products seen as poor value for money.
● No interest in customers' future needs.
● Insensitive credit control procedures.
● Infrequent sales calls.
● Low entertainment costs.

If the balance swings too heavily in either direction, the result is *loss of profit*.

Market research equals customer knowledge

Businesses change most frequently as a result of movements in their customer base. A company's marketing activity should aim to understand and quantify those movements and to achieve a continuous net growth in the size of its customer base.

Past customers are often one of the easiest prospects for improving business. Study the sales history:
● Slow buyers may show a change in quantity or regularity of purchase.
● Lost customers indicate potential product or service problems.

Existing customers' buying habits enable companies to focus on opportunities for sales extension. Ask yourself:
● Are most of our customers in one particular market segment/sector? Whom else can we sell to?
● Are there opportunities to sell other products to existing customers? How can our products be improved?
● Can customers buy larger quantities more frequently?
● Are we dealing with the right person at the right level?
● Who are the competition?

Future customers should be identified. Methods of targeting potential buyers include:
● Market research
● Prospect analysis
● Competitor research

Developing a strategy

Key elements of a marketing strategy are market segmentation, market entry and timing.

Marketing segmentation

This means breaking up the markets into parts according to customer needs. Customers may prefer a certain product make-up in one area but a slightly different one in another area. Some may value one feature of a product, others respond to another. Therefore, you should modify your product and your promotions to exploit the best competitive features in each market segment.

The purpose of dividing up the market is to identify segments which:
● Are big enough to justify committing resources.
● Have potential for growth and increased value.
● Are not completely dominated by your competitors.
● Show a genuine need for your product.

Market entry

There are a number of ways of getting into a market. For example, acquiring a company already operating there; joint ventures or some other form of collaboration with another firm; and there are sales and marketing techniques to give you a foothold.

Timing

Timing is one of the most critical elements in marketing strategy. The best product and the soundest plan will be wasted, and opportunity lost, if the timing is wrong. Ask:
● Is your product ready to compete? Have you built in a demonstrable benefit that sets your product apart?
● Is this a seasonal purchase? If so, timing is vital.
● Have you allowed enough time to promote your entry and precondition buyers to try your product?
● What are your competitors doing?
● Have you planned enough time to train your staff, set up distribution, and ensure product supply?

Marketing mix

For this piece of marketing jargon, consider a recipe which needs the right balance of ingredients mixed in the right order and cooked in the right way to satisfy the consumer.

To make your product more buyable, consider:

Product	**Place**
Position	Customer
Features	location
Quality	Distribution
Brand image	pattern
Packaging	Outlet location
Guarantees	Distribution
Service	method
	Inventories
	Sales territories
Promotion	**Price**
Communication	Level
Advertising:	Sensitivity
theme/scheme	Discount
Sales promotion	structure
Public relations	Payment terms
Selling	

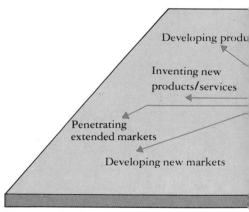

The arena in which a company operates

Developing product

Inventing new products/services

Penetrating extended markets

Developing new markets

Companies grow by:
● Developing and improving existing products and services.
● Inventing new products and services.
● Penetrating extended markets.
● Developing new markets.
● Diversifying into new products in new markets.

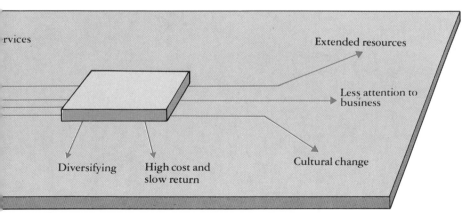

Many companies rush headlong into diversification in new markets, without fully exploiting the market for their existing products and services. Though potentially attractive, there are many pitfalls.

These include:
- Extended resources.
- Less attention to existing business.
- Cultural change necessary.
- High cost and slow return.

Success is achieved by consistently promoting and developing existing and improved products in present and extended markets.

Beware of the perils of diversification or change – stick to the existing strengths and promote them. Diversification should be carefully selected, planned, controlled and, in general, be the last resort when all other development options have been exhausted.

97

Preparing a plan

Once strategic market analysis is over and the products and markets are chosen, the next step you need to take is to produce an appropriate marketing plan.

Preparation

Successful marketing plans are developed by taking a disciplined approach to the task of preparation. Make sure that all the relevant key elements are considered.

A good marketing plan is a blend of the various aspects of a company's marketing and selling activity.

Like preparing to play a baseball game, you have to make certain that you have the following in order to be sure of success:

● The correct number of players in the appropriate positions.

● The correct blend of offensive and defensive players.

● The correct training and coaching plan.

● The right tactics to beat the opposition.

● A suitable number of competent substitutes ready on the bench to be called upon if necessary.

Implementation

Marketing plans frequently fail because companies rely too heavily on advertising and promotional campaigns without sufficient regard to the back-up service needed to respond to them.

A medium-sized car-rental company spent $1,000,000 on theme advertising that created a measured awareness of 95 percent of those sampled. The company, however, failed to capitalize on this awareness with follow-through campaigns and aggressive selling.

Growth was not sustained, and over a period of two years the company's sales fell as other competitors launched an attack on the market with heavily promoted programs, backed by service. The company's marketing plan was out of balance.

The eight-part marketing plan

Construct your marketing plan so a balance is struck.

Some sections of the eight-part marketing plan are more relevant in certain industry sectors than others. However, by going through a marketing plan in this structured way, you are forced to think of tactics and techniques which might otherwise be ignored.

1 Targets and objectives
Financial: total sales
Credit terms: units of sale (number); market share (%)

2 Product plan
Products: existing; improvement; development
Markets: existing; extensions; new

3 Pricing plan
Prices: ours vs competitors; trends
Margins
Discounts/rebates

4 Market information plan
Market research
Customer research
Competitor review

5 Sales plan
Direct: territories; distribution; prospects
Indirect: distribution; networks
Controls: budgets/targets; reports

6 Promotional plan
Advertising through the media
Printing: point of sale material; exhibitions
Public relations: free use of media; sponsorships
Direct marketing: direct mail; sales activities

7 Structure/staffing
Human resources
Training
Performance criteria
Incentives
Organization

8 Budget
To measure the performance of each of the above, linked to achievement of targets.

Promoting excellence

BMW is an example of a company with a well-formed strategy and a sound, balanced marketing plan.

BMW cars compete in the upper end of the executive car market and, in all aspects of their marketing approach, BMW promotes the technical excellence, quality engineering and reliability of their product.

Their dealer network is well supported by advertising and promotional aids. They promote an exclusive club for executives who are BMW owners. Fashion garments and regular magazines are available to owners.

By pitching their marketing effort directly at people who aspire to ownership, BMW find their price is insignificant in relation to the product and its promotion. The average lead time in 1984 for delivery of their 3-Series cars was about four to five months, yet orders kept rolling in.

The promoted features of the BMW product far outweighed any marginal price benefit so heavily featured in promotional campaigns by the other mainstream automobile manufacturers.

Taking off and crash landing

Laker Airways, "the people's airline," arrived with the spectacular low-priced, no frills transatlantic fare and departed a few years later in 1982 in an equally spectacular liquidation.

Their strategy was short-term and based largely on one feature: low price. The undoubted weakness of such a strategy was the inevitable price-cutting response from the major international airlines.

Of course, it is not that you should adopt *only* no-risk strategies. The lesson from Laker is that any low-price dominated strategy, lacking sufficient product features on which a marketing plan can be based, is highly vulnerable to forces beyond your control.

Creating a structure

An organization must be sufficiently structured to ensure that it satisfies the needs of its customers at a profit which satisfies its own needs.

The sales and marketing function in any company should be as structured as the other functions, but should not stop the development of "product champions" and "super sales people."

In creating the organization structure for a company, the sales and marketing functions are often covered simply by labelling executives "sales managers" or "marketing managers," with little thought as to the scope of their responsibilities.

The sales function
The direct sales effort should ensure that the staff covers the territory where the customers are located. The number of sales people depends on the number of calls needed to service the existing customers, regain lost customers and sell to potential customers.

Management has a responsibility to promote the use of sales techniques and make sure that a disciplined approach produces value for the company.

The marketing function
Marketing efforts should be geared toward examination, investigation and promotion of the market for a company's goods/services. The company should have sound, verifiable data on how its customers and the rest of the market are changing, and should be aware of competitors.

Marketing activity should support sales with research and promotion, and the sales people should spend as much time as possible with the customer.

Through research, marketing can also help product development.

Sales and marketing
The mix and the relative weighting of sales and marketing activity depend on the size and breadth of the market. As in any structure or model, if one element is missing or incomplete, the rest will tend to be less effective.

Market research

Marketing plans and changes in direction should be based on verifiable data.

Analyze the last five years' performance and use forecasts and published statistics to predict the behavior of customers and markets in the future. Forecast at "current prices." Remember that every forecast you make is almost certain to be wrong. Sound research-based judgment will help you to be sufficiently accurate to make key strategic decisions.

Small/medium companies often combine the sales and marketing functions under one executive or senior manager, who should see to it that the correct balance of resources and skills is working for him or her and the company.

There will tend to be greater use of resources from outside. The manager decides the need for these and how to put them to effective use.

A review of performance can take one of the following forms.

1 External audit

The market: total market, size, growth and trends (value/volume).

Market character: developments and trends, products, distribution channels, customers/consumers, communication, industry practices.

Competition: size, share, standing and reputation; marketing methods, production capabilities, profitability, key strengths and weaknesses.

2 Internal audit

Sales: by location, type, customer, product.

Market shares: profit margins, cost rates.

Marketing mix variables: product management, price, distribution, promotion, operations and resources.

3 Customer research

Customer requirements and habits: some organizations use panels of sample customers to test the acceptability of the product and its price.

In industrial marketing, research is often ignored, and questions are seldom asked of buyers about their satisfaction and future needs.

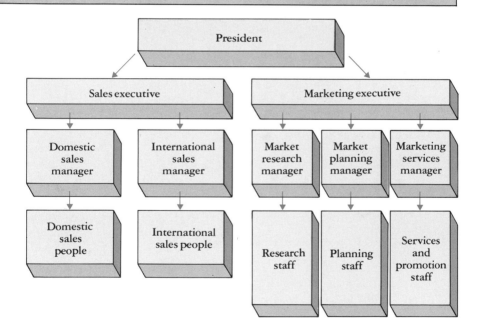

Large companies can afford the luxury of splitting up the sales and marketing activities and so manage them separately at a senior level.

In companies that have a large advertising budget, product managers take on a dominant role in sales and media campaigns.

The sales function converts interest into real purchases and can include distribution. The marketing function supports this with promotion, research and product development input from the customer and the marketplace.

Because of the extent of their resources, large companies usually enlist, but do not depend exclusively on, the help of external agencies and consultants.

Prospecting

Selling is the direct interaction between a company and its customer. Management training and material tend to be devoted to "closing the sale," "effective presentation skills," "use of visual aids," and so on. The one aspect of selling often neglected is "prospecting."

In advance of any direct selling activity or, indeed, any promotion, it is important to take time and allocate resources to mining for clients. Prospecting identifies potential buyers and their needs, likes and dislikes. It is useful in tailoring products or services, so that the quality, not quantity, of prospective buyers is what matters.

Market segmentation will show the market segment most likely to yield buyers, e.g. manufacturing companies with sales in excess of $5 million within 50 miles of your office.

Building up a prime prospect file is the most valuable activity a salesperson can do. Once achieved, canvassing is necessary only to "top up" the prospect reservoir when the level drops; that is, a prospect is converted to a customer and is replaced by another prime prospect.

The prospect file will help only if it is kept up to date and used systematically. A follow-up system will force you to plan your time effectively.

The selection of prospects can be done at the desk or by telephone. It involves a relatively low cost resource, compared with the use of a field salesperson.

The use of computers enables companies to develop a database of prospects which can be used interactively, depending on sales objectives or changes in strategy. By using a computerized marketing database, you can analyze important factors such as source of prospect/lead, date last called, change in staff.

A new sale in a market sector can open the door to acquiring a number of new prospects in this sector.

The prospecting process: Stage 1

Canvassing

The key elements in surveying potential customers are research and creativity. The research phase identifies the names of prospects, their size, location and type of business. Sources of prospects are various and often depend on product/service. Sources of data include:

- Electoral registers
- Development agency directories
- End-user lists
- Other companies' sales ledgers
- Seminars/presentations on subjects of interest
- Chambers of Commerce
- Trade Associations
- Publications

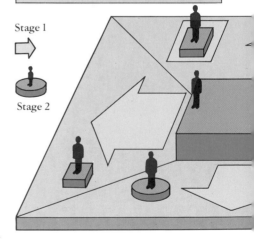

Stage 1

Stage 2

The selection process

Prospecting is based on well-researched information, but do not forget that a creative approach is always welcome.

Novel approaches to a prime prospect can often turn up a need that has been lying dormant.

The successful salesperson keeps up a continuous flow through all four stages of the process and particularly concentrates on Stage 3, i.e. hot prospects.

Stage 2

Prime prospect selection

Much time can be saved by ruthless application of the following criteria:
- Money: ability to pay for your product or service, i.e. being able to afford it and pay for it.
- Authority: you may successfully sell to a prospect, but make sure he or she has the authority to buy. Don't be misled by titles on business cards. Your time may also be profitably spent finding a star who may be a real buyer in the future.
- Need: no matter how convincing your sales talk, your time is wasted if you give it to a prospect who has no need for your product.

If any of these three criteria is not met, the prospect must be discarded.

Stage 3

Hot prospects

These are prospects who have the need to buy – now.

They must be rigorously courted and sales effort must be concentrated on the period during which they are hot.

This is the buying time, and the opportunity must not be missed.

Stage 4

Customer acquisition

The final stage of the prospecting process is when a prospect is converted to a customer and a sale is made. (NB a customer may be a *hot prospect* for other products and services).

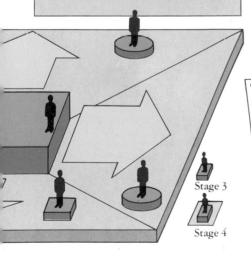

Stage 3

Stage 4

In addition to this, effective salespeople plan their time, or use research in such a way as to be encouraging prospects from Stage 2 to Stage 3. At the same time, they will be guiding customers to Stage 2 from Stage 1.

The telephone is a particularly effective tool in establishing prospects in Stage 1 and Stage 2 and in prodding customers through the various stages.

The prospect file

To enable you to make well-informed judgments and successful sales visits, a prospect file, or marketing database, must include the following information:
- Basic data: company name, address, telephone etc.
- Holding company and structure.
- Key personnel and decision-makers.
- Relationship with your company and previous contacts/jobs.
- Financial data/performance.
- Recent information/activities/appointments.

Selling

Management is fundamentally about direction and control. Selling is no different.

All salespeople, particularly those in large companies, present a basic problem: they enjoy spending their time doing what they know best, with the products that are the easiest to sell, and selling to customers who are easiest to sell to. Direction, management and control are needed to ensure that selling time and cost is spent where it is most effective – on prime and hot prospects.

Successful sales managers and directors keep the pressure on their sales force by meeting regularly with them to review:

● Performance versus budget.
● Key performance ratios.
● Follow-up procedures.
● Opportunities.
● Competitor activity.

Incentives do not figure high on this list. Many sales managers spend too much time inventing elaborate sales incentive plans, which the salesforce can manipulate to their personal benefit. Incentives must be geared toward the overall objectives of the marketing plan in terms of sales and cost. When incentives are used, they should be consistent, clear and reviewed periodically to make sure they enhance the overall sales effort but do *not* detract from it.

Sales incentive plans are often an excuse for poor management of the sales resource. There are many lasting benefits in creating an effective team relationship within a sales force: shared experience does not arise when sales people are obsessed with competing against each other.

The other forgotten standard of performance is control of credit. A sale is not a sale until the debt has been paid. The sales force should collect money owed to the company. It was responsible for the sale and should be responsible for assuring its payment.

How are we doing?

The key performance indicators of selling activity are:

Ratios
● Percentage sales : budget
● Contract/orders : quotations
● Quotations : leads
● Percentage margins : sales

Salesforce
● Number of calls
● Number of new prospects called/found
● Progress on inquiries/quotations
● Credit control
● Frequency of calls per day/week/month etc.
● Length of calls
● Percentage discounts : sales overall utilization
● Number of customers and their value
● Administration of sales reports/prospects
● Submission of itineraries

Overall
● Cost of sales force/sales
● Sales value/order
● Orders to calls ratio
● Percentage discounts : sales
● Key account development.

Know your customer base. It may be most appropriate to spend 80 percent of your selling/promotional activity with 20 percent of your clients who account for 80 percent of your sales.

Beating the competition

Always overestimate your competitors – they are not sitting back letting you make the sale at list price and in a well-ordered process. In any competitive sale, get to know the clients better than your competitors and establish what influences their attitudes. Sales are not made to companies – they are made to individual people, whose attentions are being sought. The sales call report should be used as a source of information on competitors.

The sales call report

The cornerstone of most sales control systems is the customer call report. The example can be modified to meet the needs of most companies and covers the essential ingredients. The call report can greatly aid in the communication process, and in particular:
● Assist managers to control sales staff.
● Establish customers' needs.
● Act as a follow-up reminder.
● Ensure necessary action is taken by salespeople and support staff.

1 Whom are you calling on?
This section is the basic reference which establishes if the call is being made on the decision-maker, or if it is exploratory. Salespeople are often diverted to an assistant who cannot authorize a purchase.

2 Why are you calling?
This section records the objective of the call and establishes the criteria against which results can be measured. By completing this section, the salesperson confirms that the call will represent effective use of time.

3 Result of the call
This section outlines the caller's proposal or presentation. The customer's response should be qualified, and any information, such as competitor activity or change in customer need, detailed.

4 Client/customer requirements
This section

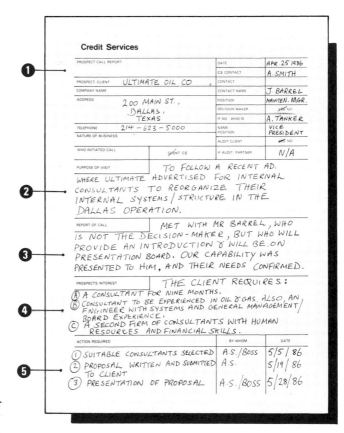

summarizes the prospect's interest and justifies the action to be taken.

5 Action required
All sales calls require action, especially those which could result in a lost order. The salesperson will normally have to follow up the call. This may involve support services to prepare detailed quotations or despatch products, and sales literature. The most important purpose is to communicate the status of a particular customer.

Promoting the business

As a manager, you will probably become involved in promoting the business. This means launching new products and services, getting the public to try them, fighting off the efforts of competing brands, and building the company's reputation as a go-getter and habitual winner in the marketplace.

To accomplish these ends, the company calls on a wide range of promotional weapons. Among them are advertising, sales promotions of infinite variety, special events, and public relations. Specialists do the work. Your role is to supply information and guidance.

Advertising – for television, radio, newspapers and magazines – is the most visible way to promote a product or service. With budgets running into millions, large companies and their advertising agencies will often survey consumers to find out which product feature has the strongest sales appeal. This then becomes the theme of the advertising. Commercials and ads are then tested among consumers to see whether they understand the message, believe it, and are motivated to buy the product.

Then comes the question of media – TV, radio, print, etc. Which medium or combination of media reaches the most prospective buyers at the lowest cost? The media expert, with the help of a computer, finds exactly who the choice prospects are for the product, where they live, how much education they have had, what they watch and read, and many other pertinent facts that help to make up the media plan. With millions at stake, the media are chosen as carefully as the message.

In the sales promotion area, one popular way to promote a new product or product improvement is to use "sampling." The company mails out small product samples to consumers or distributes them in stores or on the street. Another is to run coupons in

print ads, offering a reduced price. The idea behind these promotions is that the best way to persuade consumers to switch to your product is to give them a chance to sample it.

Some companies identify themselves with special events. They sponsor community events, support local and national causes, sponsor sporting events and similar projects that earn them publicity and the goodwill of people interested in these events.

Public relations takes many forms. It means writing publicity stories about the company, speeches by principal officers, articles by company experts. It means participating in forums on business, government, education, and so on. Such efforts keep the company name in the spotlight and foster the impression of a confident, innovative, progressive leader in its field. This helps attract good employees and

;chhh...you know who.

executives, earns respect of investors, and reinforces the public's trust in the firm and its products.

Companies also use corporate promotions – promoting the company itself instead of products and services. This is done to communicate with special noncustomer groups who are in a position to influence the affairs of the company – stockbrokers, government leaders, editors, and such.

The goal is to help these people understand how the company operates, what it stands for, its financial condition and its plans.

This is accomplished by advertising, or by testifying before government committees, making presentations to brokers and financial analysts, by holding press conferences to express the company's position on important matters, or by any other means that brings the company together with these influential groups.

Public relations involves creating news stories to announce expansion plans, appointments, new products and services, and other developments in the company. An important PR function is to maintain good relations with the press so that the company's point of view on public issues will be fully and fairly reported.

Some companies sponsor special events, such as major sports competitions, by providing financial help. Also, a company may sponsor an individual competitor or team, as Mobil sponsored Williams Honda Cars in Formula 1 racing in 1985.

The function of advertising is to persuade the public to buy a company's product or service. The American Express "Do you know me?" campaign has been so successful that the concept is now being used worldwide.

The Schweppes' ads are so designed that they only have to say "sch" and we all know to whom they are referring.

Robinson's Barley Water has become world famous through its association with the Wimbledon stars who stand beside or consume it.

Distribution

Good marketing means getting the right product to the right place at the right time. All the work done to achieve this can fail at the last moment if you do not deliver the goods or you deliver them late.

Marketing people have to balance the promotional mix to achieve the best value. This involves various trade-offs that are mirrored in delivery. Advertising moves people to products, and selling moves products to people. Physical distribution of products will link these two.

Effective distribution techniques reduce inventory levels, free working capital and reduce borrowings. The effective executive seeks to reduce the time for delivery and, at the same time, reduce the cost of transport as an element of the overall product price.

Businesses need to use their resources to the maximum. This causes a continual conflict between *time* and *capacity*. For example, it may be necessary, at times of product launch, to employ selective express carriers, but to change to distributors when a more permanent cycle of demand has been established.

There are four main channels of distribution.

Direct
Direct distribution means moving the product in sufficient bulk at a frequency that satisfies the customer and results in the lowest possible unit cost.

The main questions that arise are: method of transport; packaging of units; handling facilities at each end, and use of one's own transport or subcontractor.

The quality and reliablity of the product is in the hands of the supplier.

Owned warehouse
Distribution of the product by strategically placed warehousing allows the supplier to move large quantities of finished product at one time. The distribution warehouse may be owned by the company or may be a break-bulk distribution warehouse, where loads are broken down into a number of smaller deliveries and shared by a number of companies.

The supplier pays the price of warehousing, but gains the benefit of being able to supply in smaller quantities at more frequent intervals.

Wholesaler
As a distribution channel, the wholesaler is an intermediary who is paid a fee to distribute goods from the manufacturer to the customer. Suppliers of consumer goods, from fast-moving consumer goods, such as food, to white goods (refrigerators, washing machines) make frequent use of wholesalers as intermediaries.

Goods are *sold* to wholesalers at a discount on list price, enabling them to stock and distribute to their customers. They are assisted by the suppliers, who promote the product to their customers.

Suppliers may suffer because of the pressure of competition on wholesalers. However, the converse may be equally true.

By promoting wholesalers and distributors, suppliers can gain access to large numbers of clients. Wholesalers who are particularly effective, promote both their own business and that of the supplier.

Franchising
The ultimate channel of distribution delegates the rights to sell or manufacture, or both, to a company or an individual within a given market place. This simple, ideally low-cost form of distribution, can, on the other hand, involve a great deal of high-cost support.

Successful franchising depends on the maintenance of quality standards, a clear pricing structure and the ability to negotiate franchises while avoiding the problem of getting excessively tied up in providing a support structure.

Exporting

For most developed industrial countries, growing markets in the late 1980s will be in the developing countries. Successful exporting depends on:
- Sound marketing management.
- A firm understanding of the demand for products and services from the export market.
- Selecting the market that fits the product and the resources you are prepared to commit to it.

Explore the market in terms of:
- The country's political and economic stability.
- Recent history and forecasts of currency movements.
- Ease of communication.

Seek advice from those with experience. Most governments will help you with:
- Export-related market research.
- Export paperwork.

- Finding an agent with a successful track record.
- Creating a joint venture.
- Introductions to agents and manufacturers under license.

Many established export consultancies can help. But finding the right agent for your product can be difficult. Good agents pick and choose their clients. You will have to sell yourself to them, but beware those who seek an exclusivity agreement because you may be excluding more innovative agents in later years.

Manufacture under license agreements is often a low-risk way of penetrating a market, particularly one controlled by the importing government. But make sure you are not just transferring technology and so become vulnerable to losing a market to imitators.

The right product in the right place at the right time

Selecting the product the customer ordered requires:
1 The right inventory levels.
2 The right order processing system.
3 The right picking and packing system.

Delivering the product to the customer requires **1,2** and **3** plus:
4 The right consignment note and parcel labelling system.
5 A reliable carrier.

Delivering the product at the time the customer asked for it requires **1,2,3,4** and **5**, plus:
6 The right carrier, who can provide the required timed delivery service at the right cost.

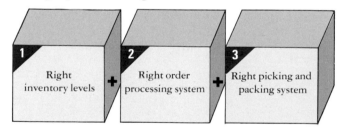

1 Right inventory levels **+** 2 Right order processing system **+** 3 Right picking and packing system

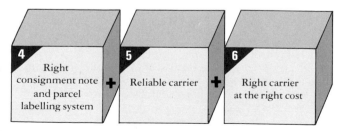

4 Right consignment note and parcel labelling system **+** 5 Reliable carrier **+** 6 Right carrier at the right cost

Getting the right balance

The materials manager ensures that there is always enough raw material and inventory available to support the forward production program and its potential variances – but only just enough.

Too little inventory can be obvious and embarrassingly public: there is no material for the workforce to use so people stand idle; customer orders fall overdue and can only then be recovered by working overtime. Therefore, most materials managers err on the side of carrying too much stock to avoid being blamed for running out of it and delaying production.

The problems of having too much stock are less apparent. Inventories have to be paid for, usually with borrowed money, which often means high interest charges. It has to be stored somewhere, and warehousing costs are expensive.

Depending on the industry and type of material, inventories either deteriorate with age or become obsolete because of design changes in the final product.

Inventory management should not be overlooked in areas where services or skills account for the major portion of costs. It can be just as costly to a business for a computer department not to have, say, adequate paper for printing out, as to have a machine operator run short of material.

Getting the right amount of stock
First, it is essential for purchasing managers to forecast what is going to be needed. This is best based on a forecast of sales of the finished product, which is then broken down to individual component levels via a bill of goods, although it can also be based on an average of how much has been used in the past.

Next, it is important to know what, and how much, is currently in stock. Obviously this changes from day to day as stock gets used and new deliveries are received. So it is essential

> **Effective materials management**
>
> To achieve this you need:
> ● An accurate sales forecast
> ● Up-to-date bill of goods
> ● Material requirements planning
> ● Inventory recording systems
> ● Routines for calculating reserve stock
> ● Constant measurement of performance against budget
> ● Regular comparison with industry standards

that purchasing managers have an *accurate* and *responsive* stock recording system.

In theory, a comparison of how much stock is available against what is required will quickly identify how much more stock needs to be bought.

However, since there is always a variable period of time between deciding to buy the goods and receiving them, an extra level of reserve stock is often required.

This is usually calculated in terms of days' usage and reflects the time needed to get the material, the distance of the supplier and the method of transport.

Finally, purchasing managers need to take into account the time needed to get material from inventory to the point of use, so a further element of reserve stock is often included.

Total inventory – system, stores and transit – can then be measured in two ways: it can be compared to previously set budget levels; or it can be measured in terms of inventory turns – the number of times the stock is used up in a year, which is probably the best yardstick.

Some firms achieve as few as two or three turns a year, but the most efficient can get up to 20 or more. The difference enables working capital to be better utilized and the business to be more profitable.

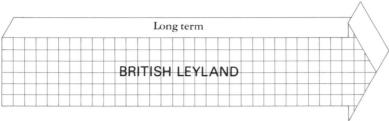

British Leyland (BL), in 1979, commissioned a firm of management consultants to overcome their storage problems at their biggest truck plant. The review recommended the building of new storage facilities, with sophisticated mechanical handling equipment, at a potential cost of several million pounds. BL decided to reduce stocks instead.

Over a two-year period, inventory was cut by half, all the rented outside stores were closed down, and the company was even able to absorb a range of vehicles from a sister plant.

Instead of spending millions, the company saved millions in working capital, reduced interest charges and eliminated costly outside warehouse hire.

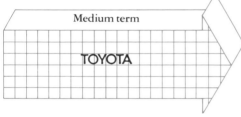

Japan provides some of the best examples of getting inventory control just right. Toyota are reported to have reduced overall stock levels to a week on average, with many items less than one shift. By calculating their requirements meticulously and organizing their suppliers properly, Toyota is often able to

hold system-fill stock only, with many parts being delivered directly to the production line by the supplier.

The end result is obvious. Toyota cars can be sold in Europe and the USA against local competition, despite the heavy freight costs, and yet the company still makes healthy profits.

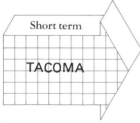

Tacoma Boatbuilding Company of Washington badly underestimated how much it would cost to fulfill customers' orders. It did not plan for the right amount of material, its cost, or how long it would take to produce the military and commercial vessels it had promised to build. It experienced a cash flow crisis

after failing to meet customer orders, and creditors clamored for repayment of $117 million in loans. In late 1985, Tacoma declared bankruptcy because expected new business failed to materialize.

111

Buying

Buying should not usually be carried out as an extra duty by the various departmental managers. A professional approach is essential: it takes just as much training, experience and flair to buy goods or services as it does to sell them.

For effective buying, you must first find out the potential suppliers of the requisite goods or services: you need to review trade journals, technical publications and directories, attend trade fairs, and keep in contact with colleagues in the buying profession.

Next, you must select a supplier, based on price, delivery time, quality, reliability and after-sales service. Price is not all-important. A supplier who fails to deliver on time or whose quality is poor can damage the company just as much, or more, than one who charges high prices.

After you have chosen the supplier and agreed on a price, you must ensure that the material *is* delivered on time and *is* the right quality.

If you are going to be buying the product over a long period, you must keep up to date with all the changing circumstances that may affect you: a new supplier may start up; technological changes may reduce manufacturing costs; fluctuations in commodity markets or exchange rates may cause price variations.

Buying also means that you must be aware of market movements that affect the supplier's costs, such as changes in raw material costs, labor costs and increases in overhead costs, so that any price increase negotiated is kept to a minimum.

Professional buying, therefore, carries a heavy responsibility. If you agree to prices which are too high, you may find that you damage your company's profitability. But if you force prices too low, the supplier may go out of business or fail to supply your needs, leaving the company short of essential materials.

What is a buyer?

Good professional buyers are likely to have many of the following characteristics:
● Experience in the trade or industry, often with an appropriate technical qualification.
● Mathematical and communication skills.
● Professional training and experience in the techniques of buying.
● Skill and credibility in negotiation.
● Entrepreneurial spirit.
● Sound understanding of own company's production process.
● Close links to sales and marketing, with a keen eye for changing customer needs.
● Willingness to become involved in lengthy and demanding relationships with suppliers, which may involve significant travel and socializing.
● Ability to manage and control established relationships.

What do buyers do?

Buyers must be sure to select the right supplier at the right price. This means identifying potential suppliers from:

● Personal experience and contacts.
● Trade directories and journals.
● Technical publications and trade fairs.
● Overseas trade visits and embassies.
● Word of mouth within the trade.

To pick the final supplier, buyers must weigh the following factors to strike the best balance.

Reliability
● Recent track record with own and other companies.
● Honesty, commitment and trustworthiness.
● Financial stability gauged from the balance sheet.
● Ability to meet imposed quality standards.

Delivery
● Reputation in the industry for holding dates.
● Type of packing and freight used.
● Relative size of own company's order in supplier's eyes.

Price
● Comparison with various other quotations/internal estimates.
● Discounts, freight costs, duty.
● Payment terms.

Responsiveness
● Ability to accept change.
● Speed of reaction to changing demand patterns.
● Supplier's after-sales service and ability to respond to problems.

Effective buying

These are the rules that ensure buying is carried out effectively:

● Never be totally reliant on a single supplier or a small number of suppliers. If more than 50 percent of purchases come from less than 5 percent of the total suppliers, your company might be at risk from supplier failure (bankruptcy, strikes etc.) or unavoidable, excessive price increases.
● Never allow any suppliers to become so reliant on your business that without it their company could no longer function.
● Make sure the finance department provides you with a listing of suppliers regularly requesting early or on account payments. This could be a sign of possible financial difficulties.
● Keep an index of material price increases and compare it regularly with indexes published by government or trade bodies.
● Obtain financial results of key suppliers to see that they maintain financial stability and do not generate excess profits.
● Keep regular statistics on rejected goods, late deliveries, discrepancies by the supplier.
● Whenever possible, get to know the suppliers and visit their premises.
● Build up your own supplier relationships to ensure that trusted members of supplying companies make and then keep personal commitments.
● Be aware of the levels and types of entertainment received by the buying staff and see that they are within accepted norms.
● A price that is significantly lower than the average for the rest of the competition can often be an indicator not to select that supplier.

113

Receiving and storing

As a manager, you need to be aware of the importance to materials management of the effective receipt and storage of goods.

Receiving goods

The layout and facilities of the goods receiving area play a significant part in a company's operating efficiency.

Ease of access to major road, rail or air networks is essential, particularly if large volumes of material are to be received frequently. Similarly, internal traffic should be running smoothly so that delivery vehicles can be turned around quickly. Drivers of supply vehicles, often bringing urgently required material, may turn away if they can see no possibility of unloading promptly.

The layout of the receiving area should be designed to ensure that off-loading can be carried out as swiftly as possible. Self-leveling docks may help the movement of fork-lift trucks; cranes or hoists may also be needed. The most important factor is to provide adequate facilities for the type of packaging material and frequency of planned deliveries.

Good operating procedures are just as important as good facilities. The first aim should be to plan a delivery schedule so that receipts are evenly phased over a given period. Suppliers who consistently leave deliveries to the last day of the month and so cause bottle-necks at the receiving end should be re-educated – or dropped!

The receiving area is where the first physical inspection checks should be made to ensure that the right goods have been sent, undamaged and in the right quantity. In some instances there may also be a need to include a full check by means of quality control inspection.

In all instances, though, deliveries must be checked and any damage or discrepancy identified immediately to the supplier and delivery agent. It is always better to reject damaged goods

---

Receiving goods

The key requirements are:
- Smooth traffic flow – external and internal.
- Adequate facilities and handling equipment.
- Delivery schedules planned to prevent bottle-necks.
- Immediate verification checks on goods delivered.
- Prompt movement of material to its final location.
- Quick and accurate data recording of goods received.

---

there and then, so that future haggling over responsibility for the damage is avoided. If this is not done, the onus may be on your company to prove that the loss or damage did not take place in your charge or on your premises.

When all checks are complete, the goods must be moved promptly to their final location. An organized receiving area is essential. Access to it should be restricted and issues made only from stores. Otherwise goods may get lost in the confusion caused by people randomly searching for the material they need.

Finally, the receipt of the goods must be entered promptly into the company's inventory recording systems. The most common means are computers, punch cards or preprinted forms. It is just as inefficient to have inventory on the premises that nobody is aware of as it is to have no inventory at all when it is urgently needed for the production process.

Storing materials

Depending on the industry, materials can be stored in a variety of ways – ranging from inventory cupboards to computer-controlled, robotically-operated warehousing systems. The succesful storage of all materials depends on the same fundamental principles.

The first consideration is the amount of space needed. Paradoxically, having too much capacity can sometimes be a greater problem in the long term than having too little. Warehousing is expensive and some companies may fill it beyond their needs to justify the cost.

If inventory holding levels are liable to rise and fall, e.g. the spirits wholesale trade before Christmas, then it may be better to consider renting temporary additional space to cover the peaks than to have a facility big enough to meet maximum demand, which occurs only once or twice a year.

Hiring space away from the company's main site and services can, however, be costly and difficult to control. So this option should not be considered as a means of overcoming long-term or permanent shortage of storage space.

Obtaining access to stock when it is required is an equally important part of the space/volume calculation. Having a full warehouse, in which it is impossible to get at the stock needed without having to shuffle pallets and cartons about is not cost effective. In the same way, having narrow aisles to utilize more storage space, where fork-lift trucks cannot pass each other or even turn round, can make stock movement expensive. It is important, therefore, to store goods in the least possible space which allows the best possible access to each and every package.

It is also crucial to know where everything is. Knowing from the inventory recording system that you have inventory, but not being able to find it, is nearly as bad as having no inventory at all. The cost of searching for it, and the disruption to production until it can be found, is often greater than the cost of going out to get more.

As part of the initial space calculations, there should be defined areas

| Running an efficient warehouse |
| A well-run warehouse requires:
• The right amount of space – not too much, not too little.
• Easy access to stock.
• Efficient stock locator systems.
• Facilities and equipment to match requirement.
• Adequate security to prevent pilferage.
• Quarantined areas to maintain quality standards. |

for all items of inventory, and it is of paramount importance that, wherever possible, each item should be stored in its designated space. This approach to storage usually comes under the heading of "inventory locator systems" and is essential for most companies.

Next, the fixed facilities and the material handling equipment should be capable of doing the job required of them. Racks, shelves, bins and pallets should be used in spaces which can accommodate them and which are allowed by the fabric of the building. Fork-lifts, tow trolleys, cranes and hoists should be readily available, when the method of packaging or the weight and volume of the material so requires.

Last, but by no means least, consideration should be given to security. If the goods stored are potentially pilferable, they should be kept in an enclosed area, securely locked and guarded. Less obvious, but almost as important, is the need to hold in a secure area reject material, or goods requiring inspection sign-off.

Such quarantined areas are essential to ensure that a company's quality standards are always maintained. They are often crucial in industries such as aerospace or defense, where one defective part can have a catastrophic effect.

Controlling inventory

The process of taking material in to a warehouse, holding it and later issuing it for use should be one of the simplest operations in any company. In practice, however, there are a number of pitfalls that can cause confusion and affect the efficient running of the company.

You, as a manager, should be aware of the problems, most of which arise from unauthorized personnel having access to the warehouse. Material collected in a panic or for a special order usually results in stock being moved about indiscriminately and either misplaced or damaged.

These casual callers rarely update the main inventory records and so, over a period of time, records become unreliable.

The first essential for good physical inventory control is, therefore, that the warehouse area should be enclosed and secure, and that access should be restricted to authorized warehouse personnel exclusively.

The next essential is accurate and up-to-date records. Every input and output, and all movements within the stores, should be accompanied by authorizing documentation, and the recording systems, including inventory location data, updated immediately.

A common danger is for inventory movements to be made hurriedly when the need is urgent, with the warehouse manager having every intention of catching up on the paperwork when convenient.

All inventory should be clearly labelled. In many warehouses, parts which look similar are stored close to each other. Inadequate or missing inventory identification can lead to the wrong material being issued or to different parts being loaded onto the same pallet.

Poor control of labelling not only leads to inaccurate inventory records but can also have a serious effect on production efficiency and quality if

---

Physical control of inventory

To maintain an efficient physical control over material held in a warehouse requires:
- A secure storage area.
- Access restricted to authorized personnel only.
- Properly authorized and updated documentation.
- Good inventory rotation.
- Meticulous attention to all the paperwork.

---

the wrong part is delivered. If material comes into the store without labelling, it should be held in a quarantined area for identification by the inspection department.

Inventory rotation is essential. Warehouse personnel should work on the FIFO principle (First In First Out) to avoid problems. If, for example, bins are continually refilled at the top and stock issues are drawn from the top, the material at the bottom will never get used and will either deteriorate with age or become obsolete.

If it is impossible to date-stamp each item, then the physical layout should be arranged so as to ensure that the oldest material is used first. (A quick check to see if material at the back of a rack is dusty or rusty can indicate the effectiveness of stock rotation.)

Other problems can arise from non-routine movements of inventory. For instance, parts may be returned from production because they were in excess of actual requirements. Or, because of material shortages, only part of a required inventory issue can be made and the remainder is to be issued when new deliveries are received.

All such movements must be supported with adequate paperwork and inventory records must be updated. The same principles apply to damaged or rejected material.

Inventory recording

The essential requirements of any stock recording system are:
- Accuracy of data.
- Promptness of updating.
- Accessibility to users.
- Updating facility limited to trained staff.
- Security.
- Regular comparison of actual quantities with recorded amounts.

Recording inventories

There are many systems used to record inventory. Nevertheless, they can usually be classified under three headings: bin card, Kardex, and computer systems.

All systems depend on the prompt and accurate recording of every physical inventory movement. This often requires sound staff training and education (particularly in the case of computerized systems) to ensure that no private or bootleg systems are operated in parallel.

Bin cards

These are used to record quantities per bin or rack and are held in the storage area itself. They consist of a series of line entries for each receipt or issue and a running balance of the remaining stock.

If bin cards are updated promptly and accurately, they provide a simple but effective picture of inventory quantities. The major drawback of this system is that the details are not readily available to other departments, such as production control, purchasing and finance.

Kardex systems

These are usually accessible to all users although they can be kept in the storage area; they are similar to bin cards but include more detail. For instance, they may contain details of suppliers or customers, inventory check reconciliations, reject reports details, unit costs or committed inventory.

Because the records are kept in a central place, rather than hung on individual storage bins or racks, Kardex systems are more readily accessible to other users, though they often suffer from the lack of ready visual checks.

If a warehouse manager sees an empty bin, where the bin card record shows there should be inventory, immediate corrective action can be taken. If, however, the only record is the Kardex, which is not routinely seen, the first sign of error is often when there is a shortage of inventory.

Computerized systems

These are the most effective methods of recording inventory. Information on inventory balances can be made readily available to users by means of a hard copy print out or computer screens. On-line systems provide instant updating of information, ensuring the proper amount of inventory is at hand.

There are numerous software and hardware packages commercially available that carry out inventory recording.

Because they are easily and quickly updated, computerized systems are more vulnerable to erroneous information being entered into memory through typing errors. It is important, therefore, to check that there is always a paper trail of transactions and that there is a regular and efficient program of physical stock reconciliation.

Care should be taken to keep security back-up copies of data files in case of malfunction or loss so that manual intervention is still possible in the event of a breakdown.

Production planning

The purpose of a production plan is to balance your requirements (orders in hand and sales forecasts) against resources (people, materials, machines) so that the company operates at maximum efficiency and profitability.

All line managers should be aware of the need to plan carefully the actual manufacture of the company's products.

Order sequencing

The first action required to formulate a production plan is to sort the orders or forecasts received into a sequence, according to the dates by which deliveries are required.

Next, the orders have to be broken down to establish what components need to be bought or made to complete the order. From this the production control department can determine what material, machines and labor hours will be needed and the earliest possible date for final production.

This is a crucial process, since, although there may be standard lead times, circumstances may alter from day to day, even hour to hour, and being short of just one component can delay the whole order, leaving the factory with excessive levels of unfinished work-in-progress.

In drawing up an order plan, it is essential to consider the capacity of individual manufacturing processes especially if the company makes a wide range of products. Unless each line is loaded evenly, one part of the factory may be working at over-capacity paying premium rates for overtime, while elsewhere people and machines will be standing idle.

In most manufacturing processes there is a period of non-productive time when different orders are changed over. Requirements for the same or similar parts should be lumped together to minimize downtime and to achieve greater output.

The final results of this balancing process should be an order schedule

---

Key elements of an order plan

- Putting the orders into a sequence according to dates desired by customers.
- Breaking down orders into constituent details.
- Balancing mix between product lines.
- Lumping orders together to achieve economies of scale.
- Keeping a balance between high and low margin orders.
- Keeping the customer informed of delays.

---

that can produce goods at a profit and satisfy the customer by the efficient use of available resources. Inevitably, there will be times when orders either cannot be produced on time, or only at an unacceptable cost. In such cases the customers must be informed.

It is better to lose a single order but keep a good customer than to gain a reputation for unreliable delivery promises and so lose customers in the long term. Obtaining the best balance of resources at the same time as satisfying customer demands is a highly complex operation.

Production scheduling

In any production process, it is usually impossible to state precisely what can be produced with given equipment, materials and manpower.

Only the industrial giants can afford computer power to formulate the best production plan, according to the wide range of possible resource allocation against a sequenced order plan. Most companies have to rely on more simple systems, coupled with the flair and experience of their managers.

However, as computerization becomes cheaper and more powerful, companies should regularly consider whether they can benefit from the mini- and micro-based systems appearing on the market.

Production scheduling is simpler if machinery is highly specialized rather than multi-purpose. Within the priorities of the order plan, production planners should ensure that all machines are loaded to the maximum possible and that downtime (because of, say, order changeover or gaps in the production sequence) is kept to the minimum.

When planning material availability, production planners should ask:
- What material is required and when?
- Is the material available in inventory now?
- Can the material be made available in time for planned start of production at an acceptable cost?

Using available labor to the maximum is a complex factor for the production planner. Particular equipment may require specialist skills that are limited to a few operatives. It may be a holiday period or a time of year when absence through sickness is traditionally high.

The workforce may also resist changes in shift patterns or levels of overtime working. In most cases, the flexibility of labor is dependent on the prevailing state of industrial relations.

When all else fails, despite the risk of encouraging potential competitors, subcontract work out. Other companies operating in the same activities may have spare machines and manpower capacity, or may have the right materials available. Reversing the process (i.e. by taking subcontracted work in) can also be a useful way of leveling out workload troughs.

The final result of balancing all the variations in resources against demand should be a clear plan for Production of what work is required to be done and when, and a clear statement to Sales of when individual orders will be completed.

Key elements of production scheduling

- Component requirements according to the priority of the order.
- Minimization of machine downtime.
- Material requirements planning based on accurate inventory recording systems.
- Maximum use of available labor hours.
- Use of subcontracting to smooth workload peaks and troughs.

Balancing resources and customer needs in a production plan

To get the right balance between customer needs and resources, you need to consider the following, broken down under four headings:

Orders
- From customers.
- From sales forecasts.
- For inventory or sub-assembly.
- Broken down into details.

Priority
- Sequenced into order of date required.
- Special requirements identified.
- Customer satisfaction maintained.
- Lumped into smaller groups.
- Evenly balanced load.

Availability
- What machinery is required?
- Is material available, or can it be procured in time?
- Is there sufficient labor with the right skills?
- Can work be subcontracted if necessary?

Cost
- Balance of high and low margin orders.
- Effect of premium payments on profitability.
- Downtime costs from excessive changeovers.
- Cost of subcontracting.

Production control

A production plan is rarely, if ever, carried out in all its details. Machines break down; suppliers' promises are broken; and people fall ill, take vacations, leave the company or go on strike.

The function of production control is twofold. First to ensure that production is maintained in line with the production plan wherever possible. Second, to respond to the things that do go wrong and rework the plan in order to get back on schedule.

The production controller monitors the supply and production process to ensure that there is always accurate up-to-date information on what per-formance has been achieved and what actions are required to maintain performance. Where deviations from the plan are spotted, corrective action can be taken at an early stage to overcome the shortfalls.

Regular checks must be made on material availability and not just on the day it is due. A supplier's promise several weeks ago may not be kept, so there should be a program of routine follow-up to keep a check on this. This should be backed up with an equally regular program of stock checks.

The production controller needs to be constantly aware of what labor hours are available, how the oper-

Things that can go wrong in production:	How to avoid or correct them
1 Machine breakdowns.	1 Service contracts; planned preventative maintenance; machine rental.
2 Poor production quality.	2 Repair and rectify; concessions from design engineering.
3 Low productivity.	3 Productivity bonuses; incentive plans.
4 Unforeseen shortages.	4 Use other materials; fresh deliveries; modify or rework other parts.
5 Rejected material.	5 Concessions from design engineering; replacement deliveries.
6 Supplier strikes.	6 Use alternative suppliers; security inventory.
7 Transport breakdowns.	7 Use alternative transport methods (e.g. air freight for sea freight).
8 Absenteeism.	8 Improved labor relations; overtime; additonal shifts.
9 Overtime bans.	9 Use temporary labor; recruitment.

"This machine's broken down. It'll take weeks to repair."

"I've run out of brackets. The buyer says they were due in yesterday."

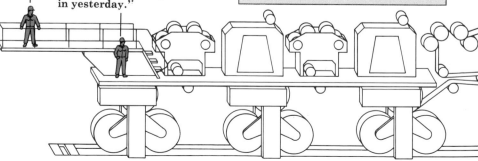

ation is performing in terms of quality and productivity, and even what social and sports events are taking place. Workers may be less amenable to working overtime during major league playoffs, for example.

If machines break down, outside contractors can be brought in to repair them quickly. If not, machines can be rented or the job may be subcontracted for completion. Materials can often be bought from other sources or other materials can be substituted.

Defects can sometimes be rectified, and design engineering may agree to the use of off-standard components if they do not materially alter the finished product. Extra overtime, additional shifts or even temporary labor may overcome problems in meeting deadlines.

Customers can often accept a later delivery date, or accept part shipment of an order, if treated correctly. In all cases, they must be made aware of the status of their orders.

The process of checking, reworking and rescheduling must be continuous to be effective.

The original plan must remain the key objective. Changes should be made only if they are absolutely necessary or unavoidable.

Maintaining production

In early 1982, an earth moving equipment manufacturer was faced with a total shut-down of its highest volume production line as a result of a protracted strike at the premises of their sole engine supplier.

By using up the extra inventory they had held in case of such an occurrence, they were able to put in a crash engineering development plan to redesign the unit to use an engine from an alternative manufacturer.

The speedy redesign combined with an extensive material procurement exercise meant the company was able to fit the new engine and so maintain the production of their vehicles.

Threatened stoppage at Ford

Ford Motor Company, in Dagenham, England, was threatened with a complete stoppage to their Cortina assembly line, which was producing 1,000 vehicles a day. A shortage of steering wheels prevented vehicles from being driven off the line.

A squad of mechanics drove cars into the park and removed the steering wheels, which were then used to drive off more cars. Although they had fields full of cars, production was not stopped, and fitting new steering wheels when they became available was relatively simple.

"I'm not working late tonight. It's the beginning of my vacation and I promised to be home on time."

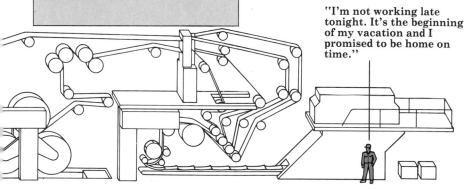

Manufacturing management

The volume, variety and complexity of day-to-day production problems, most of which require on-the-spot decisions, make manufacturing management one of the most difficult tasks a manager will face.

In most large operations, the manufacturing manager, in addition to the materials management functions described in pages 110–121, is likely to be responsible for:

● Production management.
● Machine engineering.
● Quality performance.
● Labor relations.

Production Management

The production manager must ensure that maximum output is produced for minimum cost by keeping the workforce and the machines working as close to full capacity as possible. Since production costs often form the largest part of a manufacturing company's total costs, this is clearly an important task.

Once production control has loaded each machine or process to its fullest extent, the production manager, through superintendents and foremen, must ensure that the operating performance is maintained using numerically quantifiable factors.

For machinery, this is relatively easy since actual speeds and output can be readily compared against original design standards. Measuring workforce output performance is not so easy, and usually requires a set of standards to be established as a yardstick.

There will always be problems to be dealt with, from machine breakdowns to inventory and manpower shortages. It is the production manager's skill at getting round these problems, by rearranging the details of the production plan, which will determine success or failure.

Machine engineering

Failure to produce to standard usually means that a machine needs repair or adjustment. The machine engineering department, therefore, should organize a program of regular maintenance and refurbishments to ensure that machine performance is consistently kept up to standard. It should also make certain that predictable problems are avoided.

There are, of course, always unpredictable breakdowns. In very large operations such as automated assembly lines or process systems these can be extremely expensive if not corrected immediately. To minimize such downtime it is often advisable to have a back-up squad of maintenance engineers permanently on standby to deal with any emergencies immediately.

The machine engineering department is also responsible for ensuring that the layout and flow of the factory processes are planned to give maximum efficiency, and can utilize new technological advances to improve the manufacturing process.

Quality performance

The manufacturing manager is responsible for quality performance and for quality control. There is a significant difference between these two management concepts and it is important for everyone in manufacturing to appreciate it.

Quality control is the planning and checking process by which a company aims to produce good quality products, whereas quality performance is making sure that this actually happens in practice.

It should, for instance, be obvious that quality control inspectors can only check to determine what does or does not come up to standard, but it is the production workforce that makes good or bad quality products.

The manufacturing manager is responsible for ensuring that good quality is produced regularly and that the workforce have enough pride to want to produce good quality.

Labor relations

The manufacturing manager must often be part psychologist and sociologist, as well as a trained engineer, to get the best out of his workforce. Establishing and maintaining good labor relations brings higher morale and greater productivity.

Perhaps the most important factor in this process is to establish a firm and consistent style and framework within which to operate. It is generally accepted that being too harsh in your relationships with workforce and unions leads to poor cooperation and morale.

However, being too easy-going can have a similar effect since it leads to a loss of respect for management's right to manage. Worst of all, though, is the manager who is tough one day and soft the next, because nobody knows what is expected of them. The workforce can become confused and resentful.

It is essential, therefore, that manufacturing managers develop their own effective operating style and stick to it. This will improve their ability to handle hard decisions such as dismissal and layoffs in a rational efficient way understood by everyone.

One of the major stumbling blocks in all labor relationships is remuneration. Some key rules for handling this thorny problem are:

● Low pay in relation to other local industries may encourage the most able workers to leave.

● Levels of pay that are too high may make products either over priced or unprofitable, in both cases leading to a loss of orders.

● Bonus or incentive payments should be achievable, but not automatic.

● Bonus and overtime pay should not be so large a percentage of total pay that the loss of it, at times when orders are slack, causes discontent among the workforce.

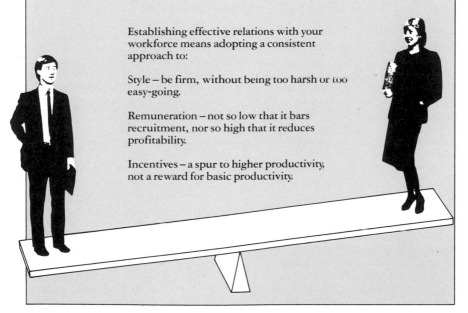

Establishing effective relations with your workforce means adopting a consistent approach to:

Style – be firm, without being too harsh or too easy-going.

Remuneration – not so low that it bars recruitment, nor so high that it reduces profitability.

Incentives – a spur to higher productivity, not a reward for basic productivity.

Manufacturing strategy

The effective manufacturing manager deals with daily problems and crises, and leaves enough time to plan medium- and long-term strategy. Most efficient companies have a long-range corporate plan. Within this plan all their subsidiary activities are carried out and collectively directed toward the achievement of the company's primary goal.

Primary objectives are most likely to be broad-based, such as increased market share, improved profit margins, introduction of new products and so on. It is the manufacturing manager's primary responsibility to develop a detailed strategic plan for the manufacturing department to support these objectives.

The manufacturing manager must take numerous factors into account, but there are some important, specific areas that should constantly be reviewed.

Automation
Buying new machines or introducing robotic techniques into the department may well improve product capacity and efficiency, but both need to be coordinated within the context of the company's overall capabilities.

For instance, there may be insufficient funding to finance the capital investment for the particular project and to pay for maintenance charges incurred. Or automation might have an adverse effect on staffing and labor relations.

As in other aspects of management, it is important to maintain a close liaison with all other departments to ensure that strategic actions are mutually compatible.

Sourcing
Significant cost savings may be made by subcontracting work to outside companies with specialist equipment and expertise, instead of replacing old plant with new capital equipment or hiring more skilled labor. Even so, this may have an adverse effect if it leads to underutilization of current plant and labor and thereby increases unit costs. Subcontracting may lead to labor-relations problems as well as additional costs if it results in layoffs.

Consolidation of facilities
If there are several different manufacturing sites all operating at less than capacity, or several underutilized machines producing similar products, it may be sensible to consolidate the work at fewer sites on machines which can then operate more productively.

Again, subsidiary factors must be considered, such as availability of specialist skills and equipment, disruptions to labor relations, closure costs and so on. The most profitable course of action may even be to reduce margins and prices in order to sell more and so produce more efficiently in greater volume.

Systems
New computerized systems may lead to improved efficiency and control but will themselves cost money and require time to be spent on training and implementation.

Horror stories abound about firms abandoning sound manual systems in favor of sophisticated computer systems only to find that they do not work as intended. It is crucial that any new systems implementation be specified and planned in minute detail, and that there are always back up plans in the event of any failures.

Purchasing
New and cheaper sources of supply should be a key objective of the purchasing department. However, before sanctioning any major resourcing action the manufacturing manager should weigh up the total costs of purchase, freight charges, quality standards, inventory carrying costs and so on, to ensure that the sourcing decision is commercially sound.

It is also essential that, when developing their own strategies, the other departments in the company are fully aware of manufacturing's plans and limitations. For example:

● Sales targets should take into account capacity constraints in order to ensure that they are both realistic and achievable.

Imagine, for instance, that part of the sales strategy is to increase the sales of Product X by 20%. But Product X is produced on a special machine already working to full capacity. Something will go dramatically wrong unless investment in new equipment is included in plans, or the target increases are reduced in sales plans.

● Design engineering will continually try to improve the design of the products made. But it should not introduce new materials, tolerances or techniques without confirming their viability.

● The finance department should be fully aware of the details of labor. relations and incentive plans before it decides to embark upon new payroll systems.

Despite the pressures of immediate daily problems, the manufacturing manager must set aside enough time in the working day to address these long-term requirements. This often involves regular planning meetings and keeping in daily contact with other heads of departments.

Similarly, the manufacturing manager must ensure that subordinate managers prepare lower level plans so that internal departmental meetings can agree the overall manufacturing strategy.

Regular meetings with your own staff are essential to formulate a strategy for the long-term development of the manufacturing function.

This strategy must contribute to the company's corporate plan. It should also be the center for all the manufacturing department's future detailed actions.

Obstacles to successful strategies

Any good strategic plan must recognize that forecasts and theories do not always turn out as predicted, and therefore should be regularly reviewed and amended in the light of changing circumstances. For the manufacturing manager some of the key areas in which problems may arise are as follows:

● New equipment or machinery may not arrive on time or may not initially perform up to specification. Putting additional contingency allowances into the overall plan can often ensure that such delays do not disrupt the overall plan.

● New computer systems often contain unforeseen bugs and operating problems that need to be ironed out out before they can work effectively. Any plan to introduce new systems should therefore include the maintenance and parallel running of the old systems until the new ones have a clean bill of health.

● Even the best of suppliers can suffer from breakdowns, strikes or even closure. The trauma that this can cause can be alleviated by ensuring that inventories of key items are held. When possible, the supply of critical components should be split between two sources.

● Internal labor relations problems can disrupt the best laid plans. The only way to prevent this happening is to work consistently, and on a daily basis, at maintaining sound labor relations.

Nationally organized disruptive action, however, may have nothing to do with a local plant but, because it affects the labor force, can seriously jeopardize its performance.

● Plant and machines may still break down, despite regular maintenance.

Innovation, research and development

All companies must look constantly to the future. They cannot afford to rely on the thinking that what works today will continue to work tomorrow. In the business chain, changes are occurring all the time – from products, workforce, suppliers and customers. New opportunities that are ignored by your company will certainly be exploited by competitors.

Every organization needs innovation. This is its life blood. While access to new technology can always be gained by negotiating licensing agreements with other companies, your organization will still need to work on stimulating innovation and creativity.

Many smaller organizations, however, cannot afford to formalize their perspectives on the future by establishing a permanent research and development (R&D) department. And even large companies with R&D departments have shown how hard it is to innovate.

RCA and Siemens, for example, tried to diversify into computers, but when they realized they were not able to move their operations in that direction, they both withdrew with expensive consequences.

Size, complexity and bureaucracy can all stifle initiative and creativity, making the passage of new ideas through the channels of organization too cumbersome.

If an R&D department is set up, its research may be pure and/or applied. Pure research has no specific end in sight except to discover more detail about a certain field, such as finding out the electroconductive properties of silicon compounds.

Applied research attempts to solve specific problems or needs that have already been identified. If controlled properly, R&D provides positive and beneficial results. Exploring the practical uses of the electroconductive properties of silicon would be an example of applied research.

The research will usually be carried out within a predetermined budget. When costs overrun budgets you will find you have to be ruthless in cutting off research projects – don't succumb to the temptation to spend just that little bit more.

Where does innovation come from? The simple and best answer is from the culture and attitudes of the people in the organization. Accepted methods and practices must be constantly analyzed and challenged. At the same time, the freedom to look for and exploit new opportunities must be positively encouraged.

Few ideas come from blinding flashes of inspiration; innovation and creativity are not simply erratic and spontaneous. The Polaroid camera, for example, was not the result of an isolated brainwave. It was the logical development of existing procedures and products, as well as the result of team work in an encouraging environment.

The stereotyped picture of R&D activity is one of people in white coats slaving away for years in laboratories on complex problems and emerging with an end-product amid cries of "Eureka!" This is not true. Remember:

● Keep R&D simple and fruitful by regularly testing new ideas in actual working practice.

● Problems such as customer complaints, incomplete production processes and the encroachment of competitors all provide opportunities for innovation.

● Don't neglect your strengths – they must be developed in tandem with problem solving. IBM, for example, woke up in time to use their strengths to dominate the personal computer market.

● Keep close to your core activities. But don't be so inward-looking that you constrain new ideas.

Sources of inspiration and innovation

Harness any ideas emerging from the core of your business. Discover what you can about your company's customers, employees and environment, by asking:

Customers:
● What are they buying and why?
● What do we do well that they like?
● What improvements or ideas for variation would they like to see?
● What complementary products or services would interest them?
● How are their needs evolving?

Employees:
● Are working methods keeping pace with new technology and materials?
● What skills are needed?
● What skills are available, but are at present underused?

● What feedback are production and sales getting on problems and quality?
● Which processes cause problems? Should they be abandoned or improved?

Environment:
● What social or demographic changes are occurring?
● What spending patterns are emerging?
● How is the public's spending power developing?
● What is happening to people's attitudes, perceptions, needs and lifestyles?
● How are our competitors developing?
● What niches in the market are our competitors exploiting?

Social and demographic changes

America's physical fitness boom, for example, provided a host of opportunities for companies like Stauffer Corporation and Pepsi Cola and Coca-Cola, which introduced popular low-calorie food and diet drinks. Similarly, companies are tailoring their products to suit regional tastes. Campbell Soup got sales of its traditional pork and beans moving in the Southwest only after it cut out the pork and added chili peppers. Demographics are constantly changing. The New York Advertising agency Ogilvy and Mather shocked clients with a 1985 survey that showed less than 10% of American families fit the "traditional" profile of father, non-working mother and two children.

Achieving the right balance

Discovering who you are, what organization will suit you and how businesses function, are the essential prerequisites to your career in management. But real management begins only when you take over your specific responsibilities and the team that will help you handle them. It is then that you start to tackle problems on a day-to-day basis.

Your ultimate responsibility as a good manager is to help the organization achieve its goals, while ensuring that your own targets, and those of the individual members of your team, are also attained. This is a tall order.

Business objectives can often be achieved only at the expense of personal aims. The result may be a high turnover of personnel.

Conversely, your people can be happy and fulfilled and not achieve corporate goals. Achieving the correct balance takes continual effort. Answers may be found, but they will need constant reassessment.

Your work will be challenging, complex and unscientific; it will demand general knowledge and specific skills. And the relentless pace of work means you will be in constant danger of being superficial, spending time on brief, varied and piecemeal activities. This is normal. Don't expect it to be any other way.

Your job has many aspects. Some of them will be compatible while others will appear conflicting. You may find yourself pulled by opposing forces.

● **Managing vs administering**
In the ebb and flow of the organization's work, you must actively shape events, determine a direction and ensure that it is followed. You need to motivate your team to follow your lead and stimulate them to find their own direction. In short, you must take responsibility.

On the other hand, you need to respond to events and interpret the actions of others. You need to be able to absorb them and ensure your team's activities stay on course. Logic, order and method mean smooth administration but you must ensure that your efforts do not stop there.

The elements of responsibility

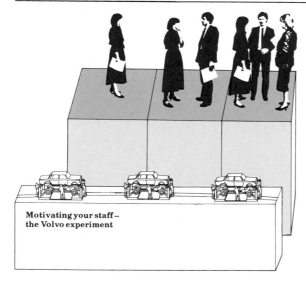

Motivating your staff –
the Volvo experiment

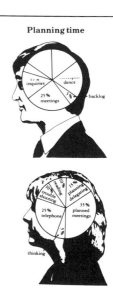

Planning time

● **Effectiveness vs efficiency**

These aspects of your work may appear similar but they are not. The effective manager tries to advance team efforts toward corporate goals. Ask yourself: "What have I added to the business today?" Progress and results are the ultimate measure.

Being efficient and busy may actually disguise a lack of real progress. Responding to daily demands and having your desk clear at the end of each day do not always mean anything worthwhile has been achieved.

● **Overseeing vs doing**

You will often be tempted into getting involved in the tasks your team has to perform – either because the tasks are exciting or familiar. However, you must manage the people, not the task.

The transition, from doing something you have always done well to organizing others to do it, will be your toughest challenge.

● **Innovating vs preserving the status quo**

You may be good at the supervision of activities, systems and processes, but managing includes creating time to think, experiment, research and generate tomorrow's ideas.

Genuine innovation relies on your ability to read all the signs in your business environment, from trends in product development and workforce practices to customer demands and competitors' progress.

A portrait of the skills of a successful manager would include a whole spectrum of qualities. The following section, *The manager's role*, gives you some ideas on how to cope better with your challenges, from leadership and communication to motivation, delegation and decision-making.

You will have your own personal aims and needs as a manager. But remember that those who work with you have also entered into a contract with the organization. They will give a lot if handled correctly. They will want something in return and not just a decent salary. They, too, seek meaning in what they do and have enduring values. These must be nurtured *by* the organization *through* you.

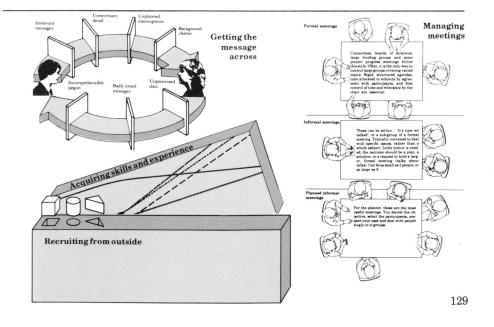

129

Leading your team

The ability to lead is vital to managerial success. Yet leadership is hard to define. Military leaders are often compared with business managers and other commercial leaders. Indeed, both types have clear objectives, roles and responsibilities and may share similar qualities, such as vision and the ability to handle a crisis. But there are important differences.

War is an extraordinary situation, requiring authoritarian leaders to command their subordinates to take required action and achieve specific objectives.

Modern business managers, on the other hand, need to be democratic, creating consensus in their teams on objectives and required action. Like their military counterparts, managers motivate their team members by encouraging ambition, the desire to achieve and a wish to contribute to the collective good of the business.

Leaders of people

Some managers may seem like born leaders. Most people have the potential to develop skills involving organizing, planning, scheduling, setting goals, making decisions, solving problems, communicating, negotiating and supervising.

However, there is no known way to train people to become leaders, although it is evident leaders need such qualities as integrity, honesty, enthusiasm and the ability to express themselves clearly. All of these qualities must be demonstrated openly and consistently.

Leadership in management necessitates pointing the way forward; leading from the front is far better than pushing from behind. While many leaders are often solitary, go-it-alone, visionaries who impose their worldview on others, managers must interact with their followers. They must work within their team to reflect its collective strength as well as their own personal view.

Effective leadership

The list of qualities a leader will need is long. While many appear daunting, most are achievable.

To lead your team you need to:
● Look for tomorrow's problems and issues to detect signs of change and pitfalls.
● Learn to adapt to change, to embrace it and turn it to your advantage.
● Set high standards as well as clear objectives.
● Think clearly but allow intuition to influence rationality.
● Create a sense of value and purpose in work, so individuals believe in what they do and do it successfully.
● Provide a positive sense of direction in order to give meaning to the lives of team members.
● Act decisively but ensure your decisions are soundly based and not just impulsive.
● Set the right tone by your actions and beliefs, thus creating a clear, consistent and honest model to be followed.
● Keep your composure and learn to wait for the right time to make decisions and take actions.
● Provide an atmosphere of enthusiasm in which individuals are stimulated to perform well, find fulfillment, gain self-respect and play an integral role in meeting the organization's overall goals.
● Be sensitive to the needs and expectations of team members. Pay regular attention to communication and ongoing training.
● Clearly define responsibilities and structures, so collective efforts are enhanced, not hindered.
● Recognize what best motivates each team member and work with these motivations to achieve standards and objectives.
● Do not constrain the team but determine the boundaries within which they can freely work.

Choosing how to lead

The idea of managers having a choice about how they lead was described by Tannenbaum and Schmidt in the Harvard Business Review (1973). They suggest that the choice relates to the amount of authority used by the manager and to the degree of freedom given to the team in making decisions.

Successful leaders are flexible in choosing a range of styles, from highly authoritative to wholly participatory, whichever is appropriate to themselves as individuals and to the teams they lead, as well as to the nature of the problem and the situation in which they operate.

1 Manager makes a decision that the team accepts.

2 Manager "sells" decision before gaining acceptance.

3 Manager presents decision but responds to questions from the team.

4 Manager presents tentative decision, subject to change after team input.

5 Manager presents problem, gets input from team, then decides.

6 Manager defines limits within which team makes decision.

7 Manager and team decide jointly.

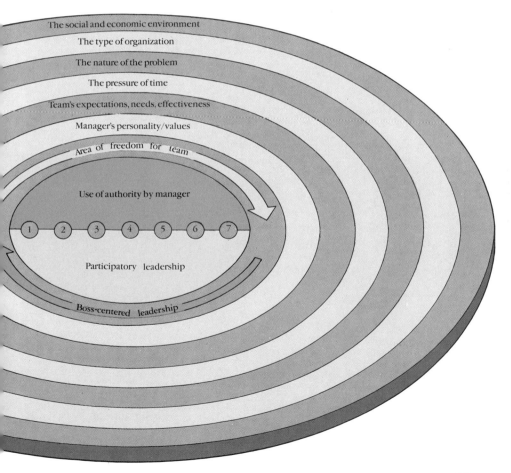

The social and economic environment

The type of organization

The nature of the problem

The pressure of time

Team's expectations, needs, effectiveness

Manager's personality/values

Area of freedom for team

Use of authority by manager

1 2 3 4 5 6 7

Participatory leadership

Boss-centered leadership

Getting it across

As a manager, you exist through your communication with colleagues and their subsequent observations about you to others inside and outside the organization. Communication has two important aspects: first, the maintenance of personal relationships, and second, the efficient transmission of messages.

You may, of course, choose not to communicate. If, for example, your opinion is sought at a particular meeting, your absence may imply lack of support. If attendance is obligatory, silence may have the same effect.

You can communicate in different ways and so it is necessary to be clear about the aim of your message before choosing a medium for it. Ask yourself: "Who needs to receive the message? What is their working environment? What do I want to happen, and how soon?"

Be clear and brief

Get into the habit of being clear and coming to the point – explanation, if it is necessary, can be provided later. Avoid verbosity, obscure language and irrelevant details in any form of communication. The same applies to jargon, statistics, or references (unless they have been specifically requested).

Written or "presentational" communications will often be received by more people than the person for whom they were intended. So write in a language that the least expert of your audience will understand.

"Get it on one piece of paper" is sensible advice. Write messages as briefly and clearly as possible. This will save your own time and the reader's, and give the message a better chance of being understood.

Don't write a memo if a telephone call will suffice. Making daily lists under headings, "see," "telephone," "write," "telex," etc, and allocating time to each, is good training for effective communication.

Think before you communicate

Before communicating ask:
● What action do I want?
● What is the main aim/purpose?
● Who will receive it?
● What is the recipient's likely attitude to the subject?
● How much do they need to know?
● Is my timing right?
● What is the main subject?
● Are the major points clear?
● Is the tone/language appropriate to the subject?
● Is there enough/too much detail?
● Is the action required clear?
● Does the recipient know what to expect?
● Is there any ambiguity?
● Have the facts been checked?
● Will I need to follow it up?
● What is the best medium for my message – memo, telephone, meeting in person?

Crossed lines

Ambiguous communication can cost the business money and waste time. It can also lead to faulty decisions as the following, perhaps apocryphal, story illustrates:

A young man was put in charge of the FBI's stores and stationery. Eager to make an impact, he decided to save on costs by reducing the size of memo paper.

One of the new sheets landed on the desk of J. Edgar Hoover himself. He disliked it on sight – the margins on both sides were too narrow for him. Across the top he wrote, in some irritation, "Watch the borders."

His purpose was misinterpreted. For the next six weeks, it became extremely difficult to enter the USA by road from either Canada or Mexico!

Irrelevant messages are counterproductive, as are irrelevancies and information which do not lead to progress or action. Repetition of main aims and objectives can be helpful. A questioning approach – "Do you have the latest sales figures?" –

establishes the receiver's state of knowledge, and gets to the point quickly.

Unnecessary detail should be avoided. Decision-makers want to know *what* will happen, and not always why. Ask yourself if the detail adds to the meaning of your

message – if not, it is "noise."

Unplanned interruptions disturb concentration and are confusing. However, if the speaker is slow to impart urgent news, such as "our competitors have just launched a new product," then interrupt.

Background chatter indicates boredom and if meetings generate a lot of it, lack of purpose is often the cause. Is the presentation meeting necessary? Is the right communication medium being used? One-to-one contact or a memo might be more effective.

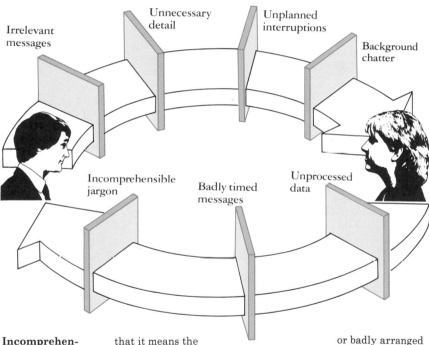

Irrelevant messages

Unnecessary detail

Unplanned interruptions

Background chatter

Incomprehensible jargon

Badly timed messages

Unprocessed data

Incomprehensible jargon is one of the more damaging forms of "noise," and can lead to faulty decisions. Avoid using jargon yourself and, if others use it, ask them to repeat it in plain English. But some jargon may be essential. If you must use it, check

that it means the same to all with whom you communicate.

Badly timed messages will prove to be unproductive. Always find out the recipient's state of readiness (by asking secretaries or others) before

giving information. Don't ask for detailed or expert advice when someone is in a hurry to leave. Always give bad news at a time when a considered response can be given.

Unprocessed data or uncoordinated

or badly arranged information is annoying to the hard-pressed manager. Technology, by increasing speed of transmission, frequently worsens the situation by making it easy to deliver information that perhaps should not have been sent at all.

One-to-one

A high proportion of an effective manager's time is always taken up with one-to-one communication with staff, peers and superiors. It is wrong to evade this responsibility through the use of written communication.

The advantage of meeting person-to-person is that you can get instant feedback about your plans and ideas. Also, you are better able to generate enthusiasm or commitment if you deal with someone face-to-face.

Show that you value others by paying attention to what they say.

Listening may seem easy but in fact it involves attention, hearing, comprehension and memory. You can check its effectiveness by asking for a summary of the conversation.

If a conversation has been wide-ranging and discursive, it is a good idea to clear up any ambiguity also by summarizing it.

Remember, you have to be especially alert when someone is communicating with you in person, in order to ensure that you give the right response. You may be asked, on the spot, to change your views to support or endorse another's proposal; to share responsibility or blame; or to make a snap decision.

You can initiate one-to-one conversations to enlist colleagues in a plan to promote change; to entreat them to help; to persuade them to relinquish power or authority; or to praise or reprimand.

Timing is important: before a one-to-one discussion, make sure there is enough time available and that other commitments will not drag you away. Spend the first part of the conversation checking your respondent's current state of mind about the issue in question. You will be in a better position to win support.

If your timing is wrong, then the best thing to do is to abort the discussion and try again at a more auspicious time.

Instant feedback

The advantage of one-to-one communication is that it enables you to gauge reactions instantly. Check understanding and ensure agreement and commitment by asking:

- Do you agree with my proposal?
- Can you meet the deadlines?
- Do you have enough relevant information?
- Have we the resources?
- Are there other aspects to the problem?
- What are implications for budgets/costs, etc.?
- Do you have an alternative proposal?
- Do you want to discuss the matter further?

By including such questions and dealing with the answers there and then you will advance important issues in the most effective way.

Communicating without words

Body language is not simply a set of standard, non-verbal signals which correspond to certain emotional states, such as fear or anger. Everyone makes individual gestures which indicate the current state of, or a change in, their emotions or attitudes.

Smart managers consciously study those they deal with to become familiar with their postures and gestures and work out what they indicate.

Body language will not give a precise insight into people's thoughts and emotions, but it may give important clues.

A salesperson who consistently fails to recognize that a customer scratches his forehead, say, before finalizing a transaction, loses a negotiating advantage.

Communicating with Jung's four types

Carl Jung observed for types of people: "thinkers," who traffic in facts and figures; "intuitors," who are creative and deal in ideas; "sensors," who are action-centred people; and "feelers," who are governed by feelings and emotions.

Obviously, the personal psychology of people should influence the way you communicate with them. Try to assess your respondent's personality and prepare your message accordingly. If you are a facts-and-figures person, you may need help in preparing a proposition for the approval of, say, an emotional, "feeling" type.

Pumping ideas across to a facts-and-figures person may not achieve the desired action or agreement. But by converting the verbal idea into a well-constructed memo you may confer the status of fact upon it and win support.

The responsibility is with you, the communicator, to shoose the right idiom or language if you wish to gain others' support. Teams will have within them very different psychological types, and you should spend time understanding these types to produce an effective group commitment. Good communicators spend a lot of time lobbying.

"Feelers" tend to be concerned with the "health" of the organization, and to gravitate toward Personnel and PR. Issues of image, reputation, environment and ethics have more appeal to them than turnover and profit. They often bring interesting alternative values and judgments to balance a purely commercial proposition.

Speak to them in terms of the values and significance of issues.

"Thinkers" are dispersed widely in organizations and specialize in analytical thought. They like order, and are suspicious of disorganized thinking and information. Often regarded as "custodians" or "regulators," their support gives respectability and adds security to a concept. They are careful, logical and rational and are attracted by arguments supported by data and measurable values.

"Intuitors" can be instinctive and intolerant of "reams of data." They enjoy being told about problems and being left to work them out. They seldom take suggestions beyond concept stage, and need back-up from those good at action. Innovation is their forte but they may be bad at getting down to details.

Timing is vital when you want to communicate with intuitors: make sure they are "switched-on."

"Sensors" are resourceful and work-orientated. They are useful members of any team, although sometimes inclined to get plans into action before they are properly completed. They tend to be more interested in the how, rather than the why, but are often highly motivated.

You can usually get to the point fairly quickly with sensors, since they are almost always in the mood to "do something."

Effective writing

The advantage of written communication is that it enables the recipient to retain and study information for as long as is necessary.

It also allows many people in different places to read the same message simultaneously. But it does lack immediacy and gives no chance for instant feedback.

Don't think you are being diligent just because you write a lot of letters and reports. Before you write something, ask yourself what it is you want to achieve. Consider whether personal contact might be more effective. Only use the written word:

● If you wish to remove the need for personal contact.

● To supply information that would otherwise take too long to reach all who need it.

● If material needs to be kept for future reference (as in a contractual letter or a report).

● If you need proof that you have taken action.

● To register or emphasize your views.

Use a structure

Organize your facts and arguments before thinking about how to express them. Then draft your material. Reduce information to manageable chunks; present your ideas in an ordered sequence. If the ideas are complex, try to clarify them with examples or analogies.

Check that the treatment and length are appropriate to the subject matter as well as to the recipient. You may be able to cut out words by using headings or summarizing points in note form.

You should be able to justify every word, sentence and paragraph. Finally, read through the finished draft, putting yourself in the place of the receiver.

For a report, the different structural elements might include: summary, findings, conclusions and your

---

Winston Churchill on brevity

Churchill issued the following memo to his government departments in August 1940:

"i The aim should be reports which set out the main points in a series of short, crisp paragraphs.

ii Often the occasion is best met by submitting not a fulldress report, but an *aide-mémoire* consisting of headings only, which can be expanded orally if needed.

iii Let us have an end of such phrases as these: 'It is also of importance to bear in mind the following consideration ...' or 'Consideration should be given to the possibility of carrying into effect ...' Most of these woolly phrases are mere padding, which can be left out altogether, or replaced by a single word. Let us not shrink from using the short expressive phrase, even if it is conversational."

---

recommendations. But these are interchangeable and dispensable, depending on the subject.

Make it readable

George Orwell wrote "Never use a long word where a short one will do ... if it is possible to cut a word out, always cut it out ... Never use a foreign phrase, a scientific word or a jargon word if you can think of an everyday English equivalent." He also had the common sense to add: "Break any of these rules sooner than say anything outright barbarous."

Remember that your written output will usually have to compete to be read, so be brief whenever you can: short reports get read; short sentences are understood. Combine the two and you are winning.

Brevity is particularly appreciated by senior management, who often have to do their reading in cars, trains and planes and do not want to be burdened with mounds of paper.

The effective report is a well set out, structured document that puts its message across succinctly.

Copy lists should be restricted to those who need to know. Otherwise, you may seem aggressive or appear to be showing off. If you want people not directly connected with the subject to know, send them a copy with a covering note.

Headings/titles enable the recipient to read quickly and efficiently. Titles can obviate the need for an introduction. The report can get straight to the point.

Origination details can be important, especially if the report is one of a sequence. Don't make the reader wait to the end to discover who wrote it.

Don't classify written communication if your message is confidential. Labelling messages as confidential makes them more tempting to the inquisitive outsider.

Categorize the report to alert readers to its purpose and help them organize their time: File report, Discussion paper, Action sheet, Meeting minutes, Report and recommendations.

Summarize each major section of a long document. Provide a summary of conclusions at the beginning or indicate in the contents where it is to be found. A busy manager will read the conclusion first.

Numbering of pages, paragraphs and notes should be consistent and simple: "page 3, para 12" is better than, say, "Findings, section 4 II (b)."

REPORT AND RECOMMENDATIONS

To: Divisional Sales Managers
Head of Purchasing
Financial Controller

From: J Smith, Marketing Department
Subject: Using our Purchasing Power to Improve Sales
Date: 6/8/85

Contents
Page 1   Background and Objectives
Page 2-3   Main Findings of Survey
Page 4-5   Summary and Recommendations
Appendix   Detailed Report

Background
The Marketing Department has conducted a survey among the suppliers of raw materials and components for our products. It has revealed that, although many of our suppliers purchase some of our products, few buy the whole range and some deal exclusively with competitors. The purpose of this report is to recommend a plan for improving the incidence of reciprocal trading with our suppliers.

Objectives
I believe we should aim to:-
a) Identify suppliers as a distinct market segment in order to direct a sales and marketing campaign at an area where we should already enjoy some goodwill. (We have more than 150 regular suppliers with an estimated sales value to us of $1.5m per year).

Subject headings direct readers to what concerns them most, makes reference easier in meetings and provide visual relief on the page.

A contents list alerts readers to what follows. Leo B. Mayer, the movie mogul, said, "Tell 'em what you're gonna tell 'em, tell 'em it, and tell 'em you've told 'em."

Wide margins on both sides of the page, generous space at the bottom and also between paragraphs allow readers to make their own notes.

Effective reading

Day by day, as a busy schedule consumes more and more of your time, a pile of reading material steadily mounts up. This growing pile may contain, for example: internal and external reports about the business and its competitors; newspaper and magazine articles; technical update material; memos, publicity and circulars; letters to be answered, and promotional material.

You may feel increasingly guilty because these remain unread, and that you may not be keeping up to date or doing your job properly. Yet even if you could find time to cope with the pile of material, you know that you could not absorb it all.

Reading effectively is a skill all managers need in their repertoire. Even though it may be true that three-quarters of our knowledge is gained through our eyes, this skill is not simply a question of reading faster. There is more to it than rapidly consuming all the reading matter arriving on your desk. It is important to understand what you decide to read.

Effective reading means quickly comprehending the essence of the printed word and interpreting it according to your needs. It takes a lot of practice to develop but it can be invaluable.

The wise manager never allows reading material to accumulate but deals with each piece as it arrives. Focus on what you or the business needs to know and then ask: Is it important or urgent, or can it be dealt with later? Important material demands that you find the time to give it proper attention. Urgent but unimportant material may be delegated.

Whatever the material, you must develop a technique of reading effectively: selecting what is essential and skimming what is not; knowing what to look for; concentrating in bursts and saving most of your energy for more important material.

Improving your reading

Adopt a positive attitude: motivate yourself to improve the effectiveness of your reading – you must want to get better at it and feel you can. Don't seek overnight improvement, but practice regularly without becoming obsessed by the problem.

Above all, accept that you cannot read everything. Constantly remind yourself to be ruthlessly selective. This may mean not being technically up-to-date in all areas of your business life. Ask yourself regularly where it is essential to stay up-to-date.

Once you have decided:
● Read the headings or index and get an idea of the essence.
● Skim the whole before reading any particular piece first.
● Review the conclusions or summary before starting on the detail.
● Read the introduction carefully: it may indicate which parts of the detail to avoid.
● Annotate as you go through. Do not wait for a second detailed reading; you may well forget what your first thoughts were.

Avoid the following bad habits:
● Don't read word for word – don't fix your eyes on one word at a time; let your sight move along the words at a constant rate and take in several words at a glance.
● Don't read aloud to yourself – don't mouth the words; let the words talk to you.
● Don't rely on every word to give you the sense of what is being said; anticipate as much as possible – effective readers require few clues to recognize what comes next in a sentence.
● Don't read the same sentence or paragraph over and over – you may legitimately discard any piece that holds no interest for you. But if there is something in the words you want to understand or absorb, by all means dwell on it.

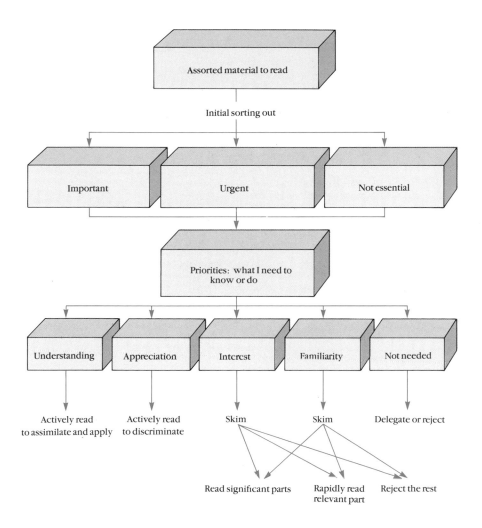

Categorizing reading matter

Try to sort your daily reading as it arrives: decide what your priorities are and then read; take notes if necessary and digest the information and ideas. Don't give up – the longer you persevere, the more you benefit.

Ask questions as you read and answer them yourself – for example:
● What is my purpose in reading this? What am I looking for?
● What is it about? What is the detail saying? What are the main ideas?
● How significant is it to me? How can I use what I am absorbing to be a better manager?

At first, it will be difficult to read and question at the same time but, with practice, the dual activity will become a habit. Keep a positive attitude and have a flexible approach – information and ideas are not readily communicated to the negative or fixed mind.

Public presentations

The public presentation of new concepts, ideas or information with visual aids involves all the communication skills: writing, speaking, body language and imaginative illustration.

An understanding of *why* the talk or presentation is being made will help decide how best to prepare for it. If the presenter knows the subject and can explain it simply, even a complex technical or financial problem can be understood by an intelligent audience, using simple visual aids such as blackboards, flip charts and overhead projectors.

If, for example, the sales force is to be briefed on a new product and motivated to achieve ambitious selling targets, then all the dramatic effects of a topline presentation are called for. In all cases, visual aids must be informative in themselves or give support to the spoken word.

Presenters have to cope with the potential indifference and inattentiveness in an audience. To help overcome these barriers, take particular care with scripting and delivery.

Scripting

For most occasions write your presentation in full and bear in mind the type of audience you aim to convince. Organize your facts in a logical sequence, choose clear language, and balance the length of your sentences. Consider where and when you want to make key points and emphasize them.

For heavily illustrated shows, detailed scripting is essential to coordinate voice and visual aids. For less complicated presentations, reduce the script to notes or to headings written on cards. Use the method with which you feel most at ease.

The script allows you to time the length of your presentation. Keep it short. The worst speakers are those who claim never to need scripting and then ramble on interminably.

Make sure your script matches the occasion and the audience.

Delivery

Your personality is the key to the success of any talk, speech or presentation. Vitality and enthusiasm count most.

A good speaking style helps. Practice, using a tape recorder to give yourself feedback and to help improve clarity and correct speech mannerisms. Face the audience and talk *to* them not *at* them; sound natural and spontaneous. Project your voice so that those at the back can hear every word. Vary the pitch and change tempo to keep the audience alert.

Signal important points by pausing before or after them. Add emphasis by raising your voice slightly or by using a gesture.

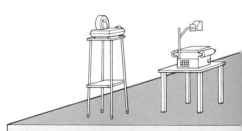

Visual aids range from simple flipcharts to computer-controlled slides or film and video programs that cost large sums to prepare and take weeks to develop. Before spending time and money, you should consider what visuals you really need.

The blackboard is a cheap and flexible visual aid: you can add and erase as you talk. Yellow chalk increases visibility. Don't use a blackboard if your writing is unclear.

Flipcharts can be prepared beforehand and information can be

140

Organizing a presentation

● Choose a venue that suits the size of the audience.
● Make sure all the audience will be able to see and hear.
● Ensure lighting is adequate.
● Check the microphones well in advance.
● Consider whether speakers need lecterns.
● Allow time for rehearsals.
● Consider how speakers will be introduced.
● Time all speakers in rehearsal, taking question time into account.
● Check that visuals don't upstage the speakers.
● Provide for coffee breaks.

Getting it across

● Write your speeches in spoken English.
● Keep on track with notes/headings written on cards.
● Allow for the loss of audience attention.
● Emphasize and repeat the main points.
● Illustrate with examples.
● Be forceful, clear and brief.
● Avoid irritating mannerisms.
● Get small audiences involved.
● Entertain large audiences with visual aids and slick presentation.
● With a small audience, take questions as you go along but stay in control and don't lose your thread.

:alled if required. They should never be ..ft on display after the speaker has moved on to another topic.

Working models are highly specialized but invaluable in the right context, e.g. showing a factory plan or an office reorganization. Don't allow the audience to become too participatory unless you want your scheme redesigned.

Overhead projection can be used both as an illuminated flip chart and as a substitute slide presentation to small audiences.

Slides can be projected to suit different-sized audiences. Professionally produced programs create superb effects. Don't let the slides compete with your script: use them for emphasis and explanation (tables, graphs and charts).

Soundtape/films/video/holograms/ lasers can all be used to add drama and impact, but take professional advice. Amateur presentations to large audiences easily go wrong or fail to communicate effectively.

Writing a memo

One of the best, and quickest, ways to establish your credentials as a manager is to cultivate the art of writing good memos. If others in your company look forward to your memos, knowing they invariably convey useful information, instead of scanning them indifferently, or ignoring them, you are well on your way to winning their respect as a leader.

The opposite is equally true. There is no quicker way to reveal a confused, jumbled mind than to put it on display in a memo where all can see it.

Are memos really all that important? Yes, because the ideas that nourish any company are almost always committed to paper, often in the form of memos. How skillfully the writer expresses them determines whether the ideas take root or vanish, produce progress or chaos.

What meager chance has a good idea – a new product, product improvement, new service, new pricing plan, new distribution scheme, any creative idea – to survive and flower in a glob of undisciplined words?

Imagine the confusion that results from a vague, incomplete, disorganized memo. And then consider how effective and efficient your operation can be if you, as the manager, transmit your ideas and instructions in clear, unmistakeable language that every reader can grasp and act upon.

If you are tempted not to trouble yourself with setting your ideas down on paper, consider the following:

● The best way to determine whether you have something worthwhile to say is to see how it looks on paper.

● The best way to organize your thoughts is to write them down.

● The best way to arrive at a logical point of view is to commit all the factors to paper where you can evaluate them together.

● The best way to keep an idea from vanishing is to preserve it on paper.

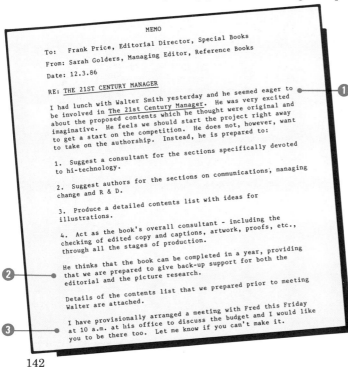

```
                              MEMO
     To:  Frank Price, Editorial Director, Special Books
     From: Sarah Golders, Managing Editor, Reference Books

     Date: 12.3.86

     RE: THE 21ST CENTURY MANAGER

     I had lunch with Walter Smith yesterday and he seemed eager to
     be involved in The 21st Century Manager. He was very excited
     about the proposed contents which he thought were original and
     imaginative. He feels we should start the project right away
     to get a start on the competition. He does not, however, want
     to take on the authorship. Instead, he is prepared to:

     1. Suggest a consultant for the sections specifically devoted
     to hi-technology.

     2. Suggest authors for the sections on communications, managing
     change and R & D.

     3. Produce a detailed contents list with ideas for
     illustrations.

     4. Act as the book's overall consultant - including the
     checking of edited copy and captions, artwork, proofs, etc.,
     through all the stages of production.

     He thinks that the book can be completed in a year, providing
     that we are prepared to give back-up support for both the
     editorial and the picture research.

     Details of the contents list that we prepared prior to meeting
     Walter are attached.

     I have provisionally arranged a meeting with Fred this Friday
     at 10 a.m. at his office to discuss the budget and I would like
     you to be there too. Let me know if you can't make it.
```

1 The first sentence of a memo is crucial because it is the one that everybody reads. Don't waste it. Get to the point fast!

2 Long, drawn-out paragraphs will turn readers off. Short ones will help to keep their attention focused on the subject.

3 Make sure you state what response or action you require from the reader. If you don't want one, then say so.

Rules for writing memos

If it is important to write a good memo, how do you go about it? Here are 15 rules:

1 Make sure you have something worth saying, something that will benefit the reader. Your goal is to establish a reputation for yourself as a manager who writes only when there is something important to communicate.

2 Get to the point fast, and stay on it. Everybody reads the first sentence, so introduce your subject in that sentence. Then immediately develop your idea.

3 Say it simply and clearly. Remember the most exciting thing in the world is an idea that works. Have faith in it. Don't blur it with obscure or over-formal language or indirection. Above all, be clear.

4 Be specific. Tell them exactly what you have in mind. Generalizations are usually worthless and boring.

5 Be complete. Don't be afraid to develop your ideas if necessary. People will read as long as the material is worth reading. Being incomplete makes it difficult to understand your message, and increases the likelihood of confusing – and losing – the reader.

6 Write to a specific reader, with his or her self-interest in mind. How is the idea in your memo going to affect that individual? That is the question the reader asks as he or she reads your memo; make sure you give an answer to it.

7 Personalize your memo. Use "you' generously, "I" sparingly. But use them.

8 Avoid pretentious language. It tends to draw attention to itself and interrupt the flow of the memo. If you are addicted to big words, technical jargon, slang, etc., use them at your peril. They may be unknown to your readers who, if so, will be both mystified and irritated. Being colorful is fine, but never at the expense of clarity.

9 Tell the reader what he or she is expected to do after reading the memo. If you expect a reply, say so. If you want the reader to take some action, be clear and specific. If the memo conveys information but requires no response, say so. The best-constructed memo imaginable is useless if it fails to produce the reaction you had in mind.

10 Learn to punctuate. Punctuation greatly affects the flow and rhythm of the written word. A misplaced comma can ruin a sentence.

11 Keep paragraphs short. Fat, blocky paragraphs look formidable. Busy readers tend to skip through them.

12 Quit when you run out of useful information.

13 If it's a long memo, summarize it at the end. This emphasizes the key points, and helps the readers fix it in their minds. It is easier for you to sort out the highlights than for the readers to do so after reading.

14 Polish, polish, polish, polish. Don't be afraid to revise your memo if you feel your first attempts do not convey the meaning you desire.

15 Never deny pride of authorship. As a manager, you are expected to produce ideas and communicate them to fellow-workers with high skill. Writing them down with meticulous care is a priceless talent and one of the reasons for your success. Take pride in doing it well.

Preparing and chairing

Well-conducted, productive meetings that deal with relevant subject matter efficiently are a sign of good teamwork, a high level of morale and commitment, and typify a healthy organization.

To the individual in such an environment, the meeting is both a challenge and an opportunity. Good performance at meetings can lead to increased responsibility and advancement. Also, the meeting provides a chance to bring group experience to bear on a particularly difficult subject.

"What do we need to know?"
Gathering or disseminating information is a crucial starting point when managing any new project. The purpose of the meeting is to share knowledge between all team members, establish lines of authority and responsibility and reinforce objectives. Often referred to as briefing, this meeting is also useful in defining problems. A strongly chaired formal style is preferable.

"How are we getting on?"
Progress reviews are essential to good project management or customer/supplier relationships. Meetings are held at regular intervals as demanded by the project. Individuals work on an agreed agenda; cross-questioning and open discussion are vital ingredients, so skilled chairing is required. Most of the participants will know each other, so a planned informal style is the most appropriate.

"What's wrong? What shall we do?"
Sometimes it is necessary to break down discussion of problems into two separate meetings if time permits: one to define, and one to solve, with an interval in between to examine alternatives. An informal style is best because the issue is often too urgent to allow elaborate preparation. Informality also helps to avoid the allocation of blame, and the time-wasting justification this often causes.

For the meeting room you may need: name cards for participants; a soundproof, air-conditioned room; telephone messages taken externally; pads and pencils; a flipchart; copying facilities; electrical sockets/extension leads; a large table, extra chairs.

If chairing the meeting:
● Be more concerned with the process than the content. Keep the meeting moving to its conclusion and stay out of the discussion. If you have a strong interest, delegate the chair during that issue.
● Protect the weak, control the strong.
● Don't watch the speaker, watch the audience for reactions.
● Ensure a result – identify the issues, and agree on the means of their solution.

Don't be in a hurry to speak. Let others make their case, then construct yours by logically summarizing their views, concluding in favor of your own.

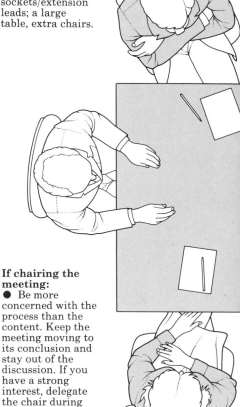

● Agree deadlines for progress reviews; set date, time and place for next meeting.
● Send good action-needed notes promptly to each participant.

Develop your skills of improvisation, be aware of what is going on and, if necessary, use your contingency plans. The unexpected may lead to a better result.

If you know that someone else shares your view, let them speak first and then follow on, supporting their strong points, and adding any points they may have missed.

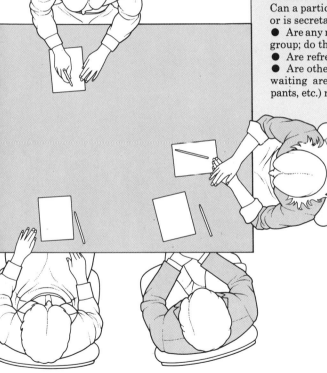

Meeting preparation

● What is the meeting's objective?
● Who needs to attend?
● When and where is convenient?
● What style should it be?
● Should information and agenda be precirculated?
● Are any special facilities (audio/visual aids) needed?
● Do topics need ranking/timing?
● Is prediscussion with individuals required?
● What kind of record/minutes/action-needed notes are most suitable? Can a participant handle recording, or is secretarial help needed?
● Are any new members joining the group; do they need briefing?
● Are refreshments needed?
● Are other facilities (car-parking, waiting area for part-time participants, etc.) needed?

The people who achieve most at meetings are often those who say least. But behind the economy of words lies detailed preparation and careful monitoring. Before the meeting it is essential to:
● Read precirculated literature carefully and question any contribution you do not understand.
● Be clear about your objective, and find out who supports and who opposes your view; lobby your supporters.
● Plan your contribution but prepare to be flexible. All plans need contingencies.

Always appear reasonable; keep a sense of humor (not flippancy); an intense approach exhausts and alienates others. Loss of cool usually means loss of argument.

Listen to all contributions; opponents may present you with openings; there may be aspects of the issue which were not covered by advance literature.

If you do not know the answer to a question, do not attempt to bluff. Promise an early reply or, if possible, ask permission to get the information at once.

Achieving results

True "brainstorming" meetings are rare because people have difficulty lifting their sights from current problems and real innovators may fear scorn from their peers.

Meetings called to generate ideas require sensitive steering but, when successful, can be of immense value; ideas are the food of business growth. Informality is invariably the right atmosphere for such meetings (lunch can provide the setting). Remember, *encourage* the ideas to emerge.

Arbitration – one of the rarest and most valuable skills – puts great responsibility on the chairman. Meetings to resolve difficulties or conflict require forethought (often careful lobbying of participants to find out attitudes and positions).

Meeting style should be a tactical decision of the person who calls the meeting, in order to achieve the desired result. Remember, consensus may not be the object if all it does is submerge conflict.

Earl Mountbatten of Burma was highly skilled at meeting technique. Alan Campbell-Johnson, his press attaché in India, recalls that he used a meeting to reach agreement on an issue, the contentious features of which had already been ironed out in personal discussion. If, during a meeting, there was unforeseen dissent, he took the matter off the agenda for personal treatment afterwards.

In this context, staff meetings, both when he was Supreme Allied Commander and Viceroy, were held on an almost daily basis, part of a continuous process of diplomacy.

How to perform well at meetings

● Listen attentively: practice this skill. It leads to good questions, improves group understanding, keeps meetings good humored.
● Give direct replies: keep the meeting to the point to avoid wasting time.
● Clarify issues: "Are you saying that you can provide this material by the end of the month...?"
● Summarize progress: "It's now 3.30 p.m., where are we...?"
● Restate important points: "So let's confirm..."
● Be prepared to change your tactics if necessary.
● Be supportive: "That sounds like a good idea..."

● Confront issues: "Are we really prepared to...?"
● Question critically: "What exactly do you mean by...?"
● Bring with you accurate supporting data.
● Make sure the meeting is not interrupted by telephone calls, except in emergencies.
● Avoid interrupting.
● Don't be afraid to make your feelings known.
● Refrain from distracting behavior such as pencil tapping.
● Don't talk to your neighbor during a presentation.
● Never lose your temper.

Formal meetings

Committees, boards of directors, large briefing groups and some progress report meetings follow this style. Often it is the only way to control large groups covering varied topics. Rigid, structured agendas, time allocated to subjects by agreement with participants, and firm control of time and relevance by the chair are essential.

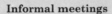

Informal meetings

These can be *ad hoc* – "It's time we talked" – or a sub-group of a formal meeting. Typically, they are convened to deal with specific issues, rather than a whole subject. Little notice is needed; the outcome should be a plan, a solution, or a request to hold a larger, formal meeting. Can be as small as two people, or as large as desirable.

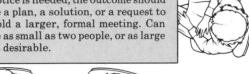

Planned informal meetings

For the planner, these are the most useful meetings. You decide the objective, select the participants, prepare your case and deal with people singly or in groups.

Using internal resources

Consultation is a way of testing what impact an action might have on others before you commit yourself to it. Consultation is used to assess risk, create consent or conduct arbitration.

Consultation is essentially a process in which one party seeks the views, knowledge or advice of another. As a manager you may want to use consultation to overcome potential resistance to a decision you have made, or to convert an action which may appear to be autocratic into one which appears more democratic.

If, as a manager, you have set the right climate for your team and your colleagues, people will feel able to consult with their bosses, peers or subordinates on a regular basis. An open style of management will promote consultation as a normal facet of business behavior and not as a sign of ignorance or weakness.

Indeed, the consultation process can have positive benefits for you and your team. People should be encouraged to seek and accept consultation, especially on issues which may have far-reaching consequences.

Benefits of consulting

Handled properly, consultation can have positive results. It helps you to:
● Test reactions to risky or threatening ideas.
● Check feasibility: if you are too close to an idea you may not be able to recognize that it just would not work in practice.
● Look for compatibility with other people's plans and projects. It is surprising how often the same idea occurs to people working in the same organization at the same time.
● Seek advice: there may well be people who are experienced or expert in something you are coming to for the first time.
● Get agreement: an idea or suggestion which meets with favorable early reaction is well on the way to agreement.
● Sharpen up your own thought processes by highlighting parts of your initial unsound thinking.
● Reveal extra pieces of the jigsaw you failed to recognize which either complement your original thoughts or reveal ideas counter to your original direction.

Direct and indirect consultation

Consultation is multi-directional: you can consult directly or indirectly with your boss, peers and subordinates. But you must be clear about what you want to achieve and whether it is feasible.

Consulting upward: if you consult your boss directly about an idea, it may give the impression that what you are really seeking is approval, not consultation. Instead, you could float the idea informally over lunch. Your boss is bound to give you an indication whether the idea is, in fact, worth pursuing or not. If the idea originated from a peer or subordinate, give him/her credit: it will encourage people to come to you with ideas and improve your reputation as the person who translates ideas into action.

Consulting sideways: when you consult peer colleagues directly, you may risk their stealing your proposal/idea: or if they oppose it, you give them time to think of ways of blocking you. If you suspect this is the case, take your idea to a superior. Get it approved and then take it to your colleagues, making sure that they know it has the superior's backing. This will give it authority and stop anyone stealing it.

Consulting downward: subordinates unused to consultative management sometimes experience confusion or suspicion if suddenly consulted directly by a superior – "Why should the boss want to consult a junior person like me?" Also, they may tell you what they think you want to hear, not what you need to hear. Even worse, they may see it as a sign of weakness on your part – "Surely you can make your own decisions without having to consult a subordinate?" Consider having your secretary, say, float your proposal for you: your subordinate is more likely to react honestly and you can act on the feedback.

Pitfalls of consulting

The risks of consultation are:
● You waste time. If an idea has been in your mind for some time, it is often impossible for someone else to understand it quickly.
● Those whom you consult may not have anything positive to contribute. The ideas you glean when you consult are often ones you have already rejected.
● You may end up antagonizing those you are consulting because they suggest ideas that you have already rejected; or because you do not follow their advice.
● Your idea may get stolen by someone else. Innovation and creativity are often in short supply and people may take your idea and call it their own.
● Consulting with your boss too frequently on minor matters may give the impression that you are not fully in control of your situation, and you probably aren't.
● Excessive consulting with subordinates will rightly be taken as a sign of weakness and diminish your standing as a leader.

Consulting successfully

Develop your skill at consultation to enhance your own solutions as a result of others' contributions.
Remember to:
● Give your good ideas time to mature in your own mind. Don't rush off to consult others every time you have a brainwave, but...
● Get used to floating your ideas at an early stage in their development.
● Don't get into consultation if you have no real options. If you are committed to an idea and are expected to implement it, don't consult on its feasibility, make it work.
● Find one or two colleagues whom you can use as regular sounding boards. In time they will come to know you better (and vice versa) and the consultation process will be speeded up.
● Be genuinely prepared to change up to the point that you commit yourself. Once committed, try not to entertain doubts.
In the last analysis, consultation does not change the basic responsibilities – the decision is always yours.

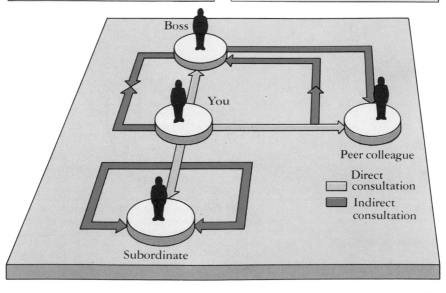

Boss

You

Peer colleague

Direct consultation

Indirect consultation

Subordinate

Seeking outside help

An organization will often bring in management consultants to deal with problems it has not either encountered before or whose solution demands resources it does not possess. Consultants are commonly thought of as having the missing piece of expertise that will complete the jigsaw or solve the problem.

But it is not simply a question of providing technical expertise. Consulting is more than that. It involves the difficult process of acclimatizing quickly to the organization and its problems, gathering information and checking its relevance, bringing together the interested parties and persuading them to make a decision. Consultation should be considered as an art, not a technique.

There are three main reasons why companies enlist the help of consultants.

The need for extra resources
There is only a finite amount of time in a working day or week and good managers need it all. This means that important projects requiring a period of concentrated effort may be delayed because of everyday demands. Bringing in consultants to deal with a specific task can be the answer to the problem.

The need for objectivity
Before making a decision on a troublesome issue, you have to weigh the pros and cons carefully. Managers may find that the issue in question has become such a bone of contention within the organization that reasonable and detached advice cannot be found internally. Equally, they may be too close to the issue to be able to stand back from it far enough and contribute usefully.

The need for expertise
Problems may arise or decisions may have to be taken which need a depth of knowledge and experience that is lacking within the organization. Good consultants can provide the necessary expertise without lengthy familiarization programs.

Apart from these three reasons, there are a number of less tangible benefits that consultants can provide:

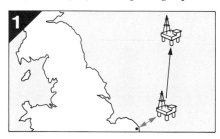

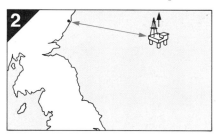

The role of consultants

Good consultants do not content themselves with solving the problems their clients ask them to solve. They try to look beneath the surface to see if there is something the clients have missed; or they question the assumptions that are at the heart of the problem.

In the early 1970s, the UK North Sea oil exploration had moved from the southern North Sea, 1, with supply bases at Yarmouth to, eventually, Aberdeen, 2. The exploration was going northward and showed no sign of stopping.

A major British finance company had the idea of establishing a supply base near where the exploration was to be concentrated. They stood to make a fortune if the base was successful.

It seemed to make good sense to invest several million pounds in building a supply base on Yell, 3, one of the Shetland islands, which had a high-quality, deep-water, protected anchorage. It seemed quite straightforward. The company enlisted the help of the British branch of Arthur Young to make a feasibility study for this project.

The study involved two parts: first, how

Reassurance

A company may want to invest a large sum of money in acquiring new machinery or other assets and may seek a second opinion from consultants to confirm it is doing the right thing.

Insurance

Say, for example, that an organization wants to spend millions on a project. Its shareholders are getting justifiably anxious as to whether the board of directors is spending the money wisely. The latter can take out an insurance policy, as it were, by enlisting the advice of top consultants. This will ease the worries of the shareholders as well as spreading the responsibility if anything goes wrong.

Sounding-board

Senior executives who have to make crucial decisions often find it difficult to consult within the organization because it might call into question their ability or competence. Nevertheless, they still need a sounding-board to assess the quality of their decisions and this need can be fulfilled by outside consultants.

Reservoirs of information

Companies and their executives are often so involved in the day-to-day running of their affairs that they cannot evaluate their own performances or compare themselves to other companies and executives. Consultants can provide a survey of industrial practice. They hold up a panoramic mirror in which the clients can then see clearly where they stand in relation to others.

Catalysts of change

The answers to clients' problems are often to be found underneath their noses and not in some magical expertise that consultants are supposed to have. In such an instance, it is the consultants' job to sift the relevant information, list the facts and get the clients to confront what they have previously been ignoring.

An internal report may give the same facts as the consultants' report. But if you are paying the consultants a lot of money for their time, you have a greater incentive to heed their advice and to take the necessary action.

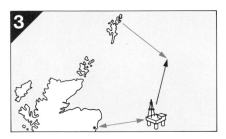

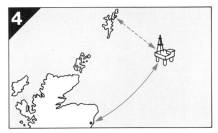

much the supply base would cost and, second, what the market was and how much business the base would do. This in turn depended on the volume of activity in the northern North Sea. These were the technical problems.

The consultants decided to interview the top executives of the oil companies that would use the supply base. This, as it turned out, gave the real answer to the feasibility study.

As a result of their investigations, the consultants decided that the crux of the problem lay in whether any of the major oil companies was committed to

using the base, 4. This, more than anything else, would determine the project's success.

Accordingly, the consultants talked to the oil companies and found that none of them, when pressed, was prepared to give a commitment to the project.

The project was therefore cancelled. The consultants had shown that the problem was more behavioral than technical and for a fee of several thousand pounds they had saved their clients several million.

The formal approach

Negotiation is the process of arriving at mutual satisfaction through discussion and bargaining. Managers negotiate to settle differences, vary agreements or terms, or to value commodities or services.

For negotiation to succeed, each party must genuinely desire agreement, which is usually expressed in some form of a contract. Agreement that cannot be applied is as useless as no agreement at all.

Solutions must be viable or the negotiators will lose their credibility and authority, and lasting agreement will be jeopardized.

Negotiators have to perform several skilled functions which make up an overall strategy. The keys to successful negotiation are flexibility and improvization. Even the best laid plans can go awry.

The case relating to each point of the negotiation must stand on its own merit. Every argument should be complete. Negotiators must be able to see both sides of an argument. This is essential to determining concessions acceptable to both parties.

Good negotiators understand how to resolve conflict. They must walk a fine line between appeasement and domination. They give way on minor points to achieve their overall aims. The firmness of a stand depends on the strength of your bargaining position and the likelihood that adopting such a stance will eventually lead to a successful conclusion.

There is no single comprehensive theory governing the complex practice of negotiation, although some of the world's foremost business education establishments – notably Harvard – devote much effort to developing strategies to help negotiators achieve positive results.

Three major theories of practice have emerged in the last two decades, namely "positional," "principled" and "situational" negotiation.

How to negotiate

The art of negotiation is to avoid reaching a fixed position too quickly. Well before meeting, messages should be exchanged.

Negotiation should then follow a well-prepared, logical sequence:

1 Introduction
Be sociable with the other party and set a tension-free atmosphere.

2 General overview
Confirm both parties' broad objectives and feelings. Assess any differences between your positions.

3 Background
Review proceedings leading up to the present negotiation. If you have different interpretations of the facts, iron out the differences.

4 Definition of issues
Specify in detail what you want to resolve, if possible starting with an issue on which agreement is probable. Link issues if advantageous. Specify if one issue can be settled only if another is also resolved.

5 Negotiate the issue
Start by asking for what you want. Both parties want as much as they can get, but both must accept that goals may have to be modified. Conflict should not be avoided – it ventilates the issues and leads to settlements.

6 Compromising
Give, to get something in return, but make sure you are consistent in valuing tradeoffs. If compromising becomes difficult, go "situational," exchanging messages outside the meeting ground through others.

7 Settlement
"Agree on what you have agreed." Unless agreement is fully understood by both parties the settlement will not last.

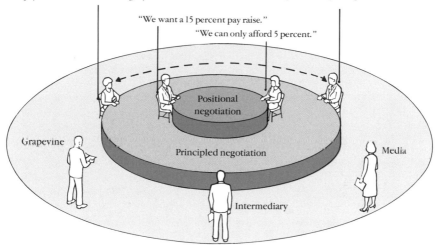

"We are prepared to accept a 10 percent pay raise if it means avoiding layoffs."

"We can afford to give a 7 percent raise if productivity is improved."

"We want a 15 percent pay raise."

"We can only afford 5 percent."

Positional negotiation

Grapevine

Principled negotiation

Media

Intermediary

Situational negotiation

Types of formal negotiation

In theory, there are three distinct types of negotiation. The distinctions are less clear in practice. For example, situational negotiation usually takes place prior to entering into principled and positional negotiations.

Situational negotiation does not require the parties to meet face to face. It is an indirect way to state your bargaining position and receive feedback from the other side. This is done through leaks to the press or via the grapevine. It can be a pre-emptive form of negotiation, as it allows both parties to come up with solutions or alternative stances before meeting, thus accelerating the negotiating process.

Principled negotiation is the "Harvard Model" whereby negotiators are encouraged to search for the underlying principles which support "positions." This is a more relaxed and creative process, since it states the objectives, but does not offer solutions. Principled negotiation requires detailed identification of all the various options. The will to succeed is often greater than in positional negotiating, because both parties feel as if they are working together to solve the dispute.

Principled negotiation degenerates into positional negotiation or deadlock if emotions are allowed to cloud the issues.

Positional negotiation is the traditional form of negotiation. Participants often work to a tight mandate. If their positions afford no compromise, the result will be deadlock. Success is usually achieved only after all aspects of opposing positions have been explored to try to find common ground.

Typical examples include, union/management bargaining, disputes between customers and suppliers and boundary or territorial difficulties.

153

Internal bargaining

Some managers may dislike the process of negotiation, believing it to be a clash of wills from which only one conclusion is certain – both parties will lose something. But negotiating is a feature of almost every bargain struck in the workplace.

Managers regularly have to negotiate – with peers, the boss and subordinates.

In theory, conflicts are resolved by agreeing on what is right for the company. Reality is much more complex, incorporating a system of favors done and owing.

Internal negotiations are much more difficult than external ones. Each person has his or her own idea of what is best for the company. This, coupled with individual needs and relationships, heightens the potential for conflict.

The loser in the negotiation may work in the same building, doing a similar job. The loser may be the winner in the next negotiation, may be a rival for promotion, a close friend or a bitter enemy.

Therefore, if you don't have to negotiate, don't. If cooperation can be achieved without bargaining or compromise, accept it. Don't believe that you have to negotiate every point, complicating the manager/subordinate relationship by encouraging negotiation of the most trivial matters. It is your duty as a manager to foster a climate of cooperation.

All parties to a negotiation perceive that they have needs which can be satisfied. If one side does not acknowledge having such needs, the other side must demonstrate that they exist. In other words, needs may have to be "sold" to the other side.

Timing is an obvious and frequently overlooked point. Two main considerations are:

● Is it the right time for the organization to accept the idea that you are trying to implement? Premature forcing of an issue weakens your negotiating position.

● Is it the right time to tackle the individual(s) to whom you must speak? Are they under pressure, busy, depressed or bad-tempered? Being sensitive to the mood and receptiveness of others can prevent sound ideas being rejected for the wrong reasons.

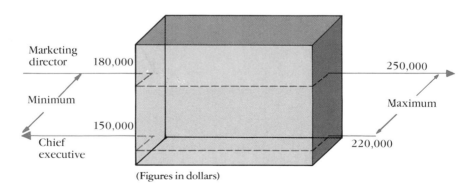

Marketing director 180,000
250,000
Minimum
Maximum
150,000
Chief executive
220,000

(Figures in dollars)

Define your objectives – most negotiations center on finding a mutually acceptable mid-point. In the annual budgeting round, for example, the marketing director's objective may be to obtain an advertising budget of $250,000, while the chief executive's objective is to keep it down to $150,000. Both parties must have a range in mind.

Settlement is likely to be reached somewhere in the blue shaded area between $180,000 and $220,000.

Achieving win/win

There is a greater need for both sides to win in internal negotiations. One danger is that argument often centers on who is doing the best job for the company.

Negotiators who adhere rigidly to a fixed position can succeed only by causing some form of damage to the other party and are, effectively, not negotiating. The damaged party will find all sorts of ways, either subtle or blatant, to get revenge. This will be to the detriment of company efficiency and staff harmony.

To arrive at a win/win solution:

● Honesty is essential. Because both sides tend to know each other very well, ploys, privileged information, strengths/weaknesses, may be difficult to exploit.

● Don't embark on negotiation with all the emphasis on your own needs – "This is what we want," "When are you going to start supporting our efforts?" Try to analyze and understand the needs of the other party. Be prepared to accommodate these other needs, unless doing so weakens your own bargaining position or jeopardizes your negotiating strategy.

● Don't deal with internal issues by full frontal confrontation. Try to don the velvet glove rather than wield the iron fist of authority.

● If you choose to be cynical and skeptical, do so only to expose the weaknesses in a position. Don't act the part of devil's advocate to repay some previous hurt or to establish a reputation with a patron.

● Remember that egos surface more readily on internal matters and often lead to power struggles to justify worth or position in the hierarchy. Don't expend effort trying to prove yourself to others, perhaps to the detriment of the point at issue.

● See the other party's need for help in accepting their losing position if a win/win situation is not achieved.

Leverage factors

The party with the greater need is in the weaker negotiating position and must analyze factors which might provide additional leverage:

● How much you need the other party.

● How much the other party needs you.

● What you know that the other party does not.

● What the other party might know that you don't.

● What you both know that you don't want exposed elsewhere.

● The time pressures on both parties.

● The extent of peer group involvement and influence.

● Fear of failure, loss of prestige, or the heaping of disgrace on either side.

● The effect on future plans (win the battle, lose the war).

● The need to be right, to win praise or recognition.

● The ability to influence formally or informally both your peers and superiors.

● The ability to make the other party feel guilty.

● Deprivation of freedom of action.

● Threat of boycott.

Having assessed as far as possible the strengths and weaknesses of both parties, ask yourself:

● What strengths does the other party have that could be a source of worry to me?

● What strengths do I have that will worry the other party?

This exercise is helpful in future negotiations as well. A previously solved problem may resurface, or a possible future problem may be identified.

Staff selection and interviewing

Recruitment of a person for your own staff is an important managerial task because you will usually have to live with the results for a considerable time.

Good managers rarely delegate the process entirely and usually stay close to all its stages. They realize that the candidates' personal commitment to them (as opposed to the department or Personnel) can be achieved only through close involvement in the appointment.

If a member of the staff leaves or is promoted, don't automatically recruit a replacement. Make sure that the work cannot be absorbed internally without affecting quality, morale or productivity.

If you have to recruit, then you must first define the job, taking into account its function, the duties and responsibilities involved, and the skill, knowledge and experience needed. Check whether past job-holders had any specific difficulties, the pay and work conditions, and the way the job interacts with those of other members of the department.

Once you have defined the job, ask:
● Is this a long-term role?
● Can it be filled internally?
● Does it demand any specialized knowledge?
● Is it likely to attract high-caliber applicants?
● Can it be merged with other responsibilities to make it more attractive?

Draw up a job specification, listing job objectives, status and reporting relationships, main tasks/responsibilities, the resources and support that are available, and any problems associated with the job.

This information can be used to issue an internal "job vacancy" memo or to produce a recruitment advertisement.

Interviewing is a time-consuming process, so make sure the information about the job is accurate and evocative of its "feel." For example, don't ask for "aggressive achievers" if the employee is to work in a conservative bureaucracy.

The interview

Read the applicants' resumes carefully prior to the interviews. If any likely sound applicant works or has worked for a company with whom you have a contact, you could make a few informal phone calls to pick up inside information.

Interviews are difficult and demanding because no two persons are alike. Some express themselves better in writing than in conversation. So if the job does not demand great speaking skills, don't be overimpressed by a candidate's eloquence. Stick to the relevant qualities that are needed for the job in question.

You will need skill, tact and understanding to make the interviewees relaxed enough to offer information that will help you assess their potential.

One indication of how the candidates will fare in your department is how they have managed their past jobs. The secret of successful interviewing is to get applicants to talk about themselves and their past employment, and then to direct the conversation into areas that are relevant to the vacant job and its particular problems.

Sympathetic listening and well-timed, but open, questions encourage honest responses; trick questions, a rigid interview structure, an impatient or bored attitude, do not.

Follow up the interview by preparing a shortlist. Write promptly to candidates who are not on it. When you have chosen a candidate, be sure to check references.

If you think a candidate who narrowly missed your job would do well elsewhere in the organization, pass on the particulars to an appropriate colleague.

Interviewer tactics

- Plan the interview but be prepared to be directed by the candidate's answers.
- Take brief notes; expand later.
- Get the interviewees to enlarge on the facts given on their resumes.
- Be alert to the interviewee embellishing the facts.
- Don't ask questions that produce only yes or no answers.
- Listen attentively.
- Ask for career aims and compare them with past experience.
- Be sure applicants have had a chance to reveal all relevant information.
- Allow candidates to question you.

Interviewee tactics

- Dress smartly and look the part.
- Support answers with examples.
- Act as if you *want* the job.
- Say *how* you have gone about your previous jobs.
- Be sure you can answer questions on career and personal objectives.
- Show, with examples, how you have handled particular challenging situations.
- Give concrete examples of your work performance.
- Be honest: falsehoods are easily discovered. It may not be worth getting a job based on untruths.
- Have questions ready to ask interviewer.

Assessing candidates

After the interview, you will have a mass of data to evaluate. You need to compare candidates both impartially and consistently. Break down their careers under the following headings:

Experience
- What experience/opportunities have the applicants had?
- What responsible positions have they held?
- What decisions have they made?
- What results have they achieved?

Motivation
- What career choices did the applicants have?
- What influenced them?
- What risks did they take?
- What did they expect to happen?
- What did they get out of it?

Achievements
- Have things gone as they/their bosses expected?
- What problems did they solve?
- Were they unaided or supported?
- How did they measure success?

Planning succession

Organizations are dynamic. Continual movement is dictated by the ever-changing demands of the marketplace, and by people's desire to improve their careers. As a manager, you have a duty to meet these changes by accepting and encouraging promotion and other opportunities.

But you should also ensure that, as you or your staff move up (or out to other jobs), the void is filled by a competent person, capable of working to the high standard you expect from your department.

What happens to you also has a bearing on your staff. If you don't plan to have your own job successfully filled as you move on in the organization, the inefficiencies that are likely to develop in your former department will call into question your ability as a leader.

Even if you have moved out of your company, your old employer's succession problems may affect your career: your new boss may be watching to make sure you don't create similar problems.

Planning subordinates' succession
The skilled and self-motivated people in your team will probably receive overtures from other companies as well as chances to move up their company's ladder.

You need to anticipate and be ready to fill the gaps left when good performers are promoted, rather than be pitched into crisis by sudden departures.

You will also have people who are not obvious candidates for promotion – staff who should not have been hired, are past their best or who are content with their level of skill/responsibility.

People may fail to live up to expectations; some will get stale and lose their motivation. You cannot afford to compromise quality and efficiency to accommodate their tarnished performance. Succession planning has a definite role to play here, too.

Anticipate and plan for staff changes

To plan succession effectively you need to look ahead at least one or two years. Planning on such a timetable will equip you to deal with departmental change and succession much better than if you tried to cope with the whole problem during a three-month notice period.

● Show you care about your subordinates' careers.
● Encourage the staff to be open with you about their ambitions.
● Be alert for signs that the staff needs or wants to move.
● Be broadminded about departures: help staff to leave pleasantly.
● Help the staff in their promotion search within the company.
● Talk frankly about the negative as well as the positive factors.
● Encourage people to seek new challenges if they have become stale or bored in your team.
● Be your own talent scout by keeping your eyes open for people who might fit into your team.

Recruiting from outside

You may need to recruit from outside to fill an important slot in your team. A different approach or new ideas and skills can be positive for your team.

The personnel department
Personnel can be helpful, if they know the market for the type of expertise you require and can support you in your search for a successor. But they may advise you to use external agencies, especially if you want to tempt someone from a competing company.

Planning your own succession

The development by you of a first-rate second-in-command is beneficial to the company because:
● Management does not waste time or money searching for and interviewing your successor.
● Departmental morale is raised by internal appointments.
● Continuity is maintained.
● If extra staff are needed, it is at a more junior level and so less costly.
● The character of the department is more likely to remain intact.

You should look for potential successors when your career is on the rise and your prospects are bright. If you put it off until you are facing setbacks and difficulties it looks like a tactical retreat or resignation.

If you have to make an appointment from elsewhere in the company or externally, you may need the help of a consultant or an agency to find the right person.

Such an appointment is better made in advance of your move; indeed, if a role can be created prior to, rather than as a result of, your move, so much the better.

John F. Akers

Successful succession

IBM has no set succession policy but still manages smooth leadership transitions. In 1974, John R. Opel was elected president under the chairmanship of Frank T. Cary. Then in 1981, Opel was named chief executive officer and two years later became chairman with John F. Akers becoming president. Carey retired that year, but remained chairman of the board's executive committee.

In 1984, Akers took on the CEO job, and appears to be heading for the chairmanship.

Register companies

These companies keep lists of people in specialist occupations (retail, electronics, food, etc.) who want to change jobs.

Such companies save the cost of advertising and can be a good source for recruiting junior management.

Recruitment agencies

Agencies offer a mixture of "register" and advertising. They screen candidates before producing a shortlist, recommending prospects, especially in middle management, for your consideration. The client pays in advance and for the advertising.

Recruitment consultancies

Consultants, retained to advise companies on how to develop their personnel, undertake the recruitment of middle and senior management.

Executive search ("headhunters")

"Headhunters" advise companies on key strategic posts. They are increasingly responsible for the most senior appointments in commerce, government, industry and the professions. They differ from other agencies in that they enter actively into the marketplace and use a network of contacts to build up a "talent list."

159

The need for training

In the early stages of your career up to manager level, training will be largely task-related: the acquisition of technical skills, professional knowledge or specific techniques.

As your career develops, and you become responsible for task-related training of others, it is crucial that you stay on top of your basic job skills. At the same time you need to acquire those business-related skills that lead to a better understanding of the management process as a whole.

Broadening your knowledge

You should become familiar with the operational activities of related functions in the organization. If, for example, you are a manager in the production department, you need to appreciate the working of the finance, marketing and sales departments. As your responsibility for others increases, so should your knowledge of the organization as a whole.

Throughout the development of your career, you should keep up to date on technology and on legislation relating to the workplace.

The acquisition of business-related skills, such as effective decision-making and problem-solving, increases with job experience so that by the time you have become established in the manager's role your ability in these areas should be well developed. People-related skills – the ability to motivate, influence and lead – are in highest demand in general corporate management.

Learning by doing

People learn to perform well from a close observation of "role models" and from being in challenging situations that require initiative and positive leadership.

You should recognize that formal training courses are a more limited source of learning. Ambitious managers actively seek learning experiences to acquire knowledge and a broader range of managerial skills.

You and those around you in the workplace are judged on performance of specific tasks. Qualifications and attendance do not guarantee a climb up the corporate ladder.

Because most of your time is spent on the job, the best way to train yourself is to seek challenging tasks and projects. Aim to get a variety of experience by transferring to well-led and pressured teams on other projects or in other departments. Don't stagnate, but don't over-specialize; build up a wide range of knowledge.

If you seek ever-greater responsibility, you will increase your management experience while improving your technical skills. A record of performance and achievement will be of greater influence in getting you promotion than any number of academic qualifications.

Formal training

Your ability to cope with specific technical skills can be helped greatly by undergoing formal training. But it is up to you to ensure that you maximize

Acquiring skills and experience

Technical skills, basic knowledge

Business related skills, eg communication, decision-making, time management

General knowledge, eg health and safety, industry/trade affairs

People-related skills, leadership, motivation, team building, delegation

Knowledge of other functions, eg finance, marketing, sales

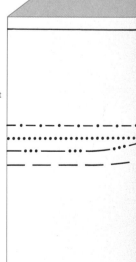

160

the usefulness of this training.

You should analyze your needs and career objectives first, and only then approach the training department, if there is one. If their proposals match your objectives, needs and timetable, then accept them. Make sure training is geared to what you want.

Make sure the courses are worthwhile. Ask former participants about content, quality and practical relevance to the job.

If the training department cannot match your needs, then consider going to an outside training organization. Many training departments augment their own work in this way. But check out the quality of an outside course thoroughly before committing your time and the company's money to it.

You should augment formal training by reading about your subject and by discussing your work, at appropriate moments, with peers or senior colleagues. Watching how acknowledged experts perform can also be helpful.

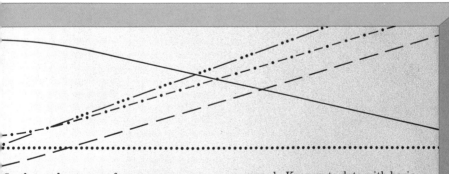

In the early stages of your career, you need to concentrate on acquiring skills that enable you to carry out specific tasks and to be given feedback on how well you have performed them.
By the time you reach first managerial level, you need to concentrate on strengthening your skills in other disciplines related to the business and to

your work. Keep up to date with basic skills so as to train others, but acquire a broad understanding of your business that will further your career.
Once you have become established as a manager, your ability to motivate, influence and lead will be in ever-greater demand. Communication skills become increasingly important.

Finding effective training

Training helps individuals, and therefore organizations, improve on their quality, competitiveness and productivity.

In a recent survey, a German manager said: "The same machines and equipment can be bought by anybody; success in the market can only be won by those who have a labor force capable of using them to their advantage, and being constantly trained to improve their performances."

This strong belief in the benefit of training is exemplified by such German companies as Bayer, Mercedes and Siemens, where half the workforce is regularly engaged in self-development training programs.

In the USA, top high-tech companies like IBM, Xerox, Boeing and McDonnell Douglas spend between 2.5 percent and 3.5 percent of sales revenue on training; and Britain's highly successful financial services industry invests a similar amount.

Benefits of training

Training should produce profitable results both for the company and the individual. But how do you know when you are being given good training advice?

The training function should essentially provide a source of experienced advice to guide you in your personal and team decisions. You should feel you are dealing with people who are close to the business, who understand the direction of its corporate development and who have access to, and the support of, senior management.

Trainers should have had recent experience running relevant parts of the business. And, indeed, they may later be expected to return to line management.

The training function should test ideas, encourage change and seek out tomorrow's issues. It should have the honesty to let you know when training is *not* the solution to your problem. Career development, organizational issues or recruitment may need attention.

There is a thriving training industry that provides specialized and general independent support for organizations that do not possess a training function or that wish to augment their existing one.

Internal or external training

There are no hard and fast rules determining whether you should go for outside training or not: you must

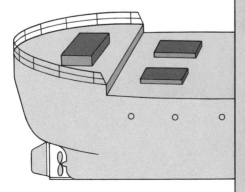

From tankers to aerospace

The Japanese company, Ishikawa-jima-Harima Heavy Industries Ltd, was the world's largest manufacturer of super tankers in the mid-seventies. The company realized that its products were vulnerable to lower price competition.

As world oil prices rocketed, depressing demand for tankers, the company looked for new markets.

Intensive research revealed that, although Japan was a world leader in shipping, it lagged behind in the international aerospace industry. Further investigation revealed that there was a significant gap in the market in the Far East for medium-sized aircraft engines.

choose according to needs.

Look at your own internal training function; try to evaluate its performance. If it scores highly with other colleagues on performance, initiative and relevance, then you would be well advised to work with them.

Internal training has its advantages; those involved will usually have accurate, up-to-date knowledge and understanding of the real problems of the business. This should mean that they are well placed to pass on realistic and relevant thoughts on how to solve the problems.

External training, on the other hand, is noted for:
● Objectivity.
● Breadth of experience (from other working environments).
● A fresh, outside view of problems.
● A proven training "product" and approach.
● Credibility with participants, based on experience, knowledge and research.

Outsiders can often deal with subjects in greater depth because they have wider experience with many companies. Your own training department should be able to recommend good organizations whose services match your needs.

For any training program to be effective, everyone in the department should be committed to it and supportive of its aims. Such commitment is essential if you are to avoid the problem of trainees arriving back from a training course, eager to apply its lessons, only to have their enthusiasm crushed by colleagues who have not undergone the same training.

If you are seeking an external training program, talk to a number of training organizations about your needs. Ask them how their product has been applied by other clients with similar needs. Talk to the other clients. Not until you are satisfied that your needs can be met should you proceed.

A trial with a test candidate may give final reassurance that the course is relevant, applicable to your industry and specialty and, above all, transferable to your workplace.

Take care that the external trainers have knowledge and insights into your actual problems and issues, and avoid the academic approach which deals with how things *should be,* rather than how they *are.*

The company at once embarked on an unprecedented restructuring exercise which involved comprehensive and in-depth retraining of the existing management and workforce, in order to teach them the new skills required to turn shipbuilders into aerospace technicians.

Some aircraft engine production expertise was brought in from other companies prominent in the field, but all IHI's staff were retrained in accordance with the Japanese "lifetime employment" principle.

The company became, by the mid-eighties, Japan's major aerospace manufacturer and a fast growing contender in the world market.

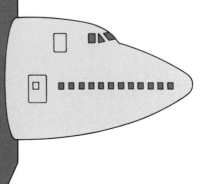

Selecting and shaping

Two types of team usually exist within an organization. The formal team is the department or section created within a recognized structure to pursue specified goals.

Informal teams are created to deal with a particular situation and they are disbanded after performing their function.

Both formal and informal teams need to be led by managers who give as much thought to team relationships as to the task the team has to perform.

Teams cannot be created simply by analyzing the demands of the project and assembling a group of people who appear to have the necessary qualifications and experience. Teams have certain features that include:
- Shared or agreed aims.
- A common working language.
- The ability to manage relationships as well as tasks.

Choosing the right team

Selecting and shaping teams to work on projects is one of the most important and interesting roles of management, and requires skill and sensitivity. Among your staff you will have people who are vague conceptual thinkers, workaholics, those who need the task spelled out, and others who can process work endlessly.

Select or build a team of people with compensating strengths and weaknesses. Make careful decisions about project teams and pairings; don't allow combinations that have worked well in the past to continue simply from force of habit. Try to match each individual's talent to his or her task.

To arrive at a good team you will need people who, for example:
- Create useful ideas.
- Analyze problems effectively.
- Get things done.
- Are good at oral and written communication.
- Have leadership qualities.
- Can evaluate logically.
- Have technical abilities.

- Can control work.

Decide in what proportion these skills are needed for the task in hand, and select staff accordingly.

If you inherit a ready-made team, go through the same process to see if you need to reshuffle or reinforce it.

Developing your team

Maintaining the health of a team and developing it demands constant attention. Put considerable effort into ensuring that differing personalities are able to relate to, communicate with and value the contribution of their colleagues.

If you are in charge of a team, you have the responsibility to develop your people. Training is not simple. You will find disparity between the time it takes people to learn new, unfamiliar skills and the time needed to develop innate skills.

As team leader, you will have the strongest influence on your team. People will not do as you *say*, they will do as you *do*, so be sure to set examples that you want followed. If, for example, you want good cost control and keen, competitive buying in your department, don't indulge in long, expensive lunches with suppliers.

Remember, too, that real life at work includes time pressure, conflict, personality clash, change and stress.

Work types

Many academics have tried to categorize the types of people who work in organizations. The chart (*right*) is based on the work of Meredith Belbin at Henley Management College, England.

When selecting a team you should be aware that these various work types have differing behavior characteristics that need to be taken into account.

Work type	Typical features	Positive qualities	Allowable weaknesses
Ideas person	Individualistic, serious-minded, unorthodox	Genius, imagination, intellect, knowledge	Up in the clouds, inclined to disregard practical details or protocol
Resource investigator	Extroverted, enthusiastic, curious, communicative	A capacity for contacting people and exploring anything new; an ability to respond to challenge	Liable to lose interest once the initial fascination has passed
Monitor-evaluator	Sober, unemotional, prudent	Judgment, discretion, hard-headedness	Lacks inspiration or the ability to motivate others
Company worker	Conservative, dutiful, predictable	Organizing ability, practical common sense, hard-working, self-discipline	Lack of flexibility, unresponsiveness to unproven ideas
Completer-finisher	Painstaking, orderly, conscientious, anxious	A capacity for follow-through, perfectionism	A tendency to worry about small things. A reluctance to "let go"
Team builder	Socially oriented, rather mild, sensitive	An ability to respond to people and to situations and to promote team spirit	Relatively indecisive at moments of crisis
Shaper	Highly strung, outgoing, dynamic	Drive and a readiness to challenge inertia, ineffectiveness, complacency or self-deception	Prone to provocation, irritation and impatience
Chairman	Calm, self-confident, controlled	A capacity for treating and welcoming all potential contributors on their merits and without prejudice; a strong sense of objectives	No more than average in terms of intellect or creative ability

Developing an approach

Changing circumstances, variable resources and constant compromise are the realities of the workplace. Systems and methods for managing teams or solving problems provide you with a starting point and a framework in which to operate.

But, as a manager, you must never forget that (most of the time) you have to get the job done with the people and resources at your disposal.

The key to any situation is the way you handle your staff. This is difficult because people's behavior is affected by numerous factors, not only by individual characteristics, ranging from timid introversion to rugged individualism, but also by cultural attributes and social skills.

All these have an important bearing on the complex web of relationships within the team. As the manager of a team you should lead rather than drive and show rather than tell. Your task is to encourage your team to practice reasonable and supportive behavior so that problems and risks are dealt with in an objective way, and

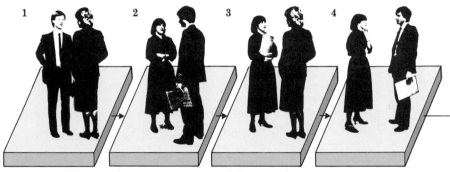

A systematic approach

To get work done, good managers develop a systematic approach like the following advocated by the Coverdale Organization, England. The process should be flexible so stages can be interchanged.

1 The assignment
Define the task before briefing your team, creating objectives or assigning responsibilities. In practice, however, it is often difficult to arrive at a conclusive definition. Don't agonize: accept your best attempt but be prepared to modify it if necessary.

2 Aims
Clarify aims by discussing with your team:
● Why is this task necessary and important?
● What is our actual objective?
● What specific criteria should we meet?
● How will we decide that our objective has been satisfactorily met?

In most instances, team commitment to the task will be higher if the members are involved in this initial process.

3 Information
When the manager and team are as clear as possible about what they need to achieve, they can then explore ways of achieving it. As this stage it is helpful to:
● Pool ideas.
● Draw on previous experience.
● Identify particular skills.
● Note skills that are lacking.
● Check available resources.
● Plan to get information.
● Explore risks/benefits of options.
This process will vary from a crisp analytical meeting to a messy but creative brainstorming session.

4 What has to be done
When it becomes clear what the preferred goal is, the team should list which steps will be involved to complete the task. This is a useful prelude to detailed planning.

5 Planning
It is your job to ensure that everyone on the team knows exactly what to do. Specify in detail who is doing what, where and by when it should be done.

the team's personal skills are engaged to their full potential. The team will have to deal with:
● The "expert" syndrome: "I know because this is my area of special knowledge."
● Relationships and circumstances constantly changing.

To manage teams successfully, you must pull back from the task at hand –

To manage teams successfully, you must pull back from the task in hand – however appealing you find it or well qualified you are to deal with it – and examine the processes that create efficient teamwork.

Find out what it is that makes your team greater than the sum of its parts. You will help the process if you:
● Have a consistent approach to solving problems.
● Take into account people's characters as well as their technical skills.
● Encourage supportive behavior in the team.
● Create an open, healthy climate.
● Make time for the team to appraise its progress.

This is a two-way process, however. Check that people understand their responsibilities as well as their tasks.

6 Action
The team carries out its tasks as separate individuals or as a group. You may feel a need to be involved with certain specific tasks, especially as you may have the best idea of how to perform them.

But you *must* maintain an overview. Monitor what is going on and check progress, spotting snags and adapting the plan to overcome them.

You cannot do this well if you are constantly involved in the action. Your team will need you to maintain a certain distance so that you can guide and direct.

7 Review
As the assignment progresses, allot time to check the quality of the work done.

When completed, carry out a detailed review on what has happened, so that future assignments can benefit from past experience. Look at the difficulties and what went well and would be worth repeating in future projects.

Supportive team practices

Listening
● Pay attention; respond positively.
● Don't interrupt; look interested.
● Build on proposals; ask clarifying questions.
● Summarize to check your understanding of the issues.

Cooperating
● Avoid coercion and acrimony.
● Encourage others to give their views; compliment good ideas.
● Give careful consideration to proposals different from yours.
● Offer new ideas openly.

Challenging
● Continually refer back to the problem-solving process and aims.
● Question assumptions in a reasonable manner.
● Review progress of objectives, team relationships and timetable.

Understanding motivation

An understanding of what motivates people is crucial to the creation of productivity and profit. Individuals' needs and desires, however, are complex and difficult to define. Priorities differ from person to person; individual aims change over time.

Money and status are important motivators but they cannot be relied on exclusively. The theories put forward by behavioral scientists provide a useful way of thinking about people's needs and desires.

In the first quarter of the century, a man named F. W. Taylor established his "scientific management" theory. This involved breaking down jobs into simple but repetitive tasks, providing a thorough training, isolating individuals from distractions and each other, and paying good wages, with bonuses for productivity over predetermined levels.

In the short term, production gains were significant; in the long run, these gains fell away as people reacted against being treated as machines.

Though the "scientific" approach has largely been discredited, some managers still give too much attention to basics, such as pay, and not enough to workers' personal needs.

In contrast to Taylor, A. H. Maslow concentrated on human needs, which he saw as five-fold:

1 Physiological – food and shelter.
2 Safety – security for home and work.
3 Social – the need for a supportive environment.
4 Esteem – status and having the respect of others.
5 Self-fulfillment – the need to realize one's potential.

As each goal is achieved, so the next is sought. Thus, at different stages of your career, you will have differing values, depending upon your progress from one need to the next.

In a publication of 1959, Frederick Herzberg added to Taylor's and Maslow's work by introducing the important idea of "hygiene" or environmental factors. If these are wanting, they can lead to dissatisfaction and so prevent effective motivation. The more obvious hygiene factors involve:
● Organizational policy and rules.
● Management style and controls.
● Retirement and sickness policies.
● Pay and recognition of status.

Herzberg thought that, although hygiene factors were important, they did not have lasting effects on motivation; other positive motivating factors must be present.

The real motivators

Money obviously plays an important role in motivation. But there are many non-financial motivators that are equally or more important:
● Achievement: most people want the satisfaction of making a meaningful contribution. They are rarely content to plod along mechanically.

Managers who recognize this and provide opportunities for others to attain their individual levels of achievement will frequently be surprised at the results.
● Recognition: it is a natural inclination to want your effort recognized. Praise and feedback stir people to achieve even more.
● Advancement: early theories suggested that people are basically uninterested in work and need a combination of carrot and stick to react. Herzberg's researches showed that this is not generally true. Most people want to move on to more challenging situations and will continue to make increased efforts to cope with them.
● Interest: the chance to practice skill or use intelligence at work motivates most people.
● Responsibility: most intelligent, skilled employees are happy to accept responsibility and authority. They do not need to be forced.

The myth of the "Organization Man"

Despite the work of behavioral scientists and a number of studies conducted in the workplace, managers persist in the belief that they are differently motivated and have a greater commitment to the organization than their staff.

This theory has been effectively debunked. Over a period of years, interviews with managers and a variety of their subordinates revealed further proof that Herzberg's results were soundly based.

The table (below) is a survey of what management, subordinates and their subordinates believe motivates themselves and others. Motivators are numbered from one to six in order of importance. There is considerable uniformity between people's views of their own motivators. But fascinating differences emerge in their views of what motivates others, both above and below them. It also shows the low priority that employees think those in authority place on the needs of the organization.

People's beliefs in what motivates themselves and others

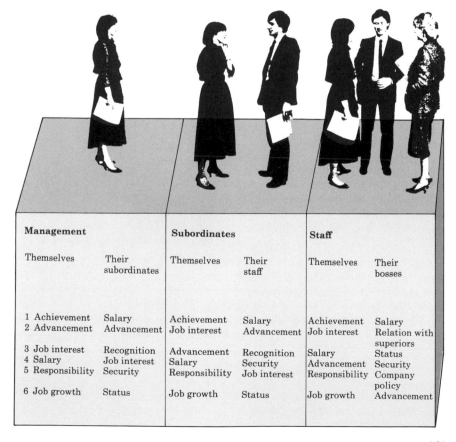

Management		Subordinates		Staff	
Themselves	Their subordinates	Themselves	Their staff	Themselves	Their bosses
1 Achievement	Salary	Achievement	Salary	Achievement	Salary
2 Advancement	Advancement	Job interest	Advancement	Job interest	Relation with superiors
3 Job interest	Recognition	Advancement	Recognition	Salary	Status
4 Salary	Job interest	Salary	Security	Advancement	Security
5 Responsibility	Security	Responsibility	Job interest	Responsibility	Company policy
6 Job growth	Status	Job growth	Status	Job growth	Advancement

Creating motivation

To motivate a team you need to investigate what motivates you. Understand this and it will help you analyze what motivates others. But remember, people will have different motivators, and these will change over time.

As a manager, it is your responsibility to ensure that your staff are well motivated and content, while making certain that they work hard and effectively and are prepared to put in extra time and effort in an emergency. Check that:

● You are doing all you can to make sure the work is interesting, challenging and demanding.
● People know what is expected of them and whether they are meeting your high standards.
● Rewards are desired and clearly linked to effort and results.

Unless these factors go some way toward fulfilling the organization's needs and the expectations of your staff, no lasting motivation can be achieved, regardless of your best efforts.

If pay and prospects within the organization are bad, you must seek to improve the system. Make sure that your part of the organization recognizes the improved performance, productivity and profit that would result from keeping motivated, effective staff longer.

The very act of interceding on behalf of your staff will help to increase their motivation and strengthen their commitment to you.

To manage staff effectively, you must get to know their circumstances, needs and aspirations, both within and outside work. Show that you can help them achieve their personal aims.

If you can coordinate your staff's aims with corporate objectives, by reconciling their personal aspirations with the organization's need to operate profitably, you will run a successful team and, at the same time, enhance your own reputation.

How to motivate your staff

● Get to know your staff individually. Keep up to date on what is happening to them.
● Understand their interests and what motivates them in and out of work. These factors will probably change, so check on how they develop.
● Provide them with increasingly challenging opportunites, but watch for signs that they may have reached the limit of their abilities.
● Analyze their strengths and weaknesses. Ensure that they have opportunities to use their strengths and that their weaknesses are compensated for.
● Coach and guide them in areas in which they are weak or are making mistakes. Ensure that they have the chance to learn from colleagues or superiors who have the strengths they lack. If appropriate, encourage them to seek formal training.
● Give immediate recognition for good job performance as well as at a formal or annual assessment.
● Tell your colleagues, superiors,

The Volvo experiment

The experiment conducted by Volvo at their car-assembly plant at Kalmar in Sweden is more than a decade old. The aim was to improve production by cutting down on absenteeism and staff turnover.

The experiment involved a radical reorganization of the production line whereby the final assembly of automobiles was done while the vehicles were stationary and not on a staff in other departments how well your team has done or is doing.

● Make sure team members get the rewards they deserve (salary, bonus, promotion, company perks, etc.). Risk giving a little too much, or a little too early, rather than too little, too late.

● Delegate more of your own work, especially those parts that are interesting or exciting. This will give your staff the incentive to do something new or more challenging. It will also give you more time to manage people and not the job. It is usually worth taking the risk of delegating a lot early, but be alert for signs that the person is not coping.

● Involve your staff in as many decisions as you can (don't overestimate how many secrets you can keep from them, anyway). Seek their views; consult them on the advisability and practicality of any potential change. They will usually reward you with greater commitment and endeavor.

● Encourage them to bring up ideas on how the job can be done better. They are closer to the action than you and will usually have better knowledge of the problems and difficulties. If they wish to change their way of working, give it serious consideration. After all, it is *their* job you are dealing with.

● Share information. They will probably hear it soon on the grapevine, so it is better if they get it directly from you.

● Get them involved in your budget development and control. Without their understanding and agreement, it will be much harder to achieve their commitment and thus any targets.

● Help them resolve their problems with other parts of the organization if their case merits it. At some point, you will want them to make sacrifices for you, so be prepared to give help when they need it.

● You can do a lot to provide the right conditions for them to work effectively and happily. However, they also have a responsibility to approach their work with a positive attitude. Make sure that they understand this.

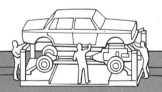 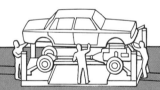

moving line. Tied in with this was a devolving of greater responsibility on workers, formation of teams to work on separate tasks, and job rotation.

After initial favorable publicity, the experiment came under increasing criticism. But an external report that monitored the first ten years indicated a qualified success. There have been problems: job rotation had not stopped staff from wanting more scope for responsibility and in-itiative; absenteeism was reduced but could have been lower still.

However, the successes included greater flexibility in production methods; the need for fewer supervisors; the lowest assembly costs of all Volvo's plants and a rise in productivity.

Volvo doubled their pre-tax profits in 1984. The initiatives begun at Kalmar have led to the introduction of similar reforms at other Volvo assembly plants.

Preparing to delegate

Delegating responsibilities to others increases your available time to carry out important work. Delegation also develops your team which, in turn, increases the effectiveness of your operation and improves your chances of achieving departmental goals.

Willingness to delegate is one of the marks of leadership, but delegation is difficult to exercise effectively. This is chiefly because it entails getting work done in a way that suits the person to whom the task is assigned, not you.

To delegate successfully, you need to know exactly what task has to be done and what motivates and satisfies the people on your staff. Effective delegation involves a continued and growing relationship between you, the manager, and those to whom you assign tasks.

As a manager, you should delegate authority but not final responsibility. This means that you must be prepared to accept responsibility for the action of your staff. That will sometimes be tough. You should also be prepared to let them have the glory when their actions are successful – and that may be even tougher.

Effective delegation is essential for the growth and development of each member of your staff. And they must know what results are expected of them and to what extent they are accountable.

People need the authority and freedom to get on with the tasks in hand, knowing that they have your confidence and that also, if it comes to it, they can come to you for help.
Delegation is not:
● Dishing out parcels of work in an indiscriminate fashion.
● Offloading tasks that you either do not have time for or do not want to do yourself.
● Merely a question of balancing the workload between individual members of staff.

Delegation inevitably involves an element of risk. A task may not be performed as well, as cheaply or as quickly as you could do it. But once your staff get the hang of it, they will eventually end up matching your own level of expertise.

Younger managers tend to hang on to too much, especially the more exciting and responsible aspects of work. So ask yourself: "What parts of my job can I *not* delegate?" Draw up a list, review it and then cut it down.

Now ask yourself: "If I were ill for a month, which tasks could not be done?" If you are honest, there should be almost nothing. But if you are still left with plenty, then you are probably not delegating enough.

Do not overestimate your abilities or underestimate your team's potential. Delegating may well create new or better ideas about how solutions can be achieved. Good managers delegate a great deal, creating a team which is constantly drawn up to the next challenge. A broad base of skill and experience is thus firmly established.

You should delegate everything you need not do personally, especially tasks that you are good at yourself and are used to doing.

You will be particularly good at training your staff to perform and take responsibility for tasks with which you are familiar. Make sure you delegate some aspects of the job that stretch your staff's ability and provide challenges. Obviously, you should delegate to staff members who have better knowledge or more up-to-date information than you.

Managers are often overworked, and effective delegation frees them for work on larger, broader projects. And when tasks are delegated to you by your boss, do not assume you are the right or only person to do them. Your desire to impress must be tempered by the need to have the work performed by a more suitable person.

Barriers to successful delegation

You may be reluctant to delegate a task for a number of reasons. The following are some of the more common ones:
● Delegated work will be done badly and you will be blamed.
● Time will be lost as you could do it quicker yourself.
● Since you have little idea how the task can be done you had better do it yourself.
● Your employees will do, and be seen doing, your job. As a result others believe your subordinates are capable of taking over from you.
● Spending time explaining to someone else how to perform a task uses up valuable time.
● Nobody else can do it as well as you can.
● There is literally nobody to delegate to. If so, who and how are you managing?
● You feel you need to be involved so as to be close to what is happening in your team.

Steps to effective delegation

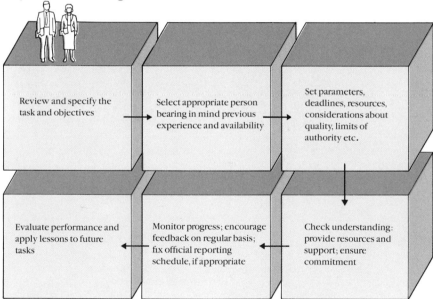

Review and specify the task and objectives

Select appropriate person bearing in mind previous experience and availability

Set parameters, deadlines, resources, considerations about quality, limits of authority etc.

Evaluate performance and apply lessons to future tasks

Monitor progress; encourage feedback on regular basis; fix official reporting schedule, if appropriate

Check understanding: provide resources and support; ensure commitment

Selecting delegates

Before delegating a job, ask yourself:
● Who would be challenged? Who would learn most? Who should not do it?
● Who has the necessary skill?
● Does the task require previous experience? Would it be useful to have someone acquire this experience to give the team greater depth?
● If time/quality allows, could the task be a training exercise for a team member?
● What particular personal qualities are needed? Who has them?
● Is more than one person needed? If so, how will they work together?
● Is it a task to be delegated upward?
● What other work-loads or priorities does your delegate have? Will you need to help to change these?
● How will you monitor progress and evaluate results?

Making delegation work

Effective management relies on proper delegation. It is wrong to say to your subordinate, "Here is the task, now do it," while you sit back and wait for results. Remember the slogan: delegate, don't abdicate.

Having decided what the task is and having selected a person to carry it out, there are three broad stages of delegation: briefing, monitoring progress and evaluating results.

Briefing
● Specify the essential parameters: details of task, deadlines, resources.
● Explain the desired outcome.
● Allow freedom to decide how to perform the task – but get the person to explain his or her plan of approach.

● Check they understand what is required – encourage discussion.
● Sell, but do not oversell, your own approach. Be enthusiastic. If you get commitment and agreement, you have a better chance of success.
● Be realistic about your expectations; do not underestimate the difficulties but set challenging targets.
● Indicate the need for progress reports, intermediate deadlines, and that the needs of all are served if you are kept closely informed.
● Discuss which areas of the task are sensitive to error or risk.

Monitoring progress
● Allow the person to proceed with the task without interference.

Briefing
Equipped with details of the assignment and tasks to be achieved, the manager delegates the role of task leader (*above*). Because it is a high-risk assignment, requiring strong commitment, she has decided to stay close throughout the process. She briefs the task leader about the aims and parameters of the assignment, and he puts forward his ideas about how he would approach and achieve it.

Planning
The task leader had decided to use a member of the team whose prior knowledge and experience would prove invaluable to this assignment. Called to a meeting with the manager and task leader (*above*), she is briefed about the task and offers her ideas in return. Delegated the specific role of "researcher," she will confer with the task leader and, with him, organize the means and timing of accomplishing of the task.

● Encourage the person to follow his or her own way of working if you are sure you are agreed on the desired result.
● Be alert for signs that things are going wrong, but be prepared to allow trivial mistakes to be made.
● Intervene only if the person does not spot errors or where sensitive areas are threatened.
● Be ready with help, advice and encouragement, but avoid doing the task yourself. Transfer the delegation only in extreme circumstances.
● Encourage frequent informal discussion rather than formal feedback.
● Stand back from the process and retain a view of the bigger picture.

Evaluation and feedback
Did the person produce the results you expected? If the task was successful, say so. Give praise, recognition and credit to the people involved.
If the result was unexpected, ask:
● Was it due to a misunderstanding between you and your people?
● Was his or her performance not up to standard?
● Was the wrong person selected?
● Were there unforeseen problems?
● Were the mistakes preventable?
Make sure everyone concerned learns from the experience. Finally, do not blame your people in public, to your boss or colleagues, but accept the responsibility yourself.

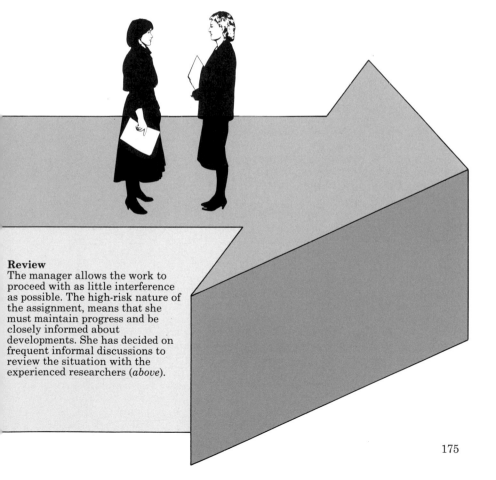

Review
The manager allows the work to proceed with as little interference as possible. The high-risk nature of the assignment, means that she must maintain progress and be closely informed about developments. She has decided on frequent informal discussions to review the situation with the experienced researchers (*above*).

Appraisal, counseling and promotion

One of the hardest managerial tasks is to appraise your staff or give performance reviews.

Reasons for assessing and appraising your staff include the need to: maximize performance, identify training needs, provide data for salary and promotion reviews and set targets for the future. You will also improve understanding between you and your staff.

Employees are naturally sensitive about any official process of scrutiny because they feel their integrity or responsibility is being questioned. But they need to have some idea of how effective they have been and whether more or different demands will be made of them.

An informal process of frequent review should be used to give your staff feedback on their performance and prospects: at the same time this encourages them to practice self-appraisal.

This approach will help you to judge your staff impartially without damaging team relationships. It will also simplify the task of meeting the formal requirements of the organization.

The added advantage of the ongoing self-appraisal system is that, by instilling trust in your team, you will get comment on *your* behavior and approach.

Counseling staff

As a manager, there are occasions when you need to discuss subordinates' problems. You may be required to give advice on how they can improve efficiency or cope with stress.

Good counseling is an exercise in good communication on a one-to-one basis. Attentive listening is important, as is the ability to talk frankly and get to the nub of the matter.

Be positive: if subordinates have come to you with problems, they will not want to go away feeling they have wasted their time and yours. Even if you cannot solve their problems, tact

Promoting staff

You are promoting employees for the right reasons if:
● They can accept more responsibility, allowing their superiors to concentrate on other tasks.
● Their particular skills can be developed to create greater productivity for the company.
● They have distinguished themselves in a series of well-managed tasks and projects; their talents should now be more widespread.
● A department has assumed greater responsibility and work, so that new employees need experienced supervision.

You are promoting employees for the wrong reasons if you argue:
● "She'll leave if we don't promote her."
● "Department X has three section managers so why shouldn't we?"
● "He's been around a long time."
● "If she's pushed upstairs she won't try to change anything."
● "He won't make any decisions without telling us first."
● "Make him management, that will curb his union activities."
● "She'll make a good manager – she never argues."

and sensitivity create trust and strengthen their loyalty to you.

Promotion and reward

If you say to your staff, "I think you are doing a great job and if it were up to me I'd give you all a 15 percent pay raise, but company policy does not..." you are passing the buck.

While you should naturally praise and encourage your staff, they will become demoralized if they see that your words are not backed up with positive results. You must devote, and be seen to be devoting, sufficient time and effort to securing appropriate rewards for your team's achievements.

"What do you think you have been able to achieve in the last year?"

The appraisal

Do ...

● Appraise frequently and in a relaxed way; you will then avoid the resentment that is felt for the formal annual review.

● Talk about strengths and weaknesses objectively; beware of overreacting to good or bad points. It is easy, but not smart, to run out of superlatives.

● Avoid saving up praise or criticism for the next appraisal. Try to deal with issues as they arise.

● Make specific criticism and illustrate the points you are trying to make. Where possible, indicate what should have been done.

● Complete the personnel department's appraisal forms carefully, and discuss them with the reviewing manager to give a fuller picture.

● Be open to changes in job description: they might lead to better job performance.

● Change the paperwork if it does not fit the individual. Let the clerks and computers adjust to the people, not vice versa.

● Remember that the purpose of appraisal is to motivate the appraised and send signals to those who decide on pay and promotion.

Don't ...

● Don't approach potentially difficult appraisals as if the employee were overpaid and unreasonable.

● Don't believe that your assessment of a bad performance will necessarily ensure that an employee improves.

● Don't fail to appreciate that team performances are interdependent and complex; a bad or good performance may not lie entirely within the control of any single team member.

● Don't dictate the way employees approach their tasks unless there is a clear reason to do so. Allow your staff to take the initiative whenever possible.

● Don't obscure criticism by talking around it. Get to the point, otherwise you may fail to get your message across.

● Don't react defensively to complaints about your management style. Rather, listen to what may be valuable feedback.

● Don't adopt standards of appraisal different from those used in everyday life.

● Don't become involved in private or emotional problems – specialized counseling may be needed. ·

Handling trouble

Teams always encounter problems. As individuals change – by, say, becoming more experienced and being promoted – so do their aims and behavior alter. This can work in the team's favor; or it can alter the equilibrium and reduce effectiveness.

Your team's health is your responsibility; it is your task to observe, diagnose and treat disaffection, disunity or demotivation.

Be on the alert for signs of trouble; in general, when your team cannot heal its own problems, you can be sure something is wrong.

If a person's bad behavior or performance threatens morale, act quickly to keep your team's respect and confidence. Look for causes, enlisting help from other team members. Then talk to the person in private. After all, if you have been working happily together for some time you will probably want to help.

Be direct about what impact the employee's attitude is having on the rest of the team. Try to identify the problem, which may be due to:
● Personal problems or illness.
● Insecurity about new structures or technology.
● Disappointment at not receiving recognition/reward.
● Significant disagreement with you or another team member.
● Failure to relate to a new team member.
● Staleness due to, say, repetitive work.
● Apparent loss of status.

Do not let the individual indulge in selfpity. Giving a rational solution to the problem is often enough to effect a reconciliation between the person and the team.

Team health is best maintained by giving individuals a variety of tasks and projects. If staleness is the problem, a change of job within the team or a move to another team may help. Differences that alienate one team member from the others call for more serious measures. First, consider whether another member of the team can help.

If the lack of commitment or the bad performance continues, confront the person again.

Give employees every chance to explain their actions; discuss ways of solving the problem. Reprimands and confrontations are a test of your fairness, objectivity and strength. You may have to broach the idea of dismissal if no alternative is available.

Once the future of the individual has been settled, communicate your decision to the rest of the team. Try to be positive. It is important for the team's recovery that the problem is not seen as a team failure.

Going ...

Your team is a self-protecting organism. Its first instinct will be to solve difficulties without involving you.

If you are aware of the problem, either because the offender is noticeable or factions have formed, show your concern.

If counseling proves ineffective, tell the individual clearly what is expected.

Danger signs

Something is wrong in a team if individuals who have been supportive and reasonable:
- Begin to perform poorly – miss deadlines, produce substandard work.
- Expect others to solve their problems.
- Do not take responsibility for their actions.
- Break up into subgroups instead of sharing work.
- Show destructive criticism or dismissive behavior toward others.
- Get involved in serious and unresolved conflicts.
- Show no interest in team activity.

Positive alternatives

"Obstinacity" is a word used by Coverdale, a U.K. training organization, to show that an employee's qualities detrimental to one environment may be helpful to another.

A quality control supervisor was taken to task for his autocratic and "nit-picking" attitude. Team spirit deteriorated so much that it was decided he had to go.

The manager prepared a balance sheet of the supervisor's good and bad points and realized that he was also accurate and painstaking. So he was transferred to a job that required him to read complex instruments. The man's lack of human skills did not affect the instruments.

Going ...

A verbal warning is the next step. Give the person a time limit in which to improve. Inform Personnel. Be reasonable and supportive; rehabilitation is your aim.

If the person fails to improve, and it is neither feasible nor appropriate to move him or her to a different team or department, then dismissal is proper.

Gone

Try to find a way of allowing the person to leave with dignity. Invite the employee to resign but be prepared to fire. Be as supportive as possible since the employee will be under a lot of stress.

Consult Personnel to make sure of compliance with notice periods, legal and trade union requirements.

Exploiting opportunities

Only a handful of successful large companies still depend exclusively on their original lines of business. They have had to respond to changing markets to survive. Former railroad operators now exploit oil and gas, while toymakers market computers.

The business world is evolving so rapidly that the watchword for the modern world is change. What once took many years to manifest itself and become part of the social fabric can now happen almost overnight. Progress in technology and communications and increasing competition have seen to that.

Changes have happened so fast that the present has hardly begun before the future is already upon us. And the indications are that the rate of change is accelerating.

This presents the manager with a demanding, but not insurmountable, problem. Change must be welcomed, embraced and turned to good effect, even though it may be threatening. Innovation and adaptability must become part of the everyday habits of managers. They must find more efficient ways of doing things, accept new developments in their industry and seek new opportunities for generating business. If they do not, competitors almost certainly will.

As a manager, you must view change and innovation as opportunities to seize rather than as threats to fear. You will learn to master change only when you encourage, welcome and incorporate it into your professional and personal lifestyle.

Businesses are microcosms of a dynamic and ever-changing environment. Legal, political, financial, technological, economic and sociological forces continually act upon companies—sometimes uncontrollably, often dramatically.

Fluctuations in international interest rates, changes in foreign exchange rates and technological innovations are just some of the external forces that daily shape the fate of many businesses.

As a manager you must play an important role in dealing with change. You have to:

● Interpret change, both outside and inside your organization, and create certainty and stability for your staff.

● Instigate and implement changes you consider essential for your part of the organization.

● Contribute to the discussions and decisions concerning the future of the organization.

Fixed ideas bring suffering not prosperity, whereas flexibility of outlook and purpose helps you to understand and adapt to changing environments.

Innovation and change are a way of life for some businesses, such as those in the high-tech arena. But others, often the more traditional ones, have a history of stability and may be resistant to change.

While doing what you have always done may be wise in an unchanging world, learning to be accomplished in a variety of ways is advisable in a world of accelerating change.

What you need is a personal strategy for managing change which:

● Enables you to assess potential change in the light of long-term improvement for the company.

● Gives you advance feedback of likely reaction to change.

● Lessens the likelihood of your being labelled an "opponent of change," thus lessening your influence.

● Makes it easier to achieve beneficial change by simplifying objectives and plans.

If you learn to deal with change, the benefits are positive – greater creativity, better performance, increased achievement. Even if you make mistakes, they will be instructive. Change also creates situations where your talents can shine and, as a result, be rewarded.

Managing change successfully

Reacting quickly to change is a key factor in the success of any business. Management at all levels needs to think in a creative and innovative way.

To help yourself and your staff to embrace change and make it work:
● Accept that dealing with continually changing situations is a normal part of your job. Don't bury your head in the sand when new or different problems arrive.
● Get routine work under control so you have time to consider the innovative aspects of your job.
● Maintain a well-informed knowledge of developments in your industry or profession. Read the part of the press relevant to you.
● Monitor the environment for signals, trends and developments in the attitudes and behavior of competitors, customers and the market.

● Stimulate a positive attitude to change by regularly discussing new ideas and issues with colleagues.
● Encourage your staff to raise issues affecting their work. Watch for signs that accepted practice is inappropriate.
● Discuss future plans and issues with your staff on a regular basis. Once every six months may be enough, but ensure it happens.
● Communicate internal changes to your staff unless there is a good reason not to do so in the short term.
● Be experimental and flexible in your approach to people's ideas.
● Try out new techniques and ideas whenever appropriate.
● Mobilize your staff quickly and boldly, but in a coordinated fashion.
● Create a working atmosphere in which ideas and issues do not fall between bureaucratic cracks.

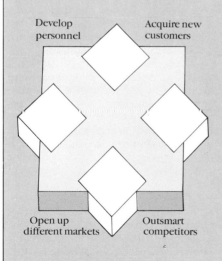

Develop personnel

Acquire new customers

Open up different markets

Outsmart competitors

Diversification

To absorb change, your organization may need to diversify new businesses or product lines. Handled correctly, diversification can:
● Produce action on new fronts and so encourage versatility, learning and development.
● Help companies adapt to changing markets and fluctuating customer requirements.
● Lead to greater understanding of weaknesses, strengths, resources, and new business potential.
● Create an environment in which managers and executives anticipate change and control it more effectively.
● Enable companies to seize more opportunities and outsmart their competitors.

Coping with crises

Managing to encourage innovation and change is quite different from managing the consequences of unexpected and dramatic change.

In the first instance, you operate in a stable environment with a relatively secure staff; you have some notion of where your organization is heading, and you control the timing of events affecting your team.

But sudden dramatic change threatens everyone in the organization and will force you to operate without direction or a controllable timeframe. You may also have to take responsibility for people whose behavior and effectiveness are impaired by stress: they will need you to create certainty at a time when little is certain.

Events leading to sudden crises may not, in themselves, be dramatic. However, the consequences of the events may often be both unexpected and far reaching. Companies can pass into crisis because habitual bad management has led to financial distress, and banks demand reductions in borrowings. Markets may change, and lack of foresight may leave the company unprepared and exposed. Mergers or take-overs can remove security, creating uncertainty and anxiety.

Common to all these situations is an apparent lack of policy or authority. The rules have not just changed, they have disappeared; and a new set needs to be imposed.

In a crisis, you may suddenly find yourself reporting to a new boss, someone brought in by the board or by the new owners of the company. In an extreme case, this person may be a receiver, appointed by the bank to return the company to profitability or to sell it as a going concern.

This new person may be sure about what has to be done and how it will be achieved. However, he or she may need time to understand fully and deal with the problem.

Your first priority, as a manager, should be to determine where you and your team stand. You may be asked to supply information about your activities, your potential, and the extent to which performance has been affected by the crisis. This is particularly important if you are in a revenue-earning position, such as sales or customer service.

Try to understand what plans there are for your organization. Ask about them, and if no answers are forthcoming, watch for signs. Action should indicate the direction in which things are moving.

Encourage your team to cooperate in the formulation of plans and new direction. Avoid adding to rumor and speculation.

The new boss may want to create a new management team, and will want to act quickly; but if the crisis is financial, there will probably be a lack of funds to recruit externally. Your performance throughout this period may determine whether you have a continuing management role or not. The period of uncertainty may be an opportunity for you to demonstrate your talent.

Be alert and cautious until the operation has returned to profitability and stability. Your part of the business may recover well, only to be undermined by continuing losses elsewhere. Crises often take longer to resolve than they do to occur.

In the end, the most sensible approach to adopt is one of project management: breaking down tasks into short-term assignments that can be managed single-mindedly.

This gives your team something specific to do and, as the list of successfully completed tasks grows, it helps to rebuild confidence.

Recognize that your team members feel threatened in a crisis. They will need reassurance throughout. Make sure they are involved and consulted.

Managing crises

The formulation of a plan, the acquisition of resources to carry it out, and the building of a new team, are the goals of crisis management.

To be a part of the team that comes together in crisis and turns round an operation can be a rewarding experience. It will test your management ability and skill – maybe even your nerve.

You should take stock of your chances of success. If you feel that your career may be endangered, it may be wise to look for another job. In a severe crisis, you must protect yourself. Be realistic, maybe even over-cautious – if in doubt, don't wait for others to make your decisions for you.

The two key areas in any crisis are, first, you and your colleagues affected by the crisis, and second, the central problem which precipitated the situation.

Regrouping
Involve key staff and resources in the construction of plans for the future. Take this outside the boundaries of your immediate operation and present your scheme to senior management.

You must ensure that you have authority in your part of the operation if you are to get the internal support essential to your team's success.

Avoid extreme reactions. Do not be rushed into hasty judgments and, above all, *look* as though you are coping.

Tending the wounded
The tasks confronting you may be daunting. People may have to change or lose their jobs.

They will need help to change or move. Act quickly and positively, if possible. The uncertainty caused by inaction can often be more painful than the eventual decision, however severe it is. Do not try to soften the blow by long explanations. Give people options and time to consider them. Then move on to the practical means of lessening the impact on the department as a whole.

The real test of a good manager is the quality of the remedies applied in a crisis. Help those who are the casualties, but ensure above all that your own and the remaining staff's futures receive your greatest attention.

Dealing with stress

Managers are responsible for making decisions that can make or break the organization. They contribute to the creation of the wealth on which the survival of a community may depend. They also significantly affect the environment in which the rest of the staff work. Those who have achieved the skills needed to manage must recognize the potential stress that goes with a challenging job. They must learn to cope with their own and others' stress in order to remain effective.

Managers need challenge to stimulate them and add zest to their lives. Challenge successfully dealt with is satisfying. Only when it cannot be met, when pressures become too great, does it become stressful. Stress reflects a failure to cope with certain situations. Reactions to stress are either predominantly related to mood and behavior or they can manifest themselves in physical symptoms such as dyspepsia, skin eruptions, headaches and so on. But, because reaction occurs at a subconscious level, the symptoms are seldom seen as directly related to the cause.

Stress is "dis-ease," involving the whole personality. Coping with it depends on a holistic approach to health. The way in which you contend with your own stress threshold depends on your basic personality, acquired skills and past experience. Thus, anxious introverts are likely to be more vulnerable to it than brash extroverts. Individual strengths and weaknesses cause different areas of vulnerability. Skillful managers thus play on their strengths and cover their weaknesses.

Coping with stress

● Know yourself: list your strengths and weaknesses; consider what you are like to work for or be married to.
● Make sure your job allows you to concentrate on your talents.
● Know what you are meant to be doing, where you are going, how you fit into the organization and what the future might hold.
● Discuss your grievances and difficulties with a sympathetic colleague or friend, or your partner. Encourage your colleagues and subordinates to do the same.
● Review your priorities regularly, change them and delegate wherever possible. Learn to say "no."
● If you are not succeeding with one approach, don't try harder. Think of a better way.
● Accept that you cannot do everything. Apply principles of time management.
● Plan holidays and days off in advance; protect this time and relinquish it only after all other possibilities have been considered. If you have to let it go, reschedule it immediately.
● List your outside activities and interests and plan them into your diary.
● Set predetermined eating and drinking "rules" for yourself. Determine your optimum weight. Take action when you stray from what you know is good for you.
● Decide your minimum sleep requirement and ensure you get it.
● Ask yourself whether you are having fun. If the answer over a long period is "no," try to work out why.
● Try to identify what is causing you to feel stressed.
● If work is a prime cause of stress, be prepared to change your job. But consult those whose opinion you respect (or who may have had the same problem) first.
● At home, stress arises from the conflict of unsolved problems. Discuss them openly with your partner and work out solutions together.

Like everyone else, managers function as whole beings and not, as they may like to think, as separate "selves" at work and at home. In practice, good relationships are the key to minimizing stress. Conflict and frustration can be work- or home-based and each affects the other. It is thus essential that your job is structured to provide defined and achievable targets. You must be willing to discuss difficulties before they become problems.

At home, as at work, understanding each other and the way people interact is the key to minimizing stress. Relaxational activities raise stress thresholds. Ask yourself what you are like as a family member and act to improve things.

A reasonable degree of physical fitness helps to keep work and home in balance, and the time needed to get fit ensures that you take time out from work. Well-balanced managers are likely to be more successful at work, happier at home and, therefore, less vulnerable to stress than narrow-minded workaholics who neglect relationships.

Equally, managers should ensure that their part of the organization provides an environment in which individuals can flourish to the benefit of the enterprise and the individuals involved. Ask yourself what you are like to work for – you should not be a cause of unnecessary stress in your subordinates. Be aware of symptoms that could be stress related. Encourage staff to achieve a balance between home and work so that they are better equipped to deal with challenge.

Stress-related symptoms

If you recognize a number of mental and physical symptoms in yourself, a member of your team, or your partner, that could be related to stress, you should tackle the problem immediately.

Danger signals at work

- Frustration over failure to get results.
- Complaints about the quality of your team's work.
- Inability to determine priorities.
- Calendar constantly full of meetings and appointments for which you are ill-prepared.
- Full in-tray, inability to decide what to tackle first.
- Personality clashes with superiors or subordinates.
- Too busy to take vacations or even a day off.
- Taking too much work home at night or weekends.
- Unwillingness to discuss problems and prospects.
- Lack of concentration and/or memory.

Danger signals at home

- Not contributing to important domestic decisions.
- Feeling that life is no fun.
- Regularly coming home late.
- Spending too little time with the family.
- Reluctance to discuss problems.
- Being too busy to exercise or eat properly.

Planning time

The manager has four major resources – people, equipment, money and time. Time is irreplaceable. One of your most challenging tasks is to discipline your own use of time and that of your colleagues and bosses.

Your purpose is not just to increase the number and quality of tasks performed, it is also to ensure that you are making the most of your career, which is, after all, a span of time devoted to the achievement of personal, financial and organizational objectives. Indeed, the most successful people often squeeze two or three different careers into one working lifetime.

Managers with domestic responsibilities need to use and respect time judiciously; career planning becomes more crucial since they may have to manage two jobs simultaneously.

Time planning depends on a methodical and disciplined approach: try breaking up your day into short segments – half-hour periods – and analyzing the main uses of time. Compare this "expenditure" with your personal and departmental objectives. If they don't match up, you are probably spending time on irrelevant details and should switch priorities.

Be ruthless with yourself and others. If you are spending time on unnecessary tasks, you are either badly organized or your superior is. Hand work back, delegate it, or question its purpose. Most time and resource waste is a result of purposeless, unquestioned activity.

First, ensure your own department is operating at maximum efficiency:
● Create demanding but realistic deadlines for tasks; otherwise work tends to expand to fill the time available.
● Never do work yourself that can be safely delegated; subordinates may not perform a task quite as well as you, but without experience, they never will.
● Try to arrange your commitments in such a way that you have a large blocks of time for difficult tasks such as planning, report writing, problem analysis or deciding on strategic direction.
● Discover your own and others' prime time and assign the most exacting tasks to it.
● Remember the right amount of pressure brings speed and high performance; too much, and things go wrong.
● Get others – secretaries, subordinates – to protect your time. If you operate an open-door policy, consider an appointments system for non-urgent staff problems.
● Make a habit of asking "How much time will we need?"
● Allow time between meetings to implement the solutions and plans produced there.

Don't assume that you can manage only your own time and that of people working for you. The greatest potential time waste can result from being badly managed by superiors.

Once your department is running like a well-oiled machine, you are ready to improve the performance of your superiors:
● List the points you want to cover in meetings with the boss.
● If possible, arrange your meeting so that there is just enough time to cover the agenda, before you or the boss, have to attend another important meeting.
● Don't try to cover too many subjects in one meeting: have short meetings more frequently.
● Always do *brief* follow-up memos; "We agreed to the following . . ." The boss will soon get the picture if long meetings produce short action lists.
● If your boss is inclined to chat, or you are collared by the office bore, you should break in at the first possible pause. Politely indicate that you have a mountain of work to do and must get back to your desk.

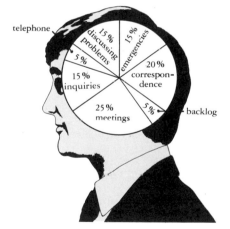

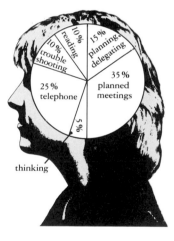

This busy manager's life is not planned. Perhaps that is why he *is* busy. His use of time indicates an entirely responsive approach to his job, with more time devoted to administration than customer service. The high level of emergency is indicative of serious problems. (Peter Drucker states in *The Effective Executive* that well-run organizations do not have crises.) This manager should ask: "What am I here to do?" "Do I delegate enough?" "Had I more time to plan, would those emergencies go away?"

This effective manager delegates correspondence to subordinates and deals with major issues in person or by telephone. Her meetings are well planned: she attends only the key parts, leaving the rest to staff, and can often fit in two meetings where a busy colleague has not completed one. She is popular with customers and suppliers because she spends time getting to know them, and her reading makes her knowledgeable about the industry. She does not merely discuss problems; she solves them. She always seems to have time...

187

Using time

Managing time is not just about enabling your team to handle increasing amounts of work. It should also ensure that events, projects, proposals and developments are timed correctly. For example, a new investment project, introduced when a similar project is late and over budget, is unlikely to be judged favorably. You need to know what is going on in the organization before making proposals that have an impact beyond your own department.

If you can manage your own time properly, then you will, by example, inspire confidence in your staff. Search for the most *relevant* and *powerful* ways of employing time, for your department and for the company.

People respond far better to well-planned surges of activity than they do to crises or to unremitting routine. Try to survey staff needs and anticipate demand to have enough time to cope with the unexpected. Vary the pace at which you and your staff work. Remember, people need recreation for their mental and physical well-being; but try to ensure that vacations do not coincide with a surge of work.

If a member of your staff is a poor time-keeper – regularly late for work or going home early – find out why. Perhaps the job is boring or personal problems need to be discussed.

If your staff are habitually working long hours, check to see if they are doing so for the right reasons. As long as it does not disrupt the team, it does not matter if the best creative work is done early or late in the day. Allow time for people to recuperate.

Committed people may work late to compare notes with colleagues or simply because they enjoy being with the team. But someone who works late from not wanting to go home could be heading for a personal crisis which then could affect the whole team. And teams who stay late because their work forces them to will soon lose their loyalty to you.

Larks and owls

Managers who ignore the body's natural clock may do so at their peril. Personal rhythms of wakefulness and rest differ from person to person and affect the timing of all mental and physical activity.

All teams consist of people who are larks (do their best work in the early morning) and owls (who peak at night). You should be aware of your own body rhythms and get to know those of your staff, colleagues and boss.

Avoid difficult meetings first thing in the morning if you are an owl. Don't waste valuable prime time doing routine tasks when you arrive at work if you are a lark. Leave them to the end of the day.

Take account of the effect of the time of day on others so you can make the best use of their abilities.

Time-related problems can be solved by a methodical approach. Analysis can lead to more than one solution.

If you choose a solution that does not work out, it could be because you chose the best method for yourself and not your staff.

Problem:
Routine review shows employee with possible time fault; this person works late, takes work home.

Action:
Discuss with person.

Tips for good time management

Does time plus money plus skill equal achievement of objectives? If not:
● Define the essentials of your job. Ensure that most of your time is spent on them.
● Frequently analyze the use of your time.
● Ration your and your staff's time.
● Plan your time so that you deal with top priority items when you are at your best.
● Gradually allow less time for tasks as experience increases, until optimum performance is reached.
● Show that you disapprove of time-wasting.
● Always question tasks – they may be irrelevant or capable of postponement.
● Before committing yourself to a task, check to see whether you can delegate it.
● Conduct *brief* meetings; set a time limit for objectives.

● Try to protect your time from intrusions.
● Make it known that your time is precious so that others compete and negotiate for it.
● Always thank those who are brief but to the point.
● Spend time understanding the organization.
● Spend time understanding your market/industry/profession.
● Minimize the time your staff spends on unpopular tasks.
● Encourage enthusiasm – it makes people work faster.
● Create surges of activity toward goals.
● Set deadlines for yourself and others, but remember that speed is not the only consideration, particularly if quality suffers.
● Constantly question whether your present activity is the best use of your time.

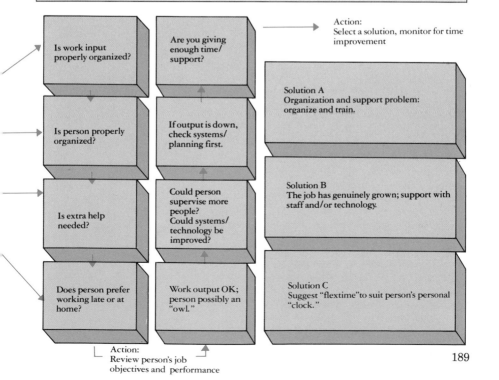

Is work input properly organized?

Are you giving enough time/support?

Action:
Select a solution, monitor for time improvement

Is person properly organized?

If output is down, check systems/planning first.

Solution A
Organization and support problem: organize and train.

Is extra help needed?

Could person supervise more people?
Could systems/technology be improved?

Solution B
The job has genuinely grown; support with staff and/or technology.

Does person prefer working late or at home?

Work output OK; person possibly an "owl."

Solution C
Suggest "flextime" to suit person's personal "clock."

Action:
Review person's job objectives and performance

189

Managing tough situations

In theory, successful managers decide objectives, identify problems, allocate resources to solve them, organize implementation and measure results. The reality is that objectives change, problems grow, resources are not always available and solutions do not necessarily work out. And, perhaps most trying of all, there is rarely enough time to accomplish everything you would like.

Furthermore, as you gain seniority, the range of subjects about which you need to have detailed knowledge broadens dramatically.

The principles of good management – proven methods of doing things – are worth knowing, but you will never have time to practice them all. They need to be coupled with a practical approach.

Although, in theory, managers plan, organize, coordinate and control, the facts may differ. You, the manager, have to cope, improvise, react and create certainty.

If you often feel so far out of your depth that if you blink you will drown, don't worry. All managers feel like that some of the time. The essential skill is to keep moving, but don't be too particular in your approach – it may cost valuable time.

Managers often have two broad priorities: consistently successful management of their department and completion of a "project X." The difference is that general management is a continuing series of problems, choices and decisions, while "project X" only happens once and has deadlines and a budget.

General management is what you do routinely all the time: meet the sales budget, complete the monthly report, supervise and support your staff. Project management, e.g. planning the new head office move, is usually imposed on an already hectic routine and must be accomplished with no disruption to normal service.

Management theories

Learn how to question the plans and projects based on management theories and ask how relevant they are within the context of your organization and your own particular situation.

● Detailed planning may be rendered obsolete when the environment changes, so back it up by knowing where you want to take your team and developing a flair for seizing opportunities.

● Print-outs from management information systems may be out of date by the time you read them. Get the latest information, even if it is just factory-floor gossip.

● Carefully planned projects may be conceived without accurate information. Develop ways of saying "Why?" to senior management until the purpose of the project is clear.

Project viability

Projects are invitations to accept risk. Do not take a project briefing at face value; it may merely be to get the problem off someone else's desk and on to yours.

Before accepting a project, be sure it is viable; if not, modify it. Never be afraid to argue for its rejection if you have tangible reasons to believe it cannot be achieved.

The trick with project management is to gain enough information and knowledge to develop an instinctive approach to the task.

● Differentiate between questioning a project to obtain time, resources and authority, and analysis paralysis produced by researching so closely that you no longer recognize a project's purpose.

● Understand the project's objectives and its value; can it be done more quickly or more cheaply?

● Does the organization really *need* the project?

● Have similar projects been done before by the organization? If so, can you have access to information?

● Can you pick your own team for the project?

● What time or budget constraints are imposed?

● Do you know all the possible snags? Are there any unstated conditions?

● Who is ultimately responsible – you or the senior manager delegating the project?

● Will you need specialized knowledge? Is it accessible?

● Seek clear indications of your expected input.

● Remember that the level of resources and the ease with which deadlines can be met are invariably underestimated.

Penguin's revival

In the early 1970s, Penguin Books, a U.K. paperback book publisher, began to lose its market share to competitors. Mounting debts and overheads, a dusty image and internal dissension conspired to make Penguin seem commercially unfit.

Managing the reality of Penguin's decline in fortunes was the task allotted to Peter Mayer, formerly publisher and vice-president of the US paperback house, Avon Books.

After becoming Penguin's chief executive in 1978, he instigated changes. Emphasis was shifted away from publishing in a traditional Penguin way and put on the books and their potential market. This involved the following changes:

● Editorial, design, production and marketing housed together.

● Staff departures or layoffs.

● Number of new titles reduced, later raised to original levels.

● Inventory reduced by four million.

● Backlist reduced by about 8 percent, later increased.

● Attention to contracts led to a lowering of royalty costs.

● Large scale promotion of books.

● Maximum publicity from book reviews, radio, TV and tours.

● Targeted advertising, promotional material and point-of-sale displays producing a new public awareness.

● New national sales manager with mass marketing background.

● Regional managers given local targets.

● Nine retail outlets opened.

● Special attention to books being sold at non-bookstore outlets – newsstands, airports, train stations and hotels.

Managing problems

All managers have to deal with the problems that arise in their jobs. The classic process of solving problems is divided into four phases: diagnosis of the problem; choosing a solution; implementing the solution; and monitoring the result.

The theory is useful but difficult to apply. As managerial responsibilities increase, so do the difficulties of managing problems. Senior managers rarely deal with isolated problems. When several exist simultaneously, the problems and the issues they raise may be interrelated.

Defining the problem

Look at the managers you know who are successful. They recognize symptoms, sensing intuitively when a problem exists or is likely to arise. They do not retreat to wrestle alone with the company's problems. They are present among those who are living the problems, observing them and other people's reactions to them.

Choosing a solution

Effective managers shepherd their teams toward solutions, maintaining flexibility in order to change course when necessary. They interrelate problems so that several can be solved at the same time. If they can, they will use progress on one problem to achieve progress on a related issue.

Solving the problem

Managers tend to rank problems according to how quickly they can be solved, tackling the easier ones first. This is a useful way to link the stages of problem analysis and problem solving into implementing the solution.

Tracking the problem

Action is often part of defining the problem, not just of implementing the solution. Look for connections among the many different problems you are dealing with. Monitor interrelated problems. Just because you have chosen one course of action, don't forget the other options.

Problem solving: some common mistakes

"I must do something because that is what a manager is employed for." Reflect and analyze the problem before taking action.

"I have seen this one before." Don't assume that this problem is the same as a previous one just because it has similarities. Mistrust solutions that are based purely on previous problems.

"I have not got all the facts, so I can't make a decision." Get moving: the action you take will give more information.

Managing problems via people

Confronted by a new problem, ask the team:
● Is this a potentially serious problem or a passing difficulty?
● Does it have an obvious possible solution? Is there someone well placed to solve it?
● Can we solve it by adjusting the way we work?

Once the team is actively addressing the problem:
● Concentrate on managing the team, not the problem.
● Be sure team members are getting accurate, timely information.
● Stay abreast of the process in case another plan is needed.
● Review progress with the team frequently.
● Encourage fresh ideas and approaches.

If the problem defies solution:
● Redefine it. Look at possible options first and see how they fit the problem.

If the problem remains insoluble, ascertain whether:
● Specialist knowledge is required. If so, acquire it, but square this with the team.
● More resources (people, time, money) are required.

Once a solution begins to emerge:
● Arrange for the team to discuss plans of action with you.
● Agree on time, resources, people to be committed.
● Ensure that the team gets recognition for solving the problem.

Remember that it is better to arrive at a solution everyone can accept than to persist in trying to apply a solution that appears to cover all aspects of the problem, but which some of the team will be reluctant to implement.

"My experience and understanding make me uniquely suited to finding the solution." You will rarely be fully qualified to deal with a problem on your own. Get more brains to help.

"I must solve my subordinates' problems for them." Encourage your team to bring to you both their problems and their ideas for solutions. Encourage subordinates to learn from their own actions.

"This problem is so urgent it must be solved immediately." Not all problems need instant solutions. Quick solutions tend to be short lived. Deliberation might lead to improvement. Sometimes, one problem may change or solve itself, so consider whether it can hold for a while.

Making decisions

Decision-making is an inescapable responsibility. No matter how good you are at generating ideas or motivating people, you will be judged by your boss and your staff on the quality of your decisions.

Quantity can be no substitute for quality. In fact, a plethora of bad or short-term decisions will lead to a serious backlog of niggling problems.

Decisions are judgments, choices between alternative courses of action, neither of which is completely right or wrong. Effective managers make:
● The minimum of decisions.
● Decisions at the right time.
● Decisions based upon the best possible information.

Managing your team's performance in a regular series of tasks and a number of special projects involves decisions relating to routine, individuals and teams. Ensure that you:
● Avoid impulsive decisions.
● Seek informal reactions to situations requiring decisions in order to gauge team response.
● Collect *all* information, not just that which supports your view.
● Do not ignore your instincts, but do use information to test them.
● Feel free to discuss decisions that will affect people with a more experienced manager – but retain responsibility for the final decision.
● Do not be tempted or forced into making premature or unnecessary decisions because someone either wants something or is passing the buck.

Decision-making about routine general management should be delegated to members of your team. Not only does this encourage their growth and development but it also frees you for strategic issues.

Certain decisions need your closest attention, for example:
● Overall direction, such as which markets to be in.
● Staff resources, such as employment of new people, promotion or the

---

Project management decisions

Managing projects means making hard decisions about money, materials and time. As projects have deadlines and budgets, they are put at risk by slow decisions. To minimize this risk:
● Ensure that all members of the project team know their roles.
● Frequently review progress to spot potential problems and note what time and resources are at hand.
● Arrange access to expert advice, if not permanently at least readily enough to help in any emergency.
● Report back to your boss frequently enough to prevent misunderstandings if things go wrong.
● Refer upward any decisions falling outside your sphere of authority and flexibility; accompany such referral with a clear statement of possible choices, together with your recommendation.

---

discipline of existing staff.
● Structure of your department, such as whether it is properly organized to meet its objectives and cope with its workload.
● Specialized skills, such as the provision of information and facilities to deliver sound technical decisions.
● Planning, such as whether your team can continue to operate cost-effectively to achieve organizational objectives. Are any new projects or budgets needed?

Never remain in the rut of one technique, one style of dealing with everything. There are no hard and fast rules to decision-making, so try to learn "unswerving flexibility." Successful decision-makers call on an ever changing blend of experience and instinct, training and insight, independence and team expertise.

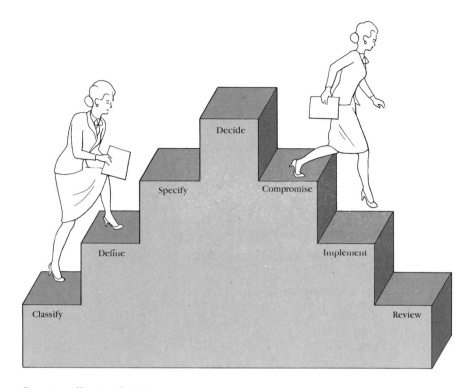

Steps to effective decisions

All managers make decisions. They are not sudden, isolated events but rather an ongoing and evolving process that can be broken down into a series of steps. These steps, based on Peter F. Drucker's sequence of effective decision-making, are outlined here.

Classify the problem: if it's generic, it is probably one of those everyday problems that has to be solved by adapting the appropriate generic rule, policy or principle. If it is extraordinary, the problem must be dealt with on its individual merits.

Define the problem: state precisely the nature of the problem and check your definition against all the observable facts. Beware of the plausible but incomplete definition that does not embrace all the known facts.

Specify the conditions: clarify exactly what the decision must accomplish. These are the so-called boundary conditions, or specifications, that must be satisfied by

the solution to the problem.

Decide the right action: decide first of all what is right to do rather than what is acceptable in the circumstances. Make the ideal decision that satisfies all the specifications.

Compromise the decision: in reality there always has to be a compromise, so make the best decision possible by adapting it to the circumstances.

Implement the decision: assign the responsibility of carrying out the decision to those people capable of doing so. Make sure everyone who needs to know about the decision is informed.

Review the effectiveness of the decision: build feedback and monitoring into the implementation process. Receive reports on how the results of decisions measure up to their expectations. Incorporate any positive facts into the classifying, defining and specifying process of making decisions.

Managing the boss

Given education, parental influences and respect for authority figures, many managers may not realize their bosses need managing and want to be managed. Though difficult and at times risky, it can and should be achieved to the benefit of both you and your boss.

Take time to find out about your boss by observing, discussing and talking to him or her and his or her colleagues. Don't worry; it is legitimate and necessary, not improper.

Do not think some areas of business are for the boss and some for you. Bosses have (arguably):
● Greater status.
● Easier access to both power and influence.
● More experience.
● More command of resources.
● Broader vision.

But you may have:
● Greater or more detailed understanding of day-to-day issues.
● More up-to-date information and closer contact with the customer.
● Easier access to the employees when a boss feels cut off from a team.

Get involved and keep close to progress on the issues your boss is dealing with. Bosses are not infallible; they will sometimes miss things, so always be on the lookout.

Don't rely on bosses for constant, detailed guidance. Provide them with ideas; give definitions of problems and your views on the solutions: don't shirk the solution part.

Always ask yourself what you would do if you were in charge and then compare your boss's solution to yours. Ask yourself which is the better course to follow and for precisely what reason.

Gradually develop a way of handling your boss by understanding what to deal with directly, what to consult on first, how to enlist his or her close involvement and when you should delegate upward.

You can legitimately expect:
● Another view on things.
● More information (bosses probably know more about the overall picture).
● Advice on tricky issues.
● Guidance on appropriate politics.
● Support, protection (but make sure you consult or clear things with the boss).

But you should provide:
● Clear definition of issues.
● Courses of action *and* your view on the one to follow.
● Reasoned arguments on how and why you have arrived at your recommendations.
● Your predictions about likely outcomes and contingencies if a recommended action is unsuccessful or of dubious worth.
● Information on group progress.

Don't forget your boss depends on you to produce results and to organize the people under you. This gives you power. And the better manager you are, the more likely it is that your boss will want others to see you as the product of his or her management.

If you are considered to be good, your boss will not want to be seen as the person who prompted you to transfer to another department, or caused you to leave the organization, or impeded your progress. He or she will want to be seen to be handling you well in the eyes of his or her own bosses and, especially, peers.

Bosses will be busy with their own issues and will want you to advance those under your control. Having watched your first successful efforts closely, they will grow to trust you more.

You will eventually get to know both when you can go ahead alone, keeping the boss informed, and when you need to check beforehand. If you are unable to determine whether to check first or not, then there could well be something wrong with the way you are managing your boss.

Analyze your boss

Develop a worthwhile relationship with your boss and get to know what makes him or her tick.

Recognize the need to exchange information and ideas constructively and remember you depend on each other for progress.

Consider your own relationship with your subordinates. When it works well, what are the reasons? Are these relevant to your relationship with your boss? If so, are they present? The following analysis assumes your boss is male, but it applies equally to female managers:

1 Aims/values
● What does he want for himself?
● Is he ambitious or concerned with protecting himself from harm and criticism?
● What are his values?
● How does he measure himself?
● How does he measure you?
● Who are the people he admires?
● Does he like open discussion?
● Is he a risk taker or a protector and controller?
● Is he autocratic, expecting you to do as he says, or intuitive, expecting you to follow broad informal indications or signs?

Analyze why situations produce conflict or stalemate. Is it because your views differ or because you both manage the situations badly?
● Does this help you decide if you have the qualities he values?
● What does he expect from you?
● Do his goals and values match yours? If not, can you live with the resulting difficulties?

2 Strengths/weaknesses
● Is he quick to see essentials, keen to resolve issues?
● Does he need time and lengthy explanations?
● Is he good at one-to-one/personal communication?
● Does he contribute good ideas and practical solutions? Or does he rely on you for that?
● Does he enjoy conflict and handle it well, or does he seek to avoid it?

Seek to complement his strengths and weaknesses. Modifying your behavior to suit your relationship with him is legitimate, not a sellout, and can be productive. But don't go too far.

Decide on your own values and how far you will go in adapting them. Avoid constant compromising of fundamentals.

3 Style
Does your boss prefer:
● Detailed written reports? If so, provide them and check orally where necessary.
● Verbal briefing? If so, provide it and confirm with a memo.
● Formal meetings with agendas?
● Preparatory memos and minutes?

4 Circumstances
● What are the pressures on him?
● What is expected of him? Where does he look for success?
● What are his own dealings with his peers and bosses?
● How are you contributing to what he is trying to achieve?
● How do his peers view him? Find out directly (by asking) or indirectly (by observing).
● What will be his reward if he succeeds? Promotion? Salary increase? Is he already a profit sharer? Does he have a bonus, riding on the results to which you are contributing?

The relationship you develop needs to recognize:
● Your individual styles, goals, strengths, circumstances.
● The need to exchange information and ideas constructively.
● Your dependence on each other for progress.

Planning your future

Success in business will never be handed to you on a plate; nor will it be achieved merely by being a good manager. You must be good at your job *and* your career.

As an excellent salesman of your company's products, you may well achieve security – with increasing financial rewards. However, if you aspire to the top corporate posts, you must start to sell yourself.

Everyone must know you possess the skills, judgment and experience to warrant promotion to the highest levels. So:

● Know your ambitions, strengths and weaknesses.

● Review your personal values and requirements (see pp. 14–15) and ask yourself whether you desire to achieve high corporate office.

You are probably right for top jobs if you enjoy responsibility, seek challenges and are obsessed with creating excellence.

● You are not right for top jobs if you leave thinking about it until a vacancy occurs.

● Start planning for your future early in your management career – 5 to 10 years is a reasonable timetable to consider.

● Don't advertise your potential bid for power. Few people like power-hungry executives.

● Keep your own counsel, be wary of placing too much of your trust in others, be careful of your reputation and study the politics of your organization.

Working hard to promote your company and career requires your family's full support. They must share your desire to achieve high corporate office because they will have to tolerate long and uncertain hours, a disrupted private life and a work-centered social life.

If you are not prepared to pay the high price or inflict it upon your family then don't aim for the top. And

---

Selling Yourself

Once you have planned a route to success your career becomes a project to be managed. The following pointers are useful:

● Encourage a positive response from everyone who meets you.

● Be well informed – read widely and discuss your industry with people you respect.

● Make friends with the PR department and encourage them to use you as a spokesman.

● Join the relevant professional, industrial or trade body.

● View membership of clubs strategically; always "trade up," not down.

● Support company social functions, but do not over-indulge.

● Get to know the person whose job you may want.

● Develop a grapevine to give you feedback on your reputation.

● Become known outside your department or firm with speech-making, community affairs, training assignments or whatever similar activity suits your temperament.

● Be interested in the company's finances – the price of the stock, shareholders and brokers.

---

if power attracts you, yet your lifestyle is important, a move to a smaller, less complex organization may be wise.

If you are happy to settle for a less senior job, select the role that best matches your positive characteristics and make sure you plan carefully to achieve it. Organizations need talented subordinates as much as leaders.

Your ambition needs a career plan and you should start charting its course early. Meteoric rises to the top are rare – executive success is more about planning, hard work, dedication, determination and, maybe, a few setbacks along the way.

David T. Chase

Chairman of a $2 billion private empire that bears his name, Chase came to Hartford, Connecticut as a gaunt survivor of a Nazi concentration camp in 1946.

He latched onto any available business opportunity – waxing cars, selling household goods – until he raised enough money to start a construction company. Legendary for his toughness, vision and generosity, Chase now controls statewide interests in real estate, broadcasting, cellular communications and insurance. And he isn't satisfied. His future projects include mass transportation and co-generation electrical plants.

David Packard

Co-founder of the computer giant Hewlett-Packard, Packard is considered America's most successful high-tech entrepreneur, one who distinguished his company as a caring employer.

As a former deputy Defense Secretary, Packard promoted military cuts to help balance the federal deficit. As chairman of the U.S.-Japan Advisory Committee, he urged joint high-tech arms production.

Conservation-minded, Packard funds a $50 million Monterey Aquarium run by his daughter. Admirers attribute his success to singlemindedly working to enact his ideas into concrete plans of action.

James Sherwood

An economics graduate from Yale, Sherwood joined the US Navy in 1955 and the United States Lines at the start of the container boom. At the age of 30, he moved to the smaller CTI and then set up his own company, Sea Cont.iners, after two years, in 1965.

Sherwood combined business acumen with personal taste, diversifying into property and leisure.

In 1977, he purchased and refurbished the most prestigious hotel in Venice, the Cipriani, followed by a ski lodge in Vail, Colorado, and the Orient Express.

The operator of the world's largest container fleet has achieved the perfect merger between business and private life.

Sandra L. Kurtzig

Unsatisfied with being a housewife, Kurtzig translated her ideas on practical "user-friendly" computer software into one of the most successful Silicon Valley companies.

She is said to retain tight control over the company she founded and heads, ASK Computer Systems. She started ASK in her apartment in 1972. In 1985, ASK was the fastest growing publicly held software company in the USA, with annual revenues running over $90. Her strength is never believing that her goals are unattainable.

Creating the right image

When a change of top executive is imminent, the successor is often waiting in the wings. The candidate has not only been pursuing a deliberate plan to get to the top but has also developed the right image for the job, the company, the industry. The development involves a reputation for:
● Achieving successful projects.
● A thorough understanding of the industry's affairs and the company's business.
● Being an able manager of people.
● Being respected by customers and industry partners.

These credentials are not in themselves enough to qualify you for the top job. You also need a touch of something special, charisma or presence, which encourages others to follow you.

Properly qualified and well-experienced candidates may be passed over in favor of someone less suited technically but better connected, someone who looks the part and projects a style and confidence fitting the company ethos.

Top jobs may differ in detail from company to company, but they share certain features:
● The exercise of power over the organization.
● The link between the organization and important external institutions.
● The barometer of corporate reputation – how the company is doing, what its challenges are, and what its responses to opportunities and dangers will be.

A major function of the job is communication – the best reputation and image command the greatest audience and confer the most business advantages on the organization.

Confident, reliable statements, for example, by a well-respected leader can positively influence dealings with business and government.

Like entertainers and politicians, top business people have to become comfortable with being public property. While there are obvious risks to this, there are also advantages.

Skilled business leaders, such as 1984 Olympic Games organizer Peter Ueberroth, find the media's reportage of their activities creates myths and legends about them.

These generate confidence, support, even fondness for a company and its products, giving it valuable prestige over its competitors.

It is essential to lay the foundations of the image you wish to project as early as possible:
● Analyze the background, culture and roots of your company and industry. Understand what your leaders feel comfortable supporting.
● Project values appropriate to your industry and support them strongly.
● Develop friendships with media people but guard against becoming their pawn.
● Evolve and be prepared to defend your stance on challenging issues and matters central to the well-being of your company.
● Build a strong team to complement your skills and give it challenging assignments crucial to your company's success. Make sure the results are well publicized.
● Get help and advice on making presentations to large audiences and the media.
● Seek appearances on radio, TV and at speaking engagements, but prepare meticulously.
● Make sure your appearance and surroundings look good when you give public interviews.
● Keep in touch with informed, influential people from related fields: it is important to be a good listener as well as a talker.
● Support the efforts of your junior managers – you will get the pick of the crop and strong loyalty.
● Never publicly deprecate your competitors for high office.

Peter Marsh

Peter Marsh started as a librarian, then joined Britain's Hull Savings Bank before becoming an actor and playwright. He made documentaries for the BBC and, in 1957, joined the largest British advertising agency outside London.

Marsh inspired the birth of the advertising agency Allen, Brady and Marsh in 1966. His belief in the work ethic, combined with a carefully nurtured reputation as Mr Advertising, has made ABM one of Britain's leading agencies.

Speaking often on radio and TV, he frequently contributes to magazines and is profiled in international publications. Eccentric and outspoken, he became, as ABM grew in status, a recognized spokesman for the rights of business in a free society.

Marsh is conscious of the value of myth and legend. Press stories tell how he kept the chairman of British Rail waiting in a small dirty room to show him how passengers suffer; and how his bizarre outfits gained impact at client presentations.

But behind the razzmatazz is a good businessman. Valuing hard work, admiring vision and singlemindedness, and caring about appearances, he is wary of over-indulgence and believes good managers are gifted individuals.

Peter Marsh is living proof of his product's excellence. Both ABM and its clients benefit from the extra edge of a carefully crafted public image.

Peter Ueberroth

Peter Ueberroth is familiar with being the right man for the job. He was selected by the board of directors of the Los Angeles Olympic Organizing Committee as president and chief executive officer of the 1984 Olympic Games because he matched the executive profile so well.

The profile, created by prominent executive search firm, Korn-Ferry International, specified a successful businessman, financially independent with experience in international events and an interest in sports.

His background of sports achievement and business acumen made him a natural choice. Following his graduation with a degree in accounting, Ueberroth worked for Trans International Airlines and expanded the company's nonscheduled airline business in Hawaii.

Ueberroth later started and built his own company – First Travel Corporation – into the second largest travel corporation in North America.

On becoming president of the Los Angeles Olympic Organizing Committee in April 1979, his mandate was to manage and stage the first-ever privately financed Olympic Games.

The result, five years later, was a wildly successful Olympic Games, operated at a surplus of $225 million. Highly regarded for entrepreneurial and negotiating skills, Ueberroth also managed 72,000 staff and volunteers at the time of the Games.

Now commissioner and chief executive officer of major league baseball, Ueberroth will devote those same skills to preserving the game's prosperity and integrity.

Changing jobs

Changing jobs is a major feature in the evolution of your career, and timing is critical to the moves you make if your plan is to proceed on schedule. Gone are the days when the concept of life-time service was admired; in some fields it can be a disqualification.

No route to the top is foolproof, however. No matter how carefully you plan to become a successful executive, you may fall foul of unforeseen factors.

Your company may be taken over by another group, making the route to the top of the new parent company, for example, too long to suit your needs. In which case you would be forced to look elsewhere in order to realize your ambitions.

In any event, do not underestimate the value of the headhunter in your strategy. Known also as executive search consultants, headhunters specialize in finding and proposing qualified candidates for important executive, managerial and technical positions.

Their services are paid for by the searching organization and fees are considerable, usually around 30 percent of the contemplated annual salary for the position they fill.

Headhunters are important to you because:
● They may be your means of escaping a company which no longer holds your interest.
● They may present an alternative strategy which gets you to your career goal faster.
● Job changes they offer may be important to gain broad-based experience in industry.
● They can be a rich source of contacts, useful in pursuing your career.

Your best interests are served by being helpful to headhunters. Their regard for you as a source, their sensitivity to your potential as an eventual client, their knowledge of your history, all make them useful friends.

When to change jobs

The route to the top of many companies often requires a spell in other industries, or even other countries, to acquire the experience deemed necessary in a top executive.

The following circumstances may indicate a change of jobs:
● If you have peaked too early in a company and face a long wait before further advancement.
● When any recent success enhances your market value.
● If you feel you are getting insufficient recognition where you are.
● If your company falls behind competitively and you cannot persuade it to respond.
● If reorganization or change has left your plan in tatters.
● If you develop new horizons.

Do not delay your decision too long. It is better to change than to stagnate.

Resume

Job applications must be backed up with recommendations from people who think highly of you, a good track record of achievements and a well thought out presentation.

A good resume may be extremely useful in advancing your chances.

You can get your resume drawn up by a professional agency at a cost, but if you compile your own remember:
● Structure facts into sections: achievements, experience, responsibilities, background, education.
● Achievement should be the focus, supported by hard facts. Give a lot of time, effort and space to this.
● Use headings, short paragraphs, margins and double-spacing.
● Be distinct – vary typefaces for copy and headings, use underlining and a summarized beginning.
● Give a chronological summary.

Carlo De Benedetti

Developing rapidly beyond his interests with a family firm, De Benedetti built up a diversified group, CIR, on an international scale. Compagnie Industriali Riunite pursues strategic and financial objectives in different fields: information technology, electromechanics, components, food and finance. Leading companies from these various sectors form part of the group.

De Benedetti is involved in managing Europe's leading information technology manufacturer, Olivetti, which he took charge of in 1978, when the company was in difficulties. Olivetti is today a highly profitable company and a world leader in sophisticated electronic office equipment.

De Benedetti has clear growth objectives, pursued with determination and efficiency, and rejects any compromise which might damage the economic bottom line.

Lee Iacocca

In 1978, Lee Iacocca was in his mid-forties, at the peak of a brilliant career as president of the Ford Motor Company, which showed record profits. Unaccountably, he was fired by an autocratic and unpredictable Henry Ford II, and the brilliant career appeared in ruins. A dying Chrysler Corporation named Iacocca chairman and he embarked on the most difficult job of his life, changing many of his management and political theories in the process.

The combination of an unstoppable "winner" mentality, a deep understanding of the automobile business and the flexibility to find solutions which matched needs, enabled him to take on a distressed corporation, reverse its fortunes and pay back over $1 billion of government-backed loans seven years early.

Jennifer Coutts Clay

The executive responsible for the implementation of British Airways corporate identity program, Jennifer Coutts Clay once worked in industrial language training for organizations such as The British Council and IBM.

Starting as a training officer in British Airways, she became sales training manager and then managed British Airways Western USA Sales and Operations – the first woman to be an overseas airline manager. She then became manager for Scotland.

Her career and many job interviews have made her realize the following are crucial when applying for jobs:

- Your salary record should show you on a steadily ascending curve.
- Don't work for third-rate bosses.
- Know the answers to "Why do you want the job?" and "Where do you see yourself in three years time?"
- Research the target company, prepare ten topics for discussion and never "wing it" in an interview.

Getting to the top

Navigating the corridors of executive power can be exceedingly complicated. The prevailing corporate behavior of each organizational level differs, and you need to fit in yet stand out at the same time. And it is no good behaving like a chairman when you get your first major department or become a junior director.

Organizational politics is the unspoken process whereby some managers achieve greatness, while others lust unproductively after power. If you are unprepared to graduate in this obscure science, forget the walnut paneling and the Rolls Royce; they will never be your natural environment.

You would in all probability be unhappy and insecure if you did achieve such power. Without the qualification or the desire, you would be far more suited to a more modest position where you could use your talents and not worry about the politics.

Appointing a top manager is a most sensitive decision, yet few organizations consistently operate a thoroughly efficient procedure for growing their own senior people.

The benefit of promoting from within is recognized by behavioral analysts and business schools, but people in power in the companies may tend to resist internal appointments which could bring change.

Ostensibly there to serve the shareholders' interests, some company executives are primarily concerned with continuing to be company executives. Hence the furious desperation with which some takeover bids, clearly in the shareholders' interest, are opposed.

Reluctant to relinquish power, such opponents are unlikely voluntarily to help an advocate of change, especially if they may suffer as a result.

As an aspiring senior executive, therefore, you must present such people with a clear political message.

Acquiring organizational power

All you have read so far about selling yourself and creating the right image must be supplemented by an objective attitude about the acquisition of organizational power. You should:

● Always work for "winners."
● Be loyal, but do not avoid "changing horses" if your career will be harmed by excessive loyalty.
● Reconcile the company's wellbeing with individual needs and be ready to make firm, if unpopular, decisions.
● Communicate the reasons for such decisions if anyone suffers.
● Recruit excellent people to cover your area of professional weakness.
● Concentrate on using your talents to benefit the organization.
● Know the strengths and weaknesses of other top executives.

On the one hand, they must see you as a way to keep their power, but on the other they must realize you are not to be thwarted.

In your organization, there may be a management training process intended to identify talented managers and expose them to a breadth of experience appropriate to a career in the upper levels of management.

Membership of this élite gives you no immunity from politics; rather it exposes you to more. For not only will you experience the acceptability barrier with each step up the corporate ladder, you will also be competing with those who share a similar ambition to yourself.

So you must know the culture of your organization and the effect it has on those around you – especially those in positions of power. But do not conclude that successful politics alone will take you to success – top managers *are* political but they also make sure they deliver.

Sir John Harvey-Jones

Sir John Harvey-Jones had a successful naval career until 1956, when he resigned for family reasons and joined ICI's work study department. In 1967, he became a director of one of ICI's biggest manufacturing divisions. He joined the main ICI Board in 1973, becoming chairman in 1982.

ICI had to change its established way of working to overcome the world recession of the early 1980s and to succeed in an increasingly competitive environment. While a divisional director, and then as chairman of the company, Sir John has long been a passionate advocate of such change. He has "reduced the number of people who can say 'no' and increased the motivation of those who can say 'yes'."

His straight-talking desire to communicate the reasons for change, his undoubted fairness and his own example of unremitting hard work have endeared him to many in ICI.

Larry Rawl

Larry Rawl started his career at Exxon Corporation in 1952 as a petroleum engineer on a drilling rig in South Texas. After assignments in both Houston and New York, Rawl became executive vice president of Exxon Company, USA, the corporation's domestic operating unit, in 1973. He later became executive vice president and a director of Exxon's Esso Europe unit in London, Exxon's regional affiliate for Europe and Africa. He returned to New York in 1980 and was elected senior vice president and director of Exxon Corporation. He was elected president of the corporation in 1985.

His formula for success, according to his colleagues, is hard work and a studied knowledge of broad business issues that affect one of America's largest companies.

Lord Weinstock

The son of a tailor, Arnold Weinstock ran Radio and Allied (Holdings) Ltd with his father-in-law in the 1950s. In 1961, this electronics company was acquired by GEC, now Britain's largest electronics and electrical group. A master of business management, Weinstock was made managing director of GEC in 1963.

He single-mindedly reorganized the electrical giant in a way which earned him plaudits as Britain's best manager.

After GEC expanded by acquisition in the late 1960s he said: "I haven't found a great increase in the size of the business imposing any additional burden." Indeed, Weinstock sits on several corporate boards including Merrill Lynch's international advisory board.

Lord Weinstock attributes GEC's success to doing "what you do more efficiently than your competitors ... you will make bigger profits and grow faster, that's what it's all about really."

Staying on top

One dilemma confronting you as you ascend to each new level of your executive career is how to stay on top. While your route is fairly steady in the earlier part of your progress, it gets more precarious as you near the summit.

Your continued occupancy of an executive position may soon be inadvisable because your vision and ambition exceed the limits of your post; or because you are stagnating through lack of challenge; or because you must move to allow up-and-coming managers scope.

Yet top posts often take a long time to become vacant. Perhaps this is because:
● Senior executives' emotional attachment to the company makes moving psychologically difficult.
● Senior executives often have a large financial stake in the company, making a move inconvenient.
● The departure of a crucial senior executive may adversely affect shareholders' confidence.

If such factors hold you back from the top job and you want neither to move nor be continually frustrated, then consider additional responsibilities and challenges, such as:
● Becoming a non-executive director of other companies.
● Getting involved in politics.
● Pursuing other personal interests, e.g. community affairs or sports.
● Starting your own company.

The ability to find other non-competitive avenues for your management talents is a mark of a successful professional. The result, if profitable, can overcome the ambition gap and round off the personality by exposure to new contacts, problems and relationships. It also enhances your claim to a senior post in your original company.

You may find, however, that your post is hard to handle because of:
● Difficulty with unfamiliar tech-

Consolidating your position

If you succeed in providing yourself with a wider sphere in which to operate, you will have created some valuable factors favoring your ability to stay on top:
● Broad internal/external support for your policies.
● Ability to use the media to carry your message.
● External sources of information concerning your rivals.
● Access to powerful influence against potential opponents.
● Wide-ranging expertise from which to draw your support.
● Fresh fields to conquer if bored.
● An escape route if you are beaten in "battle."

---

nology. Don't let technologists rule you: hire the best consultant, set firm criteria for all new high-tech projects and run them alongside people-driven ones until you can be sure that they are proven.
● Lack of experience in a professional field. Remember, specialists are available to give you advice and guidance. Depend on experts and make sure you choose experienced people carefully.
● Failure to win political battles. Information is your greatest asset, so rely on the research of your loyal supporters and gradually use it to handle all opposition.
● Inheriting an out-of-control problem. Delegate it to a team of talented experts, explain it to colleagues, update regularly. Impress upon the board it is their problem you are trying to solve.
● A "pet project" going badly wrong. Replace pet projects with a flexible series of developments, which bring benefit if successful or can be ended if they look like failing.

Sir John Cuckney

Chairman of the oldest and most respected travel firm in the world, Thomas Cook, Sir John Cuckney likes the quote: "I was brought up to spend a third of my life learning, a third earning, and a third serving." Clearly improving on the saying, he has a distinguished career in business and public service running parallel.

He was in charge of a financial group when first entering public service in 1970 as chairman of the beleaguered Mersey Docks and Harbour Board. Drastic measures, including an Act of Parliament to convert it from public ownership to a statutory company, were required to clean up the mess.

The Crown Agents, who looked after the financial and procurement interests of overseas governments and administrations, were Cuckney's next assignment – unraveling financial muddles while preserving the Agents' sound traditional business.

Chairman of Royal Insurance and of John Brown, deputy chairman of TI Group and formerly chairman of the Maritime Bureau of the International Chamber of Commerce, Sir John became chairman of the ailing British helicopter company, Westland, in the summer of 1985.

Walter Wriston

Walter Wriston gracefully retired as chairman of Citicorp at age 65 in 1984. Wriston's tenacious hold on the top seat of America's largest banking group is attributed to his visionary ideas and his unflinching faith in their merit.

Wriston relentlessly lobbied Congress to open the financial-services marketplace, and was rewarded in the last years of his tenure. He redefined the concept of a bank holding company and moved into data processing and insurance. And when he could not change the law, Wriston reinterpreted it; the group moved its credit card operation to South Dakota so it was not subject to New York's usury ceilings.

Wriston also foresaw the potential in retail consumer banking and built up the largest and most sophisticated electronic banking network. Citibank's arm now reaches into nearly 100 countries.

To attain his vision, Wriston had to weather severe criticism over Citicorp's loss of its Triple-A credit rating. He was likened to a general who survived one bloody skirmish after another. "He knew what he wanted," says one banker, "and he pulled every trick to get it."

207

Checklist to a brilliant career

Climbing the management tree to success is not an undertaking to be left to chance. You need to know yourself extremely well – strengths, weaknesses, ambitions, values – and to evolve a strong career plan that must be managed well.

Job excellence and clever career management are not enough, however. You should make sure your personality and public image match the organization in which you wish to succeed.

A brilliant career is rarely straightforward and often means moving from branch to branch of the management tree. Changing

Getting to the top

● Always work for winners.
● Recruit excellent people to cover your weaknesses.
● Be loyal, but don't jeopardize your career.
● Understand organizational politics.
● Be ready to make firm, if unpopular, decisions.
● Reconcile the company's well-being with your personal needs.
● Discover the values of each level of organization and match your achievements to them.

Changing jobs

● Never leave decisions too long; it is better to risk changing sooner than you would like or you may get blocked.
● Change jobs if you have peaked too early; if recent success enhances your market value; if your talents are not recognized; if change leaves your career

Creating the right image

● Build a strong team to complement your skills and give it assignments crucial to your company's success. Ensure the results are well publicized.
● Support the efforts of junior managers – you will help their careers and earn strong loyalty.
● Never publicly deprecate your competitors for high office.
● Make sure your values relate to your

Managing your job and your career

● Be realistic about your ambitions, strengths and weaknesses.
● Don't be overambitious.
● Start planning your progress early in your management career.
● Keep your own counsel; be wary of

trusting others unless you are sure of your trust; be careful of your reputation; study the politics of your organization.
● Stay well informed: read widely and discuss industry affairs with experts.
● Closely follow your company's results,

Staying on top

● Train your loyal supporters to help you win political battles.
● Ensure broad support for your policies.
● Use the media to carry your message.
● Seek new challenges in politics or community affairs, becoming a non-executive director of other companies or starting your own private enterprise.
● Avoid pet projects – concentrate on your business's central issues.

jobs may often be a necessary feature of success, giving you the experience and flexibility to navigate corporate power.

Reaching your goal seems to grow harder the nearer you get to it. This is when you most need your experience in organizational politics and your knowledge of what is happening in the industry.

Staying on top of the tree means seeking continued growth and avoiding stagnation. Keeping active in various fields – politics, public service, etc. – will broaden your perspective and earn respect from those who can support your climb to the top and help you stay there.

plan in tatters or with new horizons.
● Regularly update a good resume.
● Consider experiencing other industries or countries. They often allow you to acquire the breadth of knowledge deemed necessary in a top executive.
● Never underestimate the value of the headhunter in your strategy.

industry and support them strongly.
● Decide and be prepared to defend your stance on significant issues and matters central to your company.
● Develop friendships with media people but do not become their pawn.
● If you can handle them, seek appearances on TV, radio and at speaking engagements, but prepare meticulously. Get advice on making presentations to large audiences and the media.

follow the stock prices, know who the major shareholders are.
● Develop an informal network of people to give you feedback on your reputation.
● Keep close to the person whose job you may want – he or she often has a lot of say about a successor.
● Join the relevant professional, industrial or trade body and become active if you enjoy it and find it progressive.

209

Glossary

A

Accrual Accounting:
the reporting of income and expense at the time they are earned or incurred, not when they are received or paid.

Asset:
item of value that is owned by a company or person and is expected to be of economic benefit. Assets may be divided into *fixed assets* (e.g. buildings), *current assets* (e.g. inventories), or *intangible assets* (e.g. patents).

Audit:
examination of a company's financial statements by an independent third party, followed by a report to shareholders of the results. (See also *Internal auditing and Management audit.*)

Average rate of return (ARR):
measurement of the profitability of a project which averages the *cash flow* or profit over its total life.

Average total cost (ATC):
Variable costs plus fixed costs divided by the number of units produced.

B

Balance sheet:
periodic (usually annual) statement of a company's financial position which summarizes what is owned (*assets*) and owed (*liabilities*) by the business.

C

Capital:
money invested in a business by its owners in order to earn income.

Cash flow:
the inflow and outflow of cash through a company. It is used in the day-to-day management of funds to describe the cash needed to finance weekly or daily operating expenses and other obligations. (See also *Cash flow forecast* and *Cash flow statement.*)

Cash flow forecast:
estimation of expected *cash flow* used to alert management to future cash shortages or surpluses.

Cash flow statement:
summary of actual or projected *cash flow* over a particular period.

Conglomerate:
company with diverse, often unrelated, business interests.

Corporate culture:
unwritten set of values and rules within an organization that governs the behavior of those belonging to it.

Corporate strategy:
assessment of the relationship between an organization and its environment (customers, competitors, suppliers, government etc.) resulting in a plan to achieve the business objectives.

Costing systems:
the collection and classification of cost information to determine the cost of a unit of output. The most common systems are process costing and job costing in manufacturing industries, and operation costing in service industries.

Critical success factors:
those aspects of a business that need to be concentrated on to achieve a high degree of success.

Current assets:
assets of a company which are likely to be converted into cash (e.g. accounts receivable, work-in-progress) within 12 months.

D

Debenture:
long-term subordinated loan that is junior to other creditors.

Depreciation:
the amount by which a *fixed asset* is diminished in a particular year through its use in the business. This amount is charged against profits.

Direct cost:
cost directly associated with a unit of production (e.g. the amount of steel needed to make a motor car). (See also *Indirect cost*.)

Discounted cash flow (DCF):
measurement of cash flow that recognizes that future receipts or payments have less value than the same amounts received or paid today. This technique reduces all future receipts or payments to a common unit of measurement, i.e. their *net present value*.

Double entry accounting:
accountant's device for ensuring accuracy and completeness of recording transactions. All transactions are recorded twice (debit and credit) and the resulting summarized statements can be balanced, *liabilities* equalling *assets*.

Downtime:
time during which an employee or machine is not working efficiently due to maintenance work, faults, waiting for materials, etc.

E

Equity:
the *capital* invested in a company by its investors, together with *profits* from previous years that have not been distributed as dividends.

Equity capital:
the amount of money invested in a company by its risk-taking shareholders.

F

Fixed assets:
the assets of a company (e.g. equipment, land and plant), which are held, not for conversion into cash, but over long periods to further the main trading activities.

Fixed costs:
costs which are unaffected by changes in volume but tend to change over time (e.g. rent, taxes).

Glossary

Franchise:
means of distribution by which the right to sell or manufacture is sold to a company or individual within a given marketplace. The franchisee usually pays the franchisor an initial sum and thereafter a royalty in exchange for technical support and advice and the benefit of the corporate image.

H

Headhunter:
consultancy service which seeks out, interests and proposes suitable candidates for executive, managerial and technical positions.

Holding company:
company which holds, directly or indirectly, more than 50 percent of a subsidiary company or controls the composition of the board of directors. Some holding companies' business consists entirely in holding the shares or securities of other companies. (See also *Parent company*.)

I

Incorporated:
legal form of a company that protects owners from personal liability.

Indirect cost (or overhead):
cost not directly associated with a unit of production and one that will be apportioned across a number of activities or products (e.g. the cost of running a cafeteria in a car factory).

Intangible assets:
assets that are neither physical nor financial (e.g. goodwill, trademarks, licenses, etc).

Internal auditing:
review of operations by a special internal department within an organization.

Inventory:
list detailing stock that is kept for use as required – particularly raw materials, work-in-progress, supplies and finished goods.

L

Leverage:
relationship between the amounts invested in a business by its owners (*equity*) and by outsiders (*debt*).

Liability:
obligation of a company to make payment in the foreseeable future for goods or services already received.

Line manager:
employee who is responsible for the performance of a principal section of the work of the organization and for achieving its objectives.

Liquidity:
the pool of accessible funds, either in cash or in *assets* that may be transformed rapidly into cash, to meet immediate debts.

Long-term debt:
loan repayable one year or more
from date of transaction – usually
secured. (See also *Debenture* and
Secured loans.)

M
Management audit:
examination and appraisal of the
quality of management action in an
organization.

Market based pricing:
pricing decision based on the
perceived value to the customer, or
"what the market will bear."

Market research:
analysis of the changing market for
a product/service, used to formulate
marketing plans.

Marketing mix:
the balancing of a product/service
with factors such as place, promotion
and price to achieve customer
satisfaction.

Marketing plan:
the formulation of a method to
achieve profitable results from the
sale and distribution of a
product or service.

Marketing segmentation:
breaking up of the market for a
product or service into segments.

Marketing strategy:
analysis of the critical components
in the marketing of a specific
product or service and the

development of a plan to achieve
marketing objectives.

N
**National Association of Securities
Dealers Automated Quotation
System (NASDAQ):**
stock market for smaller capitalized
companies. Usually the first place a
company lists when it goes public.

Net present value (NPV):
the value today of future *cash flows*.

Net realizable value:
the price at which *assets* could be
sold minus all the cost of selling
them.

O
Overhead:
see *Indirect cost*.

Overexpansion:
trading which exceeds the financial
capacity of a business and may lead
the company into financial distress.

P
Parent company:
company that owns a majority of
shares in another company. (See also
Holding company.)

Payback period:
time taken for the initial investment
in an *asset* or project to be repaid
from profits.

Glossary

Portfolio analysis:
breakdown of the investments that a company has made in securities held for financial gain, rather than as a contribution to its operations.

Preferred shares:
form of share capital whereby the holders have a preferential right to receive a dividend out of profits of a certain percentage of the *share capital* before the owners of ordinary shares get any dividend.

Price Earnings ratio (PE):
the relationship that a company's profits bear to the publicly quoted value of its shares, usually expressed as market value of share/earnings per share.

Profit:
what remains when costs (of producing, selling, etc.) have been deducted from revenues.

Prospecting:
the identification of specific potential customers.

R

Research and development (R & D):
the search for improvements and innovations in a company's products or services and the solving of allied technical problems, with a view to creating new products or services.

S

Sale and leaseback:
form of financing by which a business sells an *asset* it owns and then leases it back at a favorable rent from the purchaser.

Sales:
the gross revenue earned from providing goods or services to customers. Sales should not be confused with *cash flow*.

Secured loans:
money loaned to a company, usually for longer than one year and against specific assets. In the event of *liquidation,* the first to be repaid.

Share premium:
money received by a company for a share issue which is in excess of its nominal value.

Solvency:
maintenance of a sufficient level of *liquid assets* by a company to meet its short-term obligations.

Standard costs:
scientifically predetermined estimates of the cost of performing a certain operation, within a given set of working conditions and for a given period.

Statement of Changes in Financial Position:
analysis of the sources of funds (financial resources) and how they have been used, showing how and why a company's cash position has changed.

Strategic management:
the discipline of managing an organization's resources to achieve defined long-term objectives.

Strategic planning:
process by which a company aims to reach a *strategic success position* by setting objectives, undertaking strategic analysis, and making strategic choices.

Strategic success position:
point from which an organization has the best opportunity to achieve above average long-term objectives.

SWOT:
acronym for strengths, weaknesses, opportunities and threats relating to a company. These are investigated as part of strategic analysis.

V

Value chain:
term coined by Michael Porter to describe the five areas in which a company's *critical success factors* lie: research/design, development, production, marketing/sales and distribution.

Variable costs:
costs that vary directly with the level of output.

W

Working capital:
the amount of short-term funds available to a business to perform its normal trading operations. Usually defined as the difference between current assets and current liabilities.

Bibliography

Armstrong, M. *How to Be a Better Manager*, Nichols Pub. 1984

Burns, T. & Stalker, G. M. *Management of Innovation*, Methuen Inc 1961

Campbell-Johnson, A. *Mission with Mountbatten*, Atheneum 1985

Collins, E. G. C. (Ed) *Executive Success*, John Wiley & Sons, Inc. 1983

Drucker, P. *The Effective Executive*, Harper & Row 1967

Drucker, P. *Managing in Turbulent Times*, Harper & Row 1980

Eyre, E. C. *Mastering Basic Management*, State Mutual Bk 1982

Goldsmith, W. & Clutterbuck, D. *The Winning Streak*, Random House 1986

Herzberg, F. *Work and the Nature of Man*, T. Y. Crowell 1966

Hickman, C. R. & Silva, M. A. *Creating Excellence*, New American Library 1984

Katz, D. & Kahn, R. L. *The Social Psychology of Organizations*, John Wiley & Sons, Inc. 1966

Levering, R., Moskowitz, M. & Katz, M. *The 100 Best Companies to work for in America*, Addison-Wesley 1984

Maslow, A. H. *Motivation and Personality*, Harper & Row 1970

Mintzberg, H. *The Nature of Managerial Work*, Harper & Row 1973

Peters, T. J. & Waterman, R. H. Jr. *In Search of Excellence*, Harper & Row 1982

Porter, M. E. *Competitive Advantage*, Collier Macmillan 1985

Pümpin, C. *Practice of Strategic Management*, Swiss Volksbank 1981

Rouche, J. La *Strategies for Women at Work*, Avon 1984

Tannenbaum, R. & Schmidt, W. H. "How to Choose a Leadership Pattern," *Harvard Business Review*, March-April 1958; also May-June 1973

Vroom, V. & Deci, E. (Eds) *Management and Motivation*, Penguin 1971

Wright, H. B. *Executive Ease and Disease*, Gower Press 1975

Arthur Young worldwide

Arthur Young is an international firm of accountants and management consultants whose history stretches back to the nineteenth century. More than 25,000 people operating from 400 cities in 80 different countries make sure that your business, wherever it is in the world, can receive prompt, efficient services of a consistently high standard.

Should your company seek advice on any one of a number of important areas, such as taxation, business strategy, personnel management, education and training, information technology or accounting systems, Arthur Young will provide you with a modern, highly coordinated response to your need.

Large and small companies, public authorities and government departments, as well as private individuals, are all well served by Arthur Young's management consultancy division – one of the largest of its kind.

By combining national strengths with worldwide coordination and quality control, Arthur Young International offers a responsive, integrated and flexible way to solving your management and accountancy problems.

Index

A

accountants 62
reliance on 78
accounting: accrual basis 62
"extraordinary items" 62
accounting, management 72
role of 73
systems 73
accounting function:
computers and 88
failure to manage 81
working with 73
accounts, analyzing 70–1
activities, grouping 51
adding machines 88
administration 42
advertising: and market
strategy 74, 98
objectives 108
advertising campaigns 106–7
A. G. Becker & Co 24
Akers, John F. 159
Allen, Brady and Marsh 201
American Express 19, 107
analysis, objective 48
strategic 48, 49
annual reports: and
corporate culture 24
information from 20, 21
Apple II 37
Apple Computers 18
and change 37
corporate culture 24
size 22
aptitudes,
analyzing/grading 11, 12
ASK Computer Systems 199
assets 64
conversion of 66
as source of funds 66
audit 66
internal 73
and sales/marketing 101
auditors 44
authority: centralized/
decentralized 54
functional organization
and 54
in organization structure
51
project-oriented 54
automation 124

B

balance sheet 62, 64
analysis 65
effects of seasonal trade 71
equation 64
information from 20
personal 16
Bank of America 18
banks 44
Bayer, and training
function 162
Becker Warburg Paribas
Group 24
Belbin, Meredith 164, 165
bin cards 117
BMW, marketing strategy
99
Boeing, and training
function 162
"brainstorming" 48, 146, 147
Branson, Richard 30
brevity 136
briefing groups, style 147
British Airways 203
British Leyland, inventory
policy 111
budgetary control 74–5
failure to operate 81
budgets/budgeting 74
advantages 75
coordination 74
flexible 74
identifying holders 74
holder's targets 74
master 74
and R & D 126
zero-based 74
Burr, Donald C. 31
business decisions,
evaluating 74
business transactions,
presentation of 72
buyers: characteristics 112
job description 113
needs/consideration 69
buying 42
effective 112, 113

C

Campbell-Johnson, Alan 146
Campbell Soup 127
canvassing 102
capital, long-term 56
return on and survival 50
capital, venture 56, 57
capital, working:
borrowing facilities 60
distribution techniques
108
increase/decrease in 66
management 58–9

capital investment
budgeting 79
career: aiming for the top
198, 199
and company size 22–3
consolidation 16–17, 206
managing 208–9
need for training 160–1
planning 198, 208–9
stages in 16–17, 168
getting to the top 206,
208, 209
cash, on balance sheet 64
cash forecasting 60–1
Chase, David T. 199
Chrysler Corporation 203
Churchill, Winston 135
Cie Financière 24
Citicorp 207
codes of behavior 30–1
colleagues, compatible 15
committees: operating 44
style of meetings 147
committees, executive 44
committees, management 44
committees, systems, and
IT plan 93
communication: advantage
of written 136–7
"crossed lines" 132
instant feedback 134
"four types" and 12, 13, 135
methods of 132–3
one-to-one 134
revolution in 89
using unofficial channels
142, 143
without words 134
Compagnie Industriali
Riunite 203
company/organization:
achieving prime
objectives 124
activity/efficiency 71
adapting to change 36–7
anatomy of 42–3, 44, 52
areas of operation 96–7
benefits from consultants
151
capital structure 70
catalysts of change 151
characteristics 48
checking on 39
choosing the right one
38–9

CIT Financial
  Corporation 35
Collier, Sophia 30
common features 40–1
and communications
  revolution 89
creating a structure 100–1
cultural identity 25, 204
differences in public
  image 18–19
diversification 180, 181
division of power 54
effective time
  management 188
environment 43
evolution 52, 53
external/internal forces 44
financial problems 80–1
first impressions 20–1
functions 44, 45
future of 39
future policy 36
growth pattern 52
heart of 34, 39
liquidity 66, 70
location and growth 52
measuring activities 62
measuring performance 72
and new technology 126
initiative/creativity 126
objectives 40, 46, 50
optimum structure 54
organization 50
Personnel policies 86–7
prime activities 41
profitability 71
promotion from within 204
promotional activity 106
public image, checking
  on 38
reaction to crises 182
and R & D 126
rules 30–1
shared values 25
signs of
  problems/success 36
size and scope 22–3, 38
stage of development 52
strategy 47, 48
strengths/weaknesses 48
success potentials 46–7
valuation of 68–9
  who has power? 26, 27
competition, beating 104
Competitive Advantage 34

computer systems, for
  inventory control 117
consultants:
  benefits from using 51
  contributions from 49
  role of 150–1
  and strategic analysis 48
consultation: advantages/
  disadvantages 148–151
  direct/indirect 148
corporate culture 24–5
  checking on 38
corporate identity, fitting
  into 204
corporate image 18–19
corporate plan,
  manufacturing
  function and 125
cost information 178
  use of 76
costing systems 76
costs, budgetary control
  and 74
Coutts Clay, Jennifer 203
Coverdale training
  organization, and
  handling trouble 179
Cuckney, Sir John 207
customers: acquisition of
  102–103
  and R & D 127
  relations with 94–5

D
data, commercial
  processing 88
De Benedetti, Carlo 203
debt, long-term 56, 57, 64
  control of 104
  distribution techniques
  and 108
  as source of funds 66
decision-making 194
  costing systems and 76
  financial evaluation and
  78
  and financial
  information 72
  steps to effective 195
delegation: barriers to 173
  briefing delegates 174–5
  evaluation and feedback
  175
  of routine decision-
  making 194
  selecting delegates 173
  stages of 174–5

successful 172, 173
department leaders 32
departments/teams/tribes
  28
  checking on 39
  close liaison with 124
  dominant 32
  function of works
  engineering 122
  handling trouble in 178–9
  how much autonomy? 54
  managing successfully
  166–7, 194
  maximum efficiency of
  186
  motivating 128
  operating codes 30
  rise and fall of 33
  stereotypes 28–9
  success of 32
  understanding 28
  winners 39
departments, finance, and
  labor relations 125
departments, purchasing,
  key objective 125
depreciation, and profit 58
directors: departmental 44
  importance of financial
  80–1
  powers of 26
  resisting change 204
  structure of board 44, 147
dismissal 178, 179
  rules of 86
distribution 34, 108–9
  time/capacity 108
  types 108
dividends, control over
  policy 68
downtime, minimizing 122
E
employees/staff: appraising/
  reviewing 176–7
  anticipating/planning
  changes 158–9
  counseling 176
  departures and personnel
  86
  functions 54
  improving understanding
  176
  maximizing performance
  176
  motivation 168

Index

and production planning
119
promotion 85, 176
and R & D 127
time-keeping problems
188
training and
development 84, 85
work types 164–5
equity finance 56–7, 64
executive search 159
expenses, checking 31
exporting 109
"extroverts" 12
Exxon Corporation 205

F

facilities, consolidation of
124
family firm, decision-
making in 52
FBI, and communications
132
"feelers" 12, 13
and communication 135
FIFO principle 116
finance functions 72–3
structure 72
financial evaluation
techniques 78–9
financial modeling 78
financial problems 80–1
financial statements 62, 64
First Travel Corporation
201
Ford Motor Company 18,
203
critical success factor 35
production control 121
franchising 108
funds/funding, sources/
applications 40, 58, 62,
66–7

G

GAAP 66
GEC: structure 22
takeovers 205

H

Harvard Business Review,
on leadership 131
Harvey-Jones, Sir John 204,
205
"headhunters" 159
importance of 202
Hertz Corporation 35
Herzberg, Frederick 168

Hewlett-Packard 199
hiring 83
Hoover, J. Edgar 132
"hygiene" factors 168

I

Iacocca, Lee 203
IBM: and change 37
corporate culture 24
staff relations 87
and training function 162
and planning succession
159
ICI 204, 205
image, creating the right
200, 208–9
income statement 62–3
industrial practice, survey
of 151
industrial relations 86
information: "briefings"
and 144
and managing teams 166
processing 88
public presentation of
140–1
transfer of 44
information technology (IT):
implementing 92–3
management 89
selection 92
innovation 126
interviewing 156
tactics 157
"introverts" 12
"intuitors" 12, 13
and communication 135
inventories 110
and cash flow 58–9
distribution techniques
and 108
inventory: controlling 116
correct amounts 110
importance of labelling
116
importance of receiving
area 114
inspection checks 114
measuring total 110
planning deliveries 114
problems of control 116
receiving/storing 114–5
recording system 110, 114
rotation 116
investment, control over
decisions 68

Ishikawajima-Harima Heavy
Industries Ltd, and
training function 162–3

J

"Jazz" software 37
JCB, production control at
121
job costing 76
job satisfaction 10, 11, 14–15
jobs: changing 208–9
managing 208–9
top 200, 206
when to change 202–3
Johnson & Johnson,
changing corporate
culture 25
Jung, Carl 12, 135
four functions 12, 13, 135

K

Kardex systems 117
K Mart 94
Kurtzig, Sandra L. 199

L

labor relations: automation
and 124
factors in 122
Laker Airways, marketing
strategy 99
"larks and owls" 188
La Rouche, Janice 31
layoffs, rules for 86
leadership, effective 130
legislation 44
leverage 57
liabilities 64
line management 54
Lisa 37
literature, company, and
corporate culture 19, 24
LM Ericsson 55

M

Macintosh 37
McDonnell Douglas, and
training function 162
management 42
appraising/reviewing
staff 176–7
approach to buying 112
aspects of 128
bad, and crises 182
company attitude to 19
developing the team 164
effectiveness vs
efficiency 128

and financial problems
80–1
importance of
communicating 132–3,
134
importance of reading
effectively 138
informal/formal teams
164–5
innovation in 128
and IT plan 92–3
lack of action 80
leadership qualities 130
overseeing vs doing 128
personnel and 82
principles of good 190
promotion of sales
techniques 100
reach of 51
"scientific" 168
selecting/shaping 164–5
and strategic analysis 48
streaming process 204
successful 50
theories 190
using consultation 148
versus admin 128
women in 24
management,
manufacturing 122–3
management, materials,
effective 110–11
management, operating, 41
policy guidance for 44
structure 44
management, production 122
management control
structure 40
and individual functions
41
managers 44
analyzing bosses 197
appointing top 204
approach to staff 166–7
broadening knowledge
160
and change/innovation
180, 181
change of top 200
choosing successor 158–9
coping with stress 184, 185
and crises 182, 183
and delegation 172
creating systems 90–1
and departures 86
duties of materials 110

effective decision-making
194, 195
and employee motivation
168, 170–1
establishing labor
relations 122
finding effective training
162–3
formal training 160–1
functional corporate 55
importance of
communication 132–3
improving performance
of superiors 186
and "four functions" 12, 13
major resources 186
managing bosses 196
and negotiation 154
and new technology 88–9
and office systems 89
and organization 50
perception/sensitivity 16
and personnel 82–3
planning personal time
186–7
priorities 190
questioning own
development 161
responsibilities 122, 128
selling yourself 198
skills required 128
solving problems 192
sources of stress 184
understanding costs 76
what type are you? 12–13
managers, manufacturing:
problems 125
and quality performance
123
responsibilities 122, 124
and sourcing decision 125
and strategy 124
manufacturing function,
long-term development
125
market analysis, strategic
96–7
market entry/timing 96
market research 95, 100
market segmentation 96, 102
marketing function 34, 100
and company objectives
94
what is it? 94
marketing mix 96
markets: crises 182

and
growth/development 43,
52
strength in 36
Marsh, Peter 200, 201
Maslow, A. H. 11
and human needs 168
McDonald's, corporate
culture 25
meetings: chairing 144–5
importance of 144
preparation for 145
regular consultative 125
techniques for 146–7
memorandum/report:
structure 136, 137
versus telephone 132
Mercedes Benz, and
training function 162
Mersey Docks and
Harbour Board 207
midlife crisis 17
Minnesota Mining &
Manufacturing
Company, and change
36
Mobil Oil Company,
success 34
motivation, creating 170–1
Mountbatten of Burma 146
N
National Association of
Securities Dealers
Automated Quotation
System 57
National Cash Register,
and change 36
National Intergroup, and
change 37
negotiations: achieving
win/win 155
approaches to formal 152
defining objectives 154
leverage factors 155
timing 154
type of formal 153
uses 152
negotiators, functions of 152
New York Stock Exchange,
and equity finance 57
O
office services function 89
Ogilvy and Mather 127
Olympic Games (1984) 200,
201

221

Index

operating codes 30
operating plan,
    development of 48
operations: costing 76
    influences on 41
    responsibility for 40–1
opportunities/threats,
    external 48, 49
order sequencing 118
organization:
    acquiring power 204
    application of principles
        50, 51
    centralized/
        decentralized 54, 55
    functional 54
    importance of 50
    line/staff 54
    matrix 54
    "Organization Man" myth
        169
organization manual,
    reading 30
organization structure,
    features 50
    requirements filled 50
"organizational politics" 204
Orwell, George 136
output performance,
    measuring 122
owners 44
    return on investment 56
    power of 26, 40

P

Packard, David 199
Pan Am 18
partnership, decision-
    making in 52
Penguin Books, revival of
    191
Personnel: development 82
    functions 83, 84–5
    government legislation
        and 86
    links with the
        organization 84
    and management process
        82
    modern 82
    and negotiating process 86
    policies 86
    and recruitment 158
Polaroid, development 126
Porter, Michael 34
power/influence 26
    holders of 27

power structure: and
    changing markets 36
    checking on 38
presentations 140–1
premises: company image
    and 19
    and isolation of tribes 28
price discrimination 76
Price Earnings ratio
    (P/E) 69
price setting: cost-based 76
    decisions 76, 77
    market-based 76
    and profitability 76
    use of 76
process costing 76
problem solving 192
    via people 193
products/services, and
    growth development 52
product, tangible 15
production 34
    employee motivation and
        168
    formulating plan 118
    maintaining 120–1
    scheduling 118–19
production controller,
    function of 120–1
profits: before taxation 62
    and funds 58
profitability: price setting
    and 76
    and success/survival 42, 50
progress reviews 144
projects: management of
        190
    progress reviews and 144
    style of progress
        meetings 147
    time management 188, 189
    viability 191
promotion, "right image"
        200, 201
prospect client call report
        105
prospect file 102, 103
prospecting, process of
        102–3
public relations 106
    effective 107
Pümpin, Professor C. 46

Q

Quaker Oats, critical
    success factor 34
quality control 123

R

Racal Electronics Group
    198, 199
Radio and Allied
    (Holdings) 205
ratio analysis 70–1
Rawl, Larry, 205
RCA: critical success
    factor 35
    diversification 126
reading, improving 138
reading material, dealing
    with 138, 139
recruitment 82, 156
    assessing candidates 157
    automation and 124
    caliber of 36
    of specialist skills 158,
        159
recruitment agencies 159
register companies 159
reprimands 178
resources: functional
    organization and 54
    managing 46
research and
    development 34, 126–7
resume: reading before
    interviewing 156
    when changing jobs 202
retirement, planning for 17

S

salary: data for
    adjustments 176
    handling problems of 123
sale and leaseback 56
sales function 100
    campaigns 94
    incentive plans 104
    and marketing 100
    promotions 107
    strategy 126
sales force: control of debt
        104
    reviewing 104
    shared experience 104
satellites 89
Sea Containers 198, 199
Sears, Roebuck and Co,
    critical success factor
        35
security, in warehouse
    area 115
self-knowledge 10–13, 208–9
    and the future 16–17

motivation 170
what do you value? 14–15
sellers, needs/
    considerations 68, 69
selling/marketing 42, 106–7
    performance indication
        104
    structured 100–1
    and communication 135
senior debt 56
"sensors" 12, 13
S. G. Warburg 24
shareholders 40
    and the audit 66
    and company valuation
        68
    power of 26, 68
    and profits 58
shares, as source of funds
    56, 66
    technical valuation of 68
Sherwood, James 198, 199
shipbuilding, and change 37
Siemens: diversification 126
    and training function 162
skills, people-related 160
social environment, and
    growth/development 52
Socrates 16
sourcing 124
sponsorship 107
Statement of Changes in
    Financial Position
    66, 67
Stock Exchange listing
    68
Strategies for Women at
    Work 31
strategy 46–7
    changes in 47
    developing/
        implementing 46, 47, 48
    manufacturing 124–5
    obstacles to successful 125
    responsibility for 44
    secret 48
strategy, marketing 96–7
    producing 94, 98–9
stress: coping with 184–5
    reactions to 184
    recognizing effects 184
    related symptoms 185
subcommittees, key 44
subcontracting 119
    and cost savings 124
subordinated debt 56

success: associating with 32
    of a business 42
    critical factors 34–5
    financial 15
    identifying potential
        46–7
    and management
        structure 41
    and marketing/sales 34
    quality of 42
    selling yourself 198–9
succession, right
    candidate? 200
    planning 158–9
superiors: analyzing 197
    managing 196
    reliance on managers 196
survival: adapting for 36–7
    factors 34, 35
SWOT 48, 49
systems: checking
    performance 90
    computer vs manual 124
    implementing 92–3
    management of 91
    reviewing 90
    security of 91
systems, office 88–9

T
Tacoma Boatbuilding
    Company, inventory
    policy 111
Tannenbaum and Schmidt
    131
tax, deferred 64
taxation, and profits 58
Taylor, F. W. 168
team practices, supportive
    167
technology, new 88–9
tendering, competitive 76
test marketing 106
"thinkers" 12, 13
    and communication 135
Thomas Cook 207
time management 188
    tips for good 189
time planning 186
timewasting 186, 187
Toshiba, staff relations 87
Toyota, inventory policy
    111
trading activity, functions 42
training functions: benefits
    162
    and delegation 172

effective 162–3
    identifying needs 176
    importance of 160
    internal/external 162–3
    for IT project 93
    task-related 160
training organizations 163
treasury departments 72, 73
treasury function 59
Triumph, and change 37
trusts, decision-making in
    52

U
Ueberroth, Peter 88, 200, 201
US Steel Corp. 18

V
value chain 34
Virgin Group 30
visual aids 140–1
Volvo, and staff motivation
    170–1

W
warehousing 108
    utilizing space 115
Weinstock, Lord 205
wholesalers 108
winning team 32–3
work-in-progress, and cash
    flow 58–9
Wriston, Walter 207
W. T. Grant & Company 36

X
Xerox, and training
    function 162

Y
Young, Arthur 150–1, 217

Acknowledgments

Picture credits

Key: *l* left *r* right *t* top *b* bottom *c* center

18/19	American Express Europe Ltd
22	Clive Coote/Daily Telegraph Colour Library
23	Richard Ellis, Chartered Surveyors
25 *t*	McDonald's Hamburgers Ltd
25 *b*	British Motor Industry Heritage Trust
30 *l*	American Natural Beverage Corp.
r	Tony Brainsby Publicity Ltd
31 *l*	Vikki Stace Associates
r	Financial Times
37 *t*	Apple Computer (UK) Ltd
ct	John Sturrock/Network Photographers
b	National Intergroup, Inc.
106 *t*	American Express Europe Limited
b	Michael King/All-Sport Photographic Ltd
107 *l*	Saatchi & Saatchi Compton Ltd
r	Tommy Hindley/Professional Sports Photography
127	Pepsi-Cola (Northern Europe) Ltd
146	Popperfoto
159	IBM United Kingdom Ltd
190	Beryl Cook/Penguin Books Ltd
199 *tl*	Chase Enterprises
tr	Hewlett Packard
bl	Sea Containers Inc.
br	ASK Computer Systems Inc.
201 *t*	Financial Times
b	Universal Pictorial Press, London
203 *t*	Ing. C. Olivetti & Co. SPA
c	Chrysler Corporation
b	People In Pictures Ltd
205 *t*	ICI PLC
c	Exxon Corp.
b	Financial Times
207 *t*	The Thomas Cook Group Ltd
b	UPI/Bettmann

The publishers and authors received invaluable help from the following people and organizations:

Ros Anstey
Sue Armitage
Janice Buswell
Alan Campbell-Johnson
Andrea Douglas
Kathie Gill
Sheila Green, Unigate PLC
The Griffin Hospital, USA
Kay Hadwick
Derek Hammond, managing director of APC International
F. C. Hayes, chairman of the Prospect Centre
Malcolm Higgs
The Industrial Society
Alison James, Headway Publications
Sue Lintern
Lotus Cars Limited
Max M. McCauslin
New York Stock Exchange
Peter O'Neill
David Robinson of the Coverdale Organization
Eric Ross
Anthony Saxton and Steven Bamfylde of John Stork and Partners
Sarah Warner
Christopher Warren-Green